AA003908

SIMUL 2017

The Ninth International Conference on Advances in System Simulation

October 8 - 12, 2017

Athens, Greece

SIMUL 2017 Editors

Arash Ramezani, The Helmut Schmidt University, Germany

Edward Williams, University of Michigan - Dearborn, USA

Marek Bauer, Politechnika Krakowska, Poland

Printed from e-media with permission by:

Curran Associates, Inc.
57 Morehouse Lane
Red Hook, NY 12571

Some format issues inherent in the e-media version may also appear in this print version.

Printed by Curran Associates, Inc. (2017)

International Academy, Research, and Industry Association (IARIA)
412 Derby Way
Wilmington, DE 19810

Phone: (408) 893-6407
Fax: (408) 527-6351

petre@iaria.org

Additional copies of this publication are available from:

Curran Associates, Inc.
57 Morehouse Lane
Red Hook, NY 12571 USA
Phone: 845-758-0400
Fax: 845-758-2633
Email: curran@proceedings.com
Web: www.proceedings.com

Table of Contents

SIMUL 2017

Forward

The Ninth International Conference on Advances in System Simulation (SIMUL 2017), held on October 8 - 12, 2017- Athens, Greece, continued a series of events focusing on advances in simulation techniques and systems providing new simulation capabilities.

While different simulation events are already scheduled for years, SIMUL 2017 identified specific needs for ontology of models, mechanisms, and methodologies in order to make easy an appropriate tool selection. With the advent of Web Services and WEB 3.0 social simulation and human-in simulations bring new challenging situations along with more classical process simulations and distributed and parallel simulations. An update on the simulation tool considering these new simulation flavors was aimed at, too.

The conference provided a forum where researchers were able to present recent research results and new research problems and directions related to them. The conference sought contributions to stress-out large challenges in scale system simulation and advanced mechanisms and methodologies to deal with them. The accepted papers covered topics on social simulation, transport simulation, simulation tools and platforms, simulation methodologies and models, and distributed simulation.

We welcomed technical papers presenting research and practical results, position papers addressing the pros and cons of specific proposals, such as those being discussed in the standard forums or in industry consortiums, survey papers addressing the key problems and solutions on any of the above topics, short papers on work in progress, and panel proposals.

We take here the opportunity to warmly thank all the members of the SIMUL 2017 technical program committee as well as the numerous reviewers. The creation of such a broad and high quality conference program would not have been possible without their involvement. We also kindly thank all the authors that dedicated much of their time and efforts to contribute to the SIMUL 2017. We truly believe that thanks to all these efforts, the final conference program consists of top quality contributions.

This event could also not have been a reality without the support of many individuals, organizations and sponsors. We also gratefully thank the members of the SIMUL 2017 organizing committee for their help in handling the logistics and for their work that is making this professional meeting a success. We gratefully appreciate to the technical program committee co-chairs that contributed to identify the appropriate groups to submit contributions.

We hope the SIMUL 2017 was a successful international forum for the exchange of ideas and results between academia and industry and to promote further progress in simulation research.
We also hope Athens provided a pleasant environment during the conference and everyone saved some time for exploring this beautiful historic city.

SIMUL Steering Committee

Hendrik Rothe, Helmut-Schmidt-Universität/ Universität der Bundeswehr Hamburg, Germany
Witold Pedrycz, University of Alberta, Canada
Ian Flood, University of Florida, USA

SIMUL 2017

Committee

SIMUL Steering Committee
Hendrik Rothe, Helmut-Schmidt-Universität/ Universität der Bundeswehr Hamburg, Germany
Witold Pedrycz, University of Alberta, Canada
Ian Flood, University of Florida, USA
Marek Bauer, Politechnika Krakowska, Poland
Mu-Chun Su, National Central University, Taiwan
Etienne Kerre, Ghent University, Belgium
Kuan Yew Wong, Universiti Teknologi Malaysia (UTM), Malaysia

SIMUL Industry/Research Advisory Committee
Tsan-sheng Hsu, Institute of Information Science | Academia Sinica, Taiwan
Michael Karner, VIRTUAL VEHICLE, Austria
Letizia Nicoletti, Cal-tek srl, Italy

SIMUL 2017 Technical Program Committee

Kareem Abdelgawad, Heinz Nixdorf Institut | Universität Paderborn, Germany
El-Houssaine Aghezzaf, Ghent University, Belgium
Ciro Alberto Amaya, University of Los Andes, Bogotá, Colombia
Frédéric Amblard, IRIT | Université Toulouse 1 Capitole, France
Boris Andrievsky, Russian Academy of Sciences, Russia
Chrissanthi Angeli, Piraeus University of Applied Sciences, Greece
Amr Arisha, Dublin Institute of Technology (DIT), Ireland
Marek Bauer, Politechnika Krakowska, Poland
Ateet Bhalla, Independent Consultant, India
Paul-Antoine Bisgambiglia, University of Corsica Pasquale Paoli, France
Paolo Bocciarelli, University of Rome Tor Vergata, Italy
Magdiel Ablan Bortone, Centro de Simulación y Modelos (CESIMO) | Universidad de los Andes, Mérida, Venezuela
Christos Bouras, University of Patras | Computer Technology Institute & Press «Diophantus», Greece
Benjamin Camus, Inria | IRISA, Rennes, France
Paula María Castro Castro, University of A Coruña, Spain
Eugene Ch'ng, University of Nottingham Ningbo, China
Federico Ciccozzi, Mälardalen University, Sweden
Franco Cicirelli, ICAR-CNR, Italy
Duilio Curcio, University of Calabria (CS), Italy
Andrea D'Ambrogio, University of Roma "Tor Vergata", Italy
Maryam Davoudpour, *Ryerson* University, Canada
Luis Antonio De Santa-Eulalia, Université de Sherbrooke, Canada
Jorge de Jesus Lozoya Santos, Universidad de Monterrey, Mexico
Tuğçe Demirdelen, Adana Science and Technology University, Turkey

Alexander Ditter, Friedrich-Alexander University Erlangen-Nürnberg (FAU), Germany
Atalan Dogan, Anadolu University, Turkey
Julie Dugdale, University Grenoble Alps, France
Vinod Dumblekar, MANTIS, India
Rémy Dupas, University of Bordeaux, France
Sabeur Elkosantini, University of Monastir, Tunisia
Diego Encinas, Informatics Research Institute LIDI – National University of La Plata (UNLP), Argentina
Zuhal Erden, ATILIM University, Turkey
Ian Flood, University of Florida, USA
Adrian Florea, 'Lucian Blaga' University of Sibiu, Romania
Romain Franceschini, University of Corsica, France
José Manuel Galán, Universidad de Burgos, Spain
Héctor Miguel Gastélum González, Tecnológico Nacional de México - Instituto Tecnológico de Tlajomulco, Mexico
Luis Gomes, Universidade Nova de Lisboa, Portugal
Antoni Grau, Technical University of Catalonia - UPC, Barcelona, Spain
Petr Hanacek, Brno University, Czech Republic
Magdalena Hańderek, Cracow University of Technology, Poland
Thomas Hanne, University of Applied Sciences and Arts Northwestern Switzerland / Institute for Information Systems, Switzerland
Houcine Hassan, Universitat Politecnica de Valencia, Spain
Celso Hirata, Instituto Tecnologico de Aeronautica, Brazil
Tsan-sheng Hsu, Institute of Information Science | Academia Sinica, Taiwan
Xiaolin Hu, Georgia State University, USA
Marc-Philippe Huget, Polytech Annecy-Chambery-LISTIC | University of Savoie, France
Mauro Iacono, Università degli Studi della Campania "Luigi Vanvitelli", Italy
Joshua Ignatius, University of Warwick, Coventry, UK
Emilio Insfran, Universitat Politecnica de Valencia, Spain
Segismundo Izquierdo, University of Valladolid, Spain
Maria João Viamonte, Institute of Engineering (ISEP) - Polytechnic Institute of Porto (IPP), Portugal
Zsolt Csaba Johanyák, Pallasz Athéné University, Hungary
Eugene B. John, The University of Texas at San Antonio, USA
Imed Kacem, LCOMS - Université de Lorraine, France
Michael Karner, VIRTUAL VEHICLE, Austria
Hamdi Kavak, Old Dominion University, USA
Peter Kemper, College of William and Mary, USA
Etienne Kerre, Ghent University, Belgium
Daria Kolmakova, Samara National Research University, Russia
Petia Koprinkova-Hristova, Institute of Information and Communication Technologies | Bulgarian Academy of Sciences, Bulgaria
Harald Köstler, Friedrich-Alexander University Erlangen-Nürnberg, Germany
Claudia Krull, Institut für Simulation und Graphik | Otto-von-Guericke-Universität Magdeburg, Germany
Anatoly Kurkovsky, Georgia Gwinnett College - Greater Atlanta University System of Georgia, USA
Massimo La Scala, Politecnico di Bari, Italy
Fedor Lehocki, Slovak University of Technology in Bratislava, Slovak Republic
Iris Lorscheid, Institute of Management Accounting and Simulation (MACCS) | Hamburg University of Technology, Germany
Edwin Lughofer, Johannes Kepler University Linz, Austria

Copyright Information

Numerical Simulation and Analysis of Enzyme-Catalysed Substrate Conversion in a Microbioreactor

Linas Petkevičius and Romas Baronas

Faculty of Mathematics and Informatics,
Vilnius University, Naugarduko st. 24, Vilnius, Lithuania
Email: {linas.petkevicius, romas.baronas}@mif.vu.lt

***Abstract*—The paper presents a non-linear mathematical model for digital simulation of an enzyme loaded porous microreactor. The model is based on a system of reaction-diffusion equations, containing a non-linear term related to the Michaelis-Menten kinetics, and involves three regions: the enzyme microreactor where the enzyme reaction as well as mass transport by diffusion take place, a diffusion limiting region (the Nernst layer), where only the mass transport by diffusion takes place, and a convective region, where the analyte concentration is maintained constant. Assuming well stirred conditions, the influence of the thickness of the Nernst layer on the behaviour of the product emission, as well as the impact of the diffusion modulus and the Biot number has been numerically investigated. The simulation results showed that the Nernst layer must be taken into consideration when modelling micro-size bioreactors. The digital simulation was carried out using the finite difference technique.**

Keywords*—*reaction-diffusion; Michaelis - Menten kinetics; microbioreactor; CSTR.

I. INTRODUCTION

Continuous-flow stirred tank reactors (CSTR) are common in chemical industries [1][2]. Although a stirred tank is a usual construction of industrial enzyme reactors, the effectiveness and optimal construction of CSTR remain open to study [3][4]. Specifically, further research is needed due to the application of the immobilized enzymes, such as biocatalysts, on a manufactoring scale that requires to use the reactors of different types, including CSTR [5][6][7].

A CSTR often refers to a model used to estimate the operation parameters when using a continuous agitated-tank reactor to reach a specified output [6]. In the last few decades, immobilized enzyme reactor models have evolved significantly with wide range of applications in food industry [8], waste cleaning [9], bacteria cells immobilization [10][11]. Rapid progress was noticed in integrating microfluidic reactors and biocatalytic reactions [12]. The combination of miniaturized technologies and microfluidics allows to increase the bioprocess efficiency. However, coupling microreactors and biocatalysis is highly complex, requiring an integrated approach addressing biocatalyst features, reaction kinetics, mass transfer and microreactors geometry [12][13].

Mathematical models have been widely used to investigate the kinetic peculiarities of the enzyme microreactors [7][12]. Models coupling the enzyme-catalysed reaction with the diffusion in enzyme microreactors are usually used. Since containing catalytic particles, the analyte in CSTR is well stirred and set in powerful motion, the mass transport by diffusion outside the microreactors is usually neglected [13][14]. In practice, the zero thickness of the diffusion shell (layer) can not be achieved [15]. We consider an array of identical spherical microreactors placed in a CSTR shown in Figure 1 [6], where area Ω_m denotes a microreactor, Ω_d denotes surrounding diffusion shell and Ω_c is a convective region.

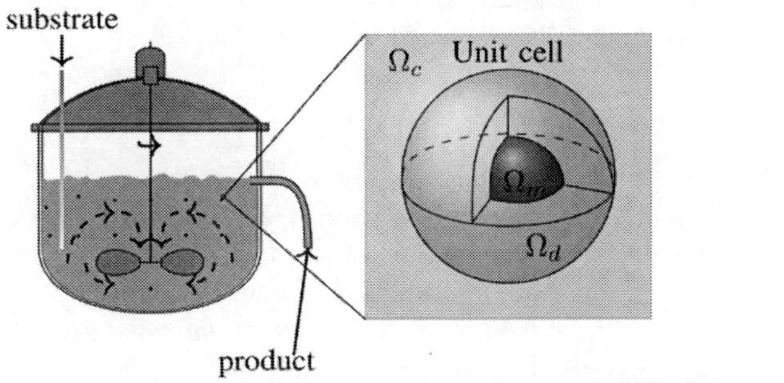

Figure 1. Continuous stirred tank reactor with enzyme-loaded microreactors (pellets) and a zoomed unit cell to be modelled.

The goal of this work was to investigate the dependencies of the internal and external diffusion limitations on the yield of the reaction product, modelled by reaction-diffusion equations, containing a non-linear term related to Michaelis-Menten kinetics [6][7][16]. The model involves three regions: the enzyme microreactor, where the enzyme reaction, as well as the mass transport by diffusion take place, a diffusion limiting region, where only the mass transport by diffusion takes place, and a convective region, where the analyte concentration is maintained constant. Due to a strong non-linearity of the reaction term, the computer simulation was carried out using the finite difference technique. [17].

The rest of the paper is organised as follows: in Section II, the mathematical model and microbioreactor characteristics are described; Section III formulates a dimensionless model and derives the main parameters of the bioreactor; Section IV describes the numerical model and the simulator; in Section V, results of numerical experiments are presented, and conclusions close the article.

II. MATHEMATICAL MODEL

We consider an array of identical spherical microreactors placed in a continuous ideally stirred-tank reactor [6]. Assuming a uniform distribution of the microreactors in the tank and a relatively great distance between adjacent microreactors, the spherical unit cell was modelled by an enzyme-loaded microreactor (pellet) and a surrounding diffusion shell (the Nernst diffusion layer). The principal structure of the tank containing uniformly distributed microreactors and a unit cell are presented in Figure 1, where Ω_m denotes a microreactor (MR), Ω_d stands for the diffusion shell and Ω_c is a convective region.

In the enzyme-loaded MR layer we consider the enzyme-catalyzed reaction

$$\mathrm{E}+\mathrm{S} \underset{k_r}{\overset{k_f}{\rightleftharpoons}} \mathrm{ES} \xrightarrow{k_{\mathrm{cat}}} \mathrm{E}+\mathrm{P}, \tag{1}$$

where the substrate (S) combines reversibly with an enzyme (E) to form a complex (ES). The complex then dissociates into the product (P) and the enzyme is regenerated [18][19].

Assuming the steady-state approximation, the concentration of the intermediate complex (ES) does not change and may be neglected when modelling the biochemical behaviour of the microreactor [6][19][20]. In the resulting scheme, the substrate (S) is enzymatically converted to the product (P),

$$\mathrm{S} \xrightarrow{\mathrm{E}} \mathrm{P}. \tag{2}$$

A. Governing Equations

Assuming the symmetrical geometry of the microreactor and homogenised distribution of the immobilized enzyme inside the porous microreactor, the mathematical model can be described in one-dimensional domain using the radial distance.

Coupling enzymatic reaction in the microreactor (region Ω_m) with the one-dimensional-in-space diffusion, described by Fick's second law, and assuming the steady-state for a system (2) lead to the following governing equations of the reaction-diffusion type ($0 < r < R_0$):

$$D_{S,m}\frac{1}{r^2}\frac{\partial}{\partial r}\left(r^2\frac{\partial S_m}{\partial r}\right) = \frac{V_{\max}S_m}{K_M+S_m}, \tag{3a}$$

$$D_{P,m}\frac{1}{r^2}\frac{\partial}{\partial r}\left(r^2\frac{\partial P_m}{\partial r}\right) = -\frac{V_{\max}S_m}{K_M+S_m}, \tag{3b}$$

where r stands for space, $S_m = S_m(r)$ and $P_m = P_m(r)$ are the concentrations of the substrate and the reaction product in the microreactor, respectively, R_0 is the radius of the microreactor, $D_{S,m}$ and $D_{P,m}$ are the diffusion coefficients, $V_{\max} = k_{cat}E_0$ is the maximal enzymatic rate and $K_M = (k_r + k_{cat})/k_f$ is the Michaelis constant (see Figure 2(a)).

In the Nernst diffusion layer Ω_d only the mass transport by diffusion takes place:

$$D_{S,d}\frac{1}{r^2}\frac{\partial}{\partial r}\left(r^2\frac{\partial S_d}{\partial r}\right) = 0, \tag{4a}$$

$$D_{P,d}\frac{1}{r^2}\frac{\partial}{\partial r}\left(r^2\frac{\partial P_d}{\partial r}\right) = 0, \quad r\in(R_0,\ R_1), \tag{4b}$$

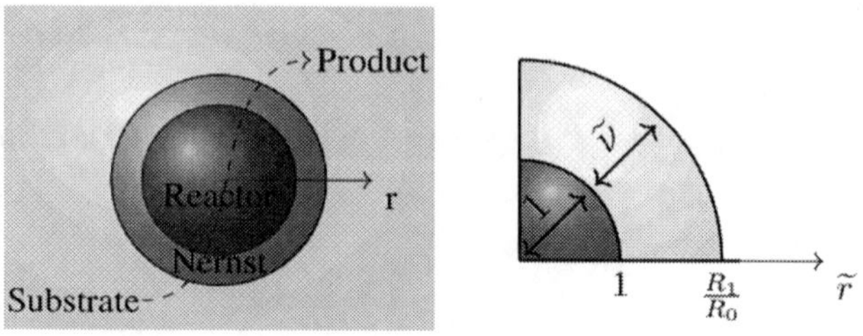

Figure 2. Principal structure of the unit cell consisting of a microbioreactor and the Nernst diffusion shell (a) and non-dimensionalized regions (b).

where $S_d = S_d(r)$ and $P_d = P_d(r)$ are the concentrations of the substrate and the reaction product in the diffusion shell, respectively, $D_{S,d}$ and $D_{P,d}$ are the diffusion coefficients of the materials in the bulk solution, R_1 is the radius of the unit cell.

B. Boundary Conditions

Fluxes of the substrate and the product through the stagnant external diffusion shell is assumed to be equal to the corresponding fluxes entering the surface of the microreactor,

$$D_{S,m}\left.\frac{\partial S_m}{\partial r}\right|_{r=R_0} = D_{S,d}\left.\frac{\partial S_d}{\partial r}\right|_{r=R_0}, \tag{5a}$$

$$D_{P,m}\left.\frac{\partial P_m}{\partial r}\right|_{r=R_0} = D_{P,d}\left.\frac{\partial P_d}{\partial r}\right|_{r=R_0}. \tag{5b}$$

The formal partition coefficient ϕ is used to describe the specificity in concentration distribution of the compounds between two neighboring regions [6][21],

$$S_m(R_0) = \phi S_d(R_0), \quad P_m(R_0) = \phi P_d(R_0). \tag{6}$$

Due to the symmetry of the microreactor, the zero-flux boundary conditions are defined for the center of the microreactor ($r = 0$),

$$D_{S,m}\left.\frac{\partial S_m}{\partial r}\right|_{r=0} = 0, \quad D_{P,m}\left.\frac{\partial P_m}{\partial r}\right|_{r=0} = 0. \tag{7}$$

According to the Nernst approach, the shell of thickness $\nu = R_1 - R_0$ remains unchanged with time [15][17]. Away from it, the solution is in motion and is uniform in concentration. Due to the continuous injection of the substrate into the stirred tank and washing off of the product, the concentration in the convective region remains unchanged:

$$S_d(R_1) = S_0, \quad P_d(R_1) = 0. \tag{8}$$

The thickness ν of the Nernst diffusion shell depends upon the nature and stirring up the buffer solution. Usually, more intensive stirring corresponds to the thinner diffusion layer (shell).

C. Microbioreactor Characteristics

In many industrial processes, especially in the production of low-value added products like biopesticides, bio-fertilizers, bio-surfactants ect. [9], it is important to continuously improve the yield and/or productivity [7]. The productivity is important, since this ensures an efficient utilization of the production capacity, i.e., the bioreactors.

The yield of the desired product on the substrate is one of the most important criteria for design and optimization of bioreactors. The economic feasibility of the process is expressed by the yield factor as the ratio of product formation rate and the substrate uptake rate [6][7].

The bioreactor construction is efficient enough when the product emission is relatively large with given substrate amount used. The product emission rate $\bar{E}_{P,O}$ can be calculated by an integration of the product flux over the outer surface of the diffusion shell [7],

$$\begin{aligned}\bar{E}_{P,O} &= \int_0^{2\pi}\int_0^{\pi} D_{P,d}\frac{\partial P_d}{\partial r}\Big|_{r=R_1} R_1^2\sin(\theta)d\theta d\varphi \\ &= 4\pi R_1^2 D_{P,d}\frac{\partial P_d}{\partial r}\Big|_{r=R_1}.\end{aligned} \tag{9}$$

The average consumption $\bar{C}_S$ of the substrate over the whole microreactor can be calculated as follows:

$$\begin{aligned}\bar{C}_S &= \int_0^{R_0}\int_0^{2\pi}\int_0^{\pi}\frac{V_{\max}S_0}{K_M+S_0}\sin(\theta)d\theta d\varphi r^2 dr \\ &= \int_0^{R_0} 4\pi\frac{V_{\max}S_0}{K_M+S_0}r^2dr \\ &= \frac{4}{3}\pi V_{\max}R_0^3\frac{S_0}{K_M+S_0}.\end{aligned} \tag{10}$$

The yield factor γ for the microreactor system, as well as for the entire tank reactor shown in Figure 1, can be defined by the ratio of the product emission rate to the substrate consumption rate,

$$\gamma = \frac{\bar{E}_{P,O}}{\bar{C}_S}. \tag{11}$$

The yield factor is equal to unity ($\gamma = 1$) when whole the consumed substrate is converted to the product and the whole the product eluted into the bulk (convective region Ω_c). The microbioreactor is absolutely inefficient ($\gamma = 0$), if no product falls into the bulk.

III. Dimensionless model

In order to define the main governing parameters of the two compartment model (3)-(8), the dimensional variable r and unknown concentrations $S_m(r), P_m(r), S_d(r), P_d(r)$ are replaced with the following dimensionless parameters:

$$\begin{aligned}&\tilde{r} = \frac{r}{R_0},\quad \tilde{S}_m = \frac{S_m}{K_M},\\ &\tilde{P}_m = \frac{P_m}{K_M},\quad \tilde{S}_d = \frac{S_d}{K_M},\quad \tilde{P}_d = \frac{P_d}{K_M},\end{aligned} \tag{12}$$

where $\tilde{r}$ is the dimensionless distance from the microreactor center and $\tilde{S}_m(\tilde{r}), \tilde{P}_m(\tilde{r}), \tilde{S}_d(\tilde{r}), \tilde{P}_d(\tilde{r})$ are the dimensionless concentrations. Having defined dimensionless variables and unknowns, the following dimensionless parameters characterize the domain geometry and the substrate concentration in the bulk:

$$\tilde{\nu} = \frac{\nu}{R_0},\quad \tilde{S}_0 = \frac{S_0}{K_M}, \tag{13}$$

where $\tilde{\nu}$ is the dimensionless thickness of the Nernst diffusion layer (see Figure 2(b)), $\tilde{S}_0$ is the dimensionless substrate concentration in the bulk solution. The dimensionless thickness of the microreactor equals one.

The governing equations (3) in the dimensionless coordinates are expressed as follows ($0 < \tilde{r} < 1$):

$$\frac{1}{\tilde{r}^2}\frac{\partial}{\partial\tilde{r}}\left(\tilde{r}^2\frac{\partial\tilde{S}_m}{\partial\tilde{r}}\right) - \sigma^2\frac{\tilde{S}_m}{1+\tilde{S}_m} = 0, \tag{14a}$$

$$\frac{D_{P,m}}{D_{S,m}}\frac{1}{\tilde{r}^2}\frac{\partial}{\partial\tilde{r}}\left(\tilde{r}^2\frac{\partial\tilde{P}_m}{\partial\tilde{r}}\right) + \sigma^2\frac{\tilde{S}_m}{1+\tilde{S}_m} = 0, \tag{14b}$$

where σ is the Thiele modulus or the Damköhler number [7][22][23] defined as:

$$\sigma^2 = \frac{V_{\max}R_0^2}{K_M D_{S,m}}. \tag{15}$$

The governing equations (4) take the following form ($1 < \tilde{r} < 1+\tilde{\nu}$):

$$\frac{D_{S,d}}{D_{S,m}}\frac{1}{\tilde{r}^2}\frac{\partial}{\partial\tilde{r}}\left(\tilde{r}^2\frac{\partial\tilde{S}_d}{\partial\tilde{r}}\right) = 0, \tag{16a}$$

$$\frac{D_{P,d}}{D_{S,m}}\frac{1}{\tilde{r}^2}\frac{\partial}{\partial\tilde{r}}\left(\tilde{r}^2\frac{\partial\tilde{P}_d}{\partial\tilde{r}}\right) = 0. \tag{16b}$$

The matching conditions (5), (6) and (8) become:

$$\frac{\partial\tilde{S}_m}{\partial\tilde{r}}\Big|_{\tilde{r}=1} = \frac{D_{S,d}}{D_{S,m}}\frac{\partial\tilde{S}_d}{\partial\tilde{r}}\Big|_{\tilde{r}=1} \tag{17a}$$

$$\frac{\partial\tilde{P}_m}{\partial\tilde{r}}\Big|_{\tilde{r}=1} = \frac{D_{P,d}}{D_{S,m}}\frac{\partial\tilde{P}_d}{\partial\tilde{r}}\Big|_{\tilde{r}=1}. \tag{17b}$$

$$\tilde{S}_m(1) = \phi\tilde{S}_d(1),\quad \tilde{P}_m(1) = \phi\tilde{P}_d(1). \tag{18}$$

$$\frac{\partial\tilde{S}_m}{\partial\tilde{r}}\Big|_{\tilde{r}=0} = 0,\quad \frac{\partial\tilde{P}_m}{\partial\tilde{r}}\Big|_{\tilde{r}=0} = 0, \tag{19a}$$

$$\tilde{S}_d(1+\tilde{\nu}) = \tilde{S}_0,\quad \tilde{P}_d(1+\tilde{\nu}) = 0. \tag{19b}$$

The dimensionless factor σ^2 essentially compares the rate of enzyme reaction ($V_{\max}/K_M$) with the diffusion through the enzyme-loaded microreactor ($D_{S,m}/R_0^2$). If $\sigma^2 \ll 1$, the enzyme kinetics controls the bioreactor action. The action is under diffusion control when $\sigma^2 \gg 1$.

The Biot number β is another dimensionless parameter widely used to indicate the internal mass transfer resistance to the external one [24][25],

$$\beta = \frac{D_{S,d}R_0}{D_{S,m}(R_1 - R_0)}. \tag{20}$$

When the Biot number is small, the effect of the external diffusion is the most marked. As the Biot number increases the effect of the external diffusion becomes less important.

The diffusion module and the Biot number are widely used in analysis and design of different bioreactors [25]. The experiment conducted by Kont et al. [10] proved the external mass-transfer limitations to be negligible for $\beta > 1$ using the first order kinetics model of CSTR and packed-bed reactors (PBR), which conducted condition (8). Typically, designers seek for bioreactors acting in the reaction-limited regime, since in this case reaction and diffusion occur on different time scales [26].

IV. Digital simulation of experiments

The non-linearity of the governing equations prevents us from solving the boundary value problem (14)-(19) analytically, hence the numerical model was constructed and solved using finite difference technique [17]. An explicit scheme was used; however since Michaelis-Menten non-linearity, further construction of equations was used:

$$D_{C,m} \cdot \frac{1}{r^2}\frac{\partial}{\partial r}\left(r^2 \frac{\partial C_m^n}{\partial r}\right) = \pm \frac{V_{\max} C_m^n}{K_M + C_m^{n-1}},$$

where $C = S, P$. Tridiagonal matrix was constructed from the equations. In the numerical simulation, scheme was run until the following loss becomes very small:

$$\mathcal{L} = ||S^n - S^{n-1}||_{l^2} + ||P^n - P^{n-1}||_{l^2} < \epsilon,$$

where decay rate value $\epsilon = 10^{-14}$ was used over l^2 norm. An explicit finite difference the scheme was built on a uniform discrete grid with 128 points in space direction [16]. The simulator has been programmed by the authors in C++ language [27].

The numerical solution of the mathematical model (14)-(19) was validated by using exact analytical solutions known for very special cases of the model parameters [22][25][6][16]. At such low concentration of the substrate as $S_0 \ll K_M$, the non-linear reaction rate in equations (3) reduces to the first order reaction rate. In very opposite case, when the substrate concentration S_0 to be measured is very high compared to the Michaelis constant K_M ($S_0 \gg K_M$), the reaction term reduces to the zero order reaction rate $V_{\max}$.

V. Results and discussion

To investigate the effects of the geometry and catalytic activity of the microreactor, the reactor action was simulated and the yield factor was calculated for very different values of the Biot number β, the Thiele module σ and the substrate dimensionless concentration S_0.

A. Concentration profiles

Figure 3 shows the profiles of the product concentration P calculated from the microreactor model (14)-(19) changing the Thiele module σ as well as the Biot number β, and keeping unchanged the following model parameters:

$$D_{S,m} = D_{P,m}, \quad D_{S,d} = D_{P,d}, \quad \phi = 0.5, \quad \widetilde{\nu} = 1. \qquad (21)$$

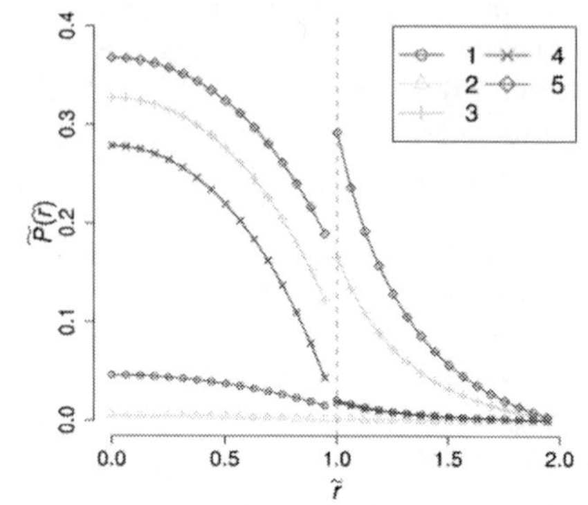

Figure 3. Concentration profiles of the product in the microreactor simulated at the substrate concentration $\widetilde{S}_0 = 1$ and different values of the Thiele module σ^2: 0.1 (2), 1 (1), 10 (3-5), as well as the Biot number β: 0.5 (5), 1 (1-3), 10 (4), the other parameters are as defined in (21). Dashed line shows boundary between the microreactor and the diffusion layer.

One can be seen in Figure 3, that low Thiele modulus values $\sigma < 1$ or high Biot number values, which means that the species passes the Nernst diffusion layer fast, give the concentrations approach to straight line because of linearity of governing equations in the area $r \in (1, 1 + \widetilde{\nu})$. On the other hand, high Thiele modulus values ($\sigma^2 \geq 10$) lead to significant differences in concentration distribution across the outer boundary of the microreactor.

B. Impact of the substrate concentration

To investigate the dependence of the yield factor γ on the substrate concentration $\widetilde{S}_0$, γ was calculated by simulating the microreactor action at three characteristic values of the Thiele module σ^2: 0.1, 1 and 10, as well as at three values of the Biot number β: 0.5, 1 and 10. The effect of the substrate concentration was investigated in a wide range of $\widetilde{S}_0$ values $[10^{-3}, 10^3]$. Calculation results are presented in Figure 4.

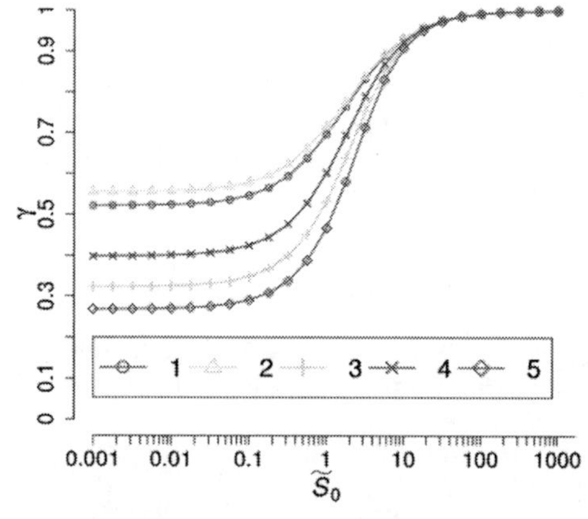

Figure 4. The yield factor γ vs. the substrate concentration $\widetilde{S}$. The notation and values of the parameters are the same as in Figure 3.

One can see (Figure 4) a non-linear impact of the substrate concentration on the yield factor.

As a function of $\widetilde{S}_0$, the yield factor γ is a monotonous increasing function with limit of one. At low concentrations of the substrate $\widetilde{S}_0 < 1$, the yield factor increases with decreasing the Thiele modulus and increasing the Biot number β.

The yield factor γ is, practically, invariant to changes in the substrate concentration $\widetilde{S}_0$ when the Michaelis-Menten kinetics approaches the first order ($\widetilde{S}_0 \ll 1$) or zero order kinetics ($\widetilde{S}_0 \gg 1$). At intermediate values of $\widetilde{S}_0$, when the kinetics changes from the first to zero order, the yield factor γ noticeably increases with increasing the substrate concentration. Increasing the substrance concentration does not influence the increase in the product yield for $\widetilde{S}_0 > 100$.

C. Impact on product rate

Figure 5 presents the dependence of the product emission rate on the thickness of the Nernst diffusion layer. Values of $\bar{V}_{P,0}$ were calculated changing the dimensionless thickness $\widetilde{\nu}$ of the Nernst diffusion layer from $10^{-0.5}$ up to $10^{0.75}$. At lower values of $\widetilde{\nu}$ the two compartment model (14)-(19) reduces to a notably simpler one layer model [22][25]. The reactor behaviour at larger values of $\widetilde{\nu}$ is not so important due to the product emission at very low rate.

As one can see in Figure 5, the rate $\bar{V}_{P,0}$ is a decreasing function of $\widetilde{\nu}$, which confirms a hypothesis about the importance of the Nernst layer for the reactors productivity [25]. The decrease in $\bar{V}_{P,0}$ with increasing $\widetilde{\nu}$ is especially noticeable at relatively high substrate concentrations ($\widetilde{S}_0 = 10$, curve 4), as well as high values of the Thiele module ($\sigma^2 = 2$, curve 2), i.e. in the case of the first order kinetics or when the reactor is under the diffusion control.

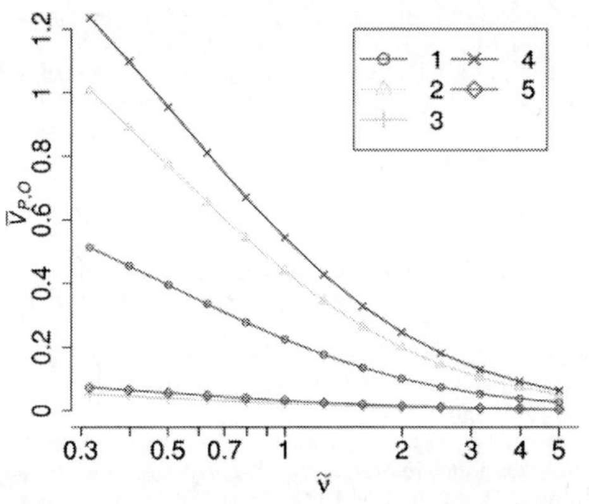

Figure 5. The product emission rate $\bar{V}_{P,0}$ vs. the dimensionless thickness $\widetilde{\nu}$ of the Nernst diffusion layer at $\widetilde{S}_0$: 0.1 (5), 1 (1-3), 10 (4), σ^2: 0.1 (3), 1 (1, 4, 5), 2 (2), the other parameters are as defined in (21).

The impact of the thickness $\widehat{\nu}$ on the product rate $\bar{V}_{P,0}$ gives us tendencies on thickness $\widehat{\nu}$ selection. However, reducing the thickness of Nernst layer is a serious problem. Since microreactor is soaking and mixing to create layer and zero thickness of the diffusion shell can not be achieved [15], the impact of other model parameters on the microreactor efficiency is also important.

D. Impact of the Biot number

To investigate the dependence of the yield factor γ on the Biot number β, the factor γ was calculated at different values of the Thiele module σ^2 (0.1, 1 and 10) and the substrate concentration $\widetilde{S}_0$ (0.1, 1 and 10), changing the Biot number in a range of $[10^{-1}, 10^2]$. The results of the calculations are depicted in Figure 6.

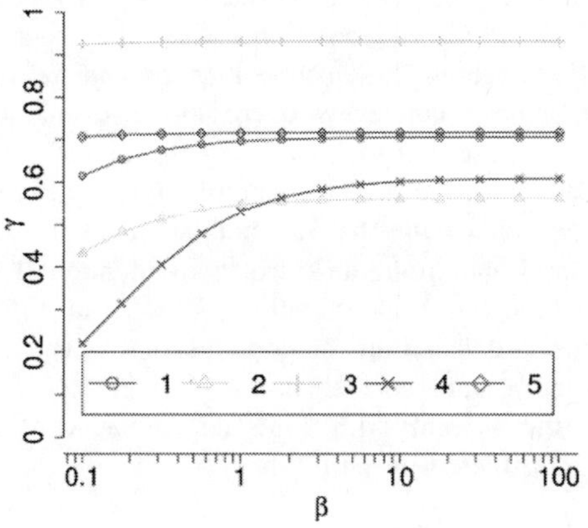

Figure 6. The yield factor γ vs. the Biot number β at $\widetilde{S}_0$: 0.1 (2), 1 (1, 4, 5), 10 (3), σ^2: 0.1 (5), 1 (1-3), 10 (4), the other parameters are as in (21).

Figure 6 shows the product yield γ as an increasing function of the Biot number β. However, the yield factor γ rapidly grows only when β values are relatively small ($\beta < 1$), and the reactor action is under the diffusion control ($\sigma > 1$). The yield factor, practically, does not depend on β when the microreactor acts under the enzyme kinetics control ($\sigma < 1$) or the substrate concentration is high ($\widetilde{S}_0 > 10$). On the other hand, the Nernst diffusion layer may be neglected when the Biot number is higher than around 20 [25][28].

E. Impact of the Thiele Module

The dependence of the yield factor γ on the Thiele modulus was investigated by calculating the factor γ at different values of the Biot number β, as well as of the substrate concentration $\widetilde{S}_0$ and changing modulus σ from 10^{-3} up to 10^5. Figure 6 shows the yield factor γ as a monotonous decreasing function of σ at very different values of β and $\widetilde{S}_0$.

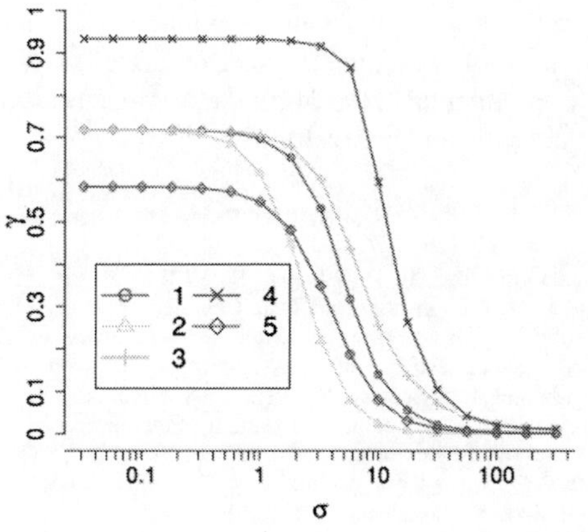

Figure 7. The yield factor γ vs. the Thiele modulus σ at β: 0.1(2), 1(1, 4, 5), 10(3), S_0: 0.1(5), 1(1-3), 10(4), the other parameters are as in (21).

It can be seen in Figure 7 that the yield factor γ, practically, does not depend on σ and approaches to zero when the bioreactor acts notably under the diffusion control ($\sigma > 100$). The yield factor γ is also invariant to changes in the modulus σ when the enzyme kinetics controls the bioreactor action ($\sigma < 0.01$). At mixed conditions when the reactor action is influenced by both the enzyme kinetics and the diffusion, the yield factor γ noticeably decreases with increasing the modulus σ. Figure 7 also shows that the factor γ increases with increasing the substrate concentration (as in Figure 4), as well as when increasing the Biot number β (as in Figure 6).

There are some limitations worth to mention that might be used for the future investigations. First of all, in physical experiments, pellets will not be perfect spheres, which requires modelling more sophisticated domains in 2D and 3D space. Secondly, the system with time dependent characteristics should be considered in the future work.

VI. Conclusion and Future Work

The mathematical model (3)-(8) of the microbioreactor can be successfully used to investigate the behaviour of the catalytic microreactor and to optimize its configuration.

The thickness of the Nernst diffusion layer (shell) noticeably effects the reaction product emission (Figures 5, 6). The production rate $\widetilde{V}_{P,0}$ as well as the yield especially decreases when the thickness is more than two times greater than the radius of the microreactor, $\widetilde{\nu} > 2$, $\beta < 0.5$. This property becomes important when the size of microbioreactors used in industrial applications continuously reduces, while the Nernst diffusion layer is still often neglected.

The yield of the product increases with increasing the substrate concentration (Figure 4) and with decreasing the Biot number (Figure 6). However, an increase in the substrate concentration becomes ineffective when the enzyme reaction apporaches the zero order kinetics $\widetilde{S}_0 > 10$ (Figure 4). The high yield can be achieved only when the enzyme kinetics controls the bioreactor action $\sigma < 1$ (Figure 7).

Such formulation can be useful to find optimal parameters of such biosystem construction [11]. More importantly, it might improve the design and production of microbioreactors.

More precise and sophisticated computational models, implying the multiple reactions of microreactor, as well as the observed experimental data of the microreactors for model validation are still under development.

References

[1] A. Regalado-Mndez, R. R. Romero, R. N. Rangel, and S. Skogestad, "Biodiesel Production in Stirred Tank Chemical Reactors: A Numerical Simulation," in *New Trends in Networking, Computing, E-learning, Systems Sciences, and Engineering*. Springer, 2015, pp. 109–116.

[2] O. N. Ada and D. T. Sponza, "Anaerobic/aerobic treatment of municipal landfill leachate in sequential two-stage up-flow anaerobic sludge blanket reactor (UASB)/completely stirred tank reactor (CSTR) systems," *Process Biochemistry*, vol. 40, no. 2, pp. 895–902, 2005.

[3] A. Miyawaki, S. Taira, and F. Shiraishi, "Performance of continuous stirred-tank reactors connected in series as a photocatalytic reactor system," *Chemical Engineering Journal*, vol. 286, pp. 594–601, 2016.

[4] M. A. Dareioti and M. Kornaros, "Effect of hydraulic retention time (HRT) on the anaerobic co-digestion of agro-industrial wastes in a two-stage CSTR system," *Bioresource Technology*, vol. 167, pp. 407–415, 2014.

[5] A. J. Straathof and P. Adlercreutz, *Applied Biocatalysis*. CRC Press, 2000.

[6] P. M. Doran, *Bioprocess Engineering Principles*. Academic Press, 1995.

[7] J. Villadsen, J. Nielsen, and G. Liden, *Bioreaction Engineering Principles*. Dordrecht: Springer, 2011.

[8] S. K. Dubey, A. Pandey, and R. S. Sangwan, *Current Developments in Biotechnology and Bioengineering: Crop Modification, Nutrition, and Food Production*. Elsevier, 2016.

[9] J. W. Wong, R. D. Tyagi, and A. Pandey, *Current Developments in Biotechnology and Bioengineering: Solid Waste Management*. Elsevier, 2016.

[10] A. Konti, D. Mamma, D. G. Hatzinikolaou, and D. Kekos, "3-Chloro-1, 2-propanediol biodegradation by Ca-alginate immobilized Pseudomonas putida DSM 437 cells applying different processes: mass transfer effects," *Bioprocess and Biosystems Engineering*, vol. 39, no. 10, pp. 1597–1609, 2016.

[11] D. Cacaval, A. C. Blaga, and A.-I. Galaction, "Diffusional effects on anaerobic biodegradation of pyridine in a stationary basket bioreactor with immobilized Bacillus spp. cells," *Environmental Technology*, pp. 1–13, 2017.

[12] R. Karande, A. Schmid, and K. Buehler, "Applications of multiphasic microreactors for biocatalytic reactions," *Organic Process Research & Development*, vol. 20, no. 2, pp. 361–370, 2016.

[13] F. M. Pereira and S. C. Oliveira, "Occurrence of dead core in catalytic particles containing immobilized enzymes: analysis for the michaelis–menten kinetics and assessment of numerical methods," *Bioprocess and Biosystems Engineering*, vol. 39, no. 11, pp. 1717–1727, 2016.

[14] M. B. Kerby, R. S. Legge, and A. Tripathi, "Measurements of kinetic parameters in a microfluidic reactor," *Analytical Chemistry*, vol. 78, no. 24, pp. 8273–8280, 2006.

[15] J. Wang, *Analytical Electrochemistry*, 3rd ed. Joboken, New Jersey: John Wiley & Sons, 2006.

[16] R. Baronas, F. Ivanauskas, and J. Kulys, *Mathematical Modeling of Biosensors*. Dordrecht: Springer, 2010.

[17] D. Britz and J. Strutwolf, *Digital Simulation in Electrochemistry*, 4th ed., ser. Monographs in Electrochemistry. Springer, 2016.

[18] M. F. Chaplin and C. Bucke, "The large-scale use of enzymes in solution," *Enzyme Technology*, pp. 138–166, 1990.

[19] H. Gutfreund, *Kinetics for the Life Sciences*. Cambridge: Cambridge University Press, 1995.

[20] L. A. Segel and M. Slemrod, "The quasi-steady-state assumption: a case study in perturbation," *SIAM Review*, vol. 31, no. 3, pp. 446–477, 1989.

[21] M. Velkovsky, R. Snider, D. E. Cliffel, and J. P. Wikswo, "Modeling the measurements of cellular fluxes in microbioreactor devices using thin enzyme electrodes," *Journal of Mathematical Chemistry*, vol. 49, no. 1, pp. 251–275, 2011.

[22] T. Schulmeister, "Mathematical modelling of the dynamic behaviour of amperometric enzyme electrodes," *Selective Electrode Reviews*, vol. 12, no. 2, pp. 203–260, 1990.

[23] D. J. Fink, T. Na, and J. S. Schultz, "Effectiveness factor calculations for immobilized enzyme catalysts," *Biotechnology and Bioengineering*, vol. 15, no. 5, pp. 879–888, 1973.

[24] R. Aris, *Mathematical Modeling: a Chemical Engineer's Perspective*. Academic Press, 1999, vol. 1.

[25] M. E. Davis and R. J. Davis, *Fundamentals of Chemical Reaction Engineering*. New York: MGraw-Hill, 2003.

[26] D. A. Edwards, B. Goldstein, and D. S. Cohen, "Transport effects on surface-volume biological reactions," *Journal of Mathematical Biology*, vol. 39, no. 6, pp. 533–561, 1999.

[27] W. T. Vetterling, *Numerical Recipes Example Book (C++): The Art of Scientific Computing*. Cambridge University Press, 2002.

[28] R. Baronas, "Nonlinear effects of diffusion limitations on the response andsensitivity of amperometric biosensors," *Electrochimica Acta*, vol. 240, pp. 399–407, 2016.

Simulation Improves Material Handling in General Assembly

Improvement of Material Flow, Work Apportionment, and Equipment Usage

Julio Pérez, Gabriel Carreño, Ozge Çivit
Simulation Analysis
PMC
Dearborn, Michigan, USA
{e-mail: jperez, gcarreno, ocivit}@pmcorp.com

Edward J. Williams
Business Analytics, College of Business
University of Michigan - Dearborn
Dearborn, Michigan, USA
e-mail: williame@umich.edu

***Abstract*—Discrete-event process simulation has long since achieved distinction as a powerful tool for the improvement of all aspects of manufacturing operations, including but not limited to equipment selection, maintenance policies, inventory management, buffer sizing and location, production scheduling, and work flow. The study documented here used simulation to analyze and improve the material handling operations responsible for delivering raw material to the line and taking finished product away for subsequent shipment. The improvements addressed important metrics such as reliability of supply, timeliness of supply, equipment utilization, worker utilization, and cost.**

Keywords- Material Handling; Material Flow; Assembly; Manufacturing; Discrete-Event Process Simulation.

I. Introduction

Historically, the first highly important commercial application of discrete-event simulation modelling was manufacturing operations [1]. Along with more recent and current simulation applications such as call centers [2], health care delivery [3], supply chains [4], retail stores [5], urban transport [6], and others, manufacturing remains a highly important application area.

In this paper, we document the successful use of simulation to analyze and improve material handling operations in the context of a large and complex manufacturing operation. This manufacturing operation undertakes the assembly of motor vehicles. The scope of the study included the assembly lines themselves, docks, material handling equipment (e.g., fork trucks and tuggers), the employees responsible for material-handling work, and the design of workflow. The client managers and engineers sought improvement of vital performance metrics such as timeliness and reliability of deliveries, worker and equipment utilization, inventory levels, and aggregate costs (labor, equipment, and operations). Simulation studies such as this one are often very useful for researchers and practicing industrial engineers seeking productivity improvements not only in manufacturing operations, but also in warehouses [7] and in shipping terminals such as those in railroad freight yards [8] and oceangoing ports.

The organization of this paper is as follows: Section II provides an overview of the manufacturing and material-handling operations. Next, in Section III, we provide a summary of operational data required to build, verify, and validate the model, with commentary on methods of collecting those data. The following Section IV describes the building, verification, and validation of the simulation model. Next, in Section V, we describe the execution of the model and summarize the conclusions drawn from that experimentation. We conclude, in Section VI, by describing our recommendations to the client company, along with indications for likely future work.

II. Overview of Operations

The manufacturing plant in question fabricates automotive vehicle bodies; indeed, it is referred to colloquially as a "body shop." As such, it has many subassembly lines and therefore extensive material-handling requirements. This body shop has supply docks on both its east side (having four bay doors) and its west side (having two bay doors). These docks collectively contain three production hours' worth of inventory, comprising many (hundreds) of small lot parts, bulk parts, and unique part types. As the study began, the east side was served by six tuggers and four fork lift trucks; the west side, by five tuggers and three fork lift trucks. Dolly preparation occurs in front of the dock receiving doors, and empty dollies are subsequently returned to these dolly preparation areas.

At this plant, manufacturing operations were chronically plagued by tardy deliveries (idling expensive machines and highly paid production workers), frequent congestion of the material-handling equipment (the tuggers and fork lift trucks) in various aisles (leading to increased fuel costs and downtimes for battery recharging), and, derivatively, increased inventory levels and hence costs (consisting of both excessive accumulation of raw materials at the receiving docks and tardy delivery of finished goods to outgoing shipping docks, each of which worsened the client company's cash flow position). Motivated by these difficulties, the client company's engineers and managers requested an extensive consultation using the methods of industrial engineering. As is typically the case, the analytical methods of industrial engineering (e.g., process simulation, work flow analysis, ergonomics, value stream mapping, etc.) collaborated synergistically to provide suggestions for process and operational improvements.

Specifically, the objectives of this simulation project, defined collaboratively by plant managers, plant engineers, and the consultant's analysts, were to:

- Verify and update the existing material data for the current status of operations
- Update the "Plan for Every Part" (PFEP), the in-plant logistics database); this proprietary database comprises information about part storage locations, containers and racks used in storage, and in-plant replenishment systems
- Perform a material flow study to analyze the receiving of parts, staging of parts, delivery of parts (or containers there) to the assembly lines, and shipment of finished product
- Determine current-state material handling requirements
- Undertake a material flow analysis.

Having defined these objectives, the client company and the consultants then agreed on a division of responsibilities, most particularly including: providing complete documentation of plant operations; collection of data; analysis of data; model construction, verification, and validation; analysis of results, and presentation and documentation of results.

III. DATA COLLECTION AND ANALYSIS

Data collection began with confirmation of these basic assumptions, as provided by client engineers and managers:

- 1290 available minutes of work per calendar day
- Workers' walking speed 4.8 feet/second (English units used throughout study)
- 8.8 feet/second maximum fork truck speed and maximum tugger speed
- 2.28 feet/second/second fork truck and tugger acceleration (and matching deceleration)
- 626 unique part types in the PFEP
- 133 distinct delivery locations alongside the assembly lines
- 423 distinct locations for containers to be stored immediately after unloading from a truck

A PFEP, as mentioned in the previous section, was provided by the client company; each of these comprised a part description (sufficient to uniquely identify each part), storage location, location(s) of usage, daily volume required at these locations, container type, density, and physical dimensions. Using the numerous and powerful library of Microsoft Excel® functions – particularly those operating on text strings -- the consultant team sorted and filtered these data in various ways in search of errors in the client's originally supplied PFEP. Several such errors – primarily due to volatile data, which routinely become out-of-date – were called to the attention of client engineers. Therefore, the simulation project could and did begin with currently correct and audited data comprising details pertinent to all parts used in the manufacturing operations. An example subset of these data appears in the Appendix as Table 1.

Likewise, these initial observations of current plant operations determined the precise apportionment of material-handling tasks between tuggers and fork trucks, confirmed the carrying capacities of both, and mapped their routes through all parts of the operation. For the purpose of model run initialization, the assumption of three hours' initial inventory at the docks was made. For the tuggers, loading time of dollies was 29 seconds and unloading time was 47 seconds. For the fork trucks, both load and unload times were calculated based on the location and dimensions of the containers being loaded or unloaded. Consultant engineers travelled to the plant site for direct observation; their observation and data collection confirmed, with minor amendments agreed to by the client, for these and other detailed data items. In view of extensive worker involvement in the material-handling operations (as contrasted with extensively automated work tasks), great care was taken, largely by unobtrusive observation methods, to guard against the Hawthorne effect [9]. Given this detailed overview of operational procedures, it will be readily appreciated that (a) guarding against the Hawthorne effect was vitally important and (b) data collection (as opposed to model construction) was on the project critical path [10]. For the purposes of this study, no stochastic variation was incorporated in the values quoted above, in view of the "capacity planning" objective of the study.

IV. MODEL CONSTRUCTION, VERIFICATION, AND VALIDATION

After considerable discussion, the client managers and engineers, jointly with the consultants, decided on the use of Flow Planner®, which works within and compatibly with the well-known AutoCAD® tools, as an analytical software tool highly appropriate for this project. This software, like many of its worthy competitors [11], provides ease of use, high analytical power, the ability to analyse multiple alternatives, and extensive graphics and animation. The tool provides all of these capabilities in the context of manufacturing simulation. As such, it represents an advance over similar software tools often used for projects, such as this one, which aim to improve efficiency via manufacturing plant design [12]. A relatively recent application of Flow Planner® is documented in [13].

After visually analysing the material flow throughout the facility, the consultants worked with client engineers and plant operations supervisors to create flow diagrams. Material-handling methods (fork truck, tugger, or manual transport by an operator) varied with the part types, and each part flow was identified and checked based on both client-supplied data and the consultants' observations. Next, using information from the PFEP and the newly constructed flow diagrams, the consultants created a large Microsoft Excel® comma-separated-variable (".csv") file, as required by Flow Planner®. Much of the actual construction of this file involved repetitive and tedious tasks. Therefore, the consultants decided to, in large measure, automate it by investment of time in the creation of and debugging of a macro written in Visual Basic for Applications (VBA) [14]. Versus completely manual operations, the consultant team estimated that development of the macro returned a 5:1 benefit ratio of time required, and also greatly reduced the risk of "clerical" errors in organization of the data. A separate Microsoft

Excel® workbook, incorporating multiple worksheets, contained additional information of products, their method of transport, and their locations of storage and use.

Explicit verification and validation steps undertaken by the modeling engineers included the following [15]:

- Inserting one entity into the model and following it step-by-step (a "trace").
- Provisionally removing all randomness from the model and checking results against hand computations.
- Performing directional analysis – e.g., when the rate at which entities enter the model is increased, the lengths of queues must either remain the same or increase.
- Ensuring the client engineers and managers watched the animation and concurred in its representation of current operations.
- Building the model incrementally with the precautions above successfully performed upon the completion of each increment, before proceeding to model the next segment of the system.

After running Flow Planner®, the consultants collected the calculated parts-movement distances. Using these distances, loading and unloading times, and speed of transport method used, the consultants built a Microsoft Excel® file calculating expected time for all parts transport for all point pairs (A,B), considering "A" as the point of storage and "B" as a point of use. Similar calculations were performed for transport return trips "running empty." Then, with available work time per day being readily available, the utilizations of each class of transport equipment were calculated. Furthermore, these utilizations were readily subdivided into "definitely value-added" (transporting parts to where they were needed) and "inevitably necessary" (returning empty for another load). All these results were verified and validated against client data and experience.

V. RESULTS AND CONCLUSIONS

Many of the results of this study were most usefully visualized in the output graphics routinely provided by the Flow Planner® software. For example, Figure 1 in the Appendix depicts "straight-flow" aggregate data. In this figure, a particular line color represents an assignment of the vehicle to a plant zone (west, east, or LRS [a nickname for the stamping area, the origin of this nickname would reveal confidential information]). Straight flow paths are typically the best for viewing, understanding, and verifying where flows originate from and travel to, as they (mythically) go straight from the origin to the destination regardless of obstacles. By contrast, Figure 2 (Appendix), derived from the same input data as Figure 1, represents the part transport flows grouped by aisle. These flows are geometrically realistic, inasmuch as the vehicles do not "magically" penetrate physical obstacles. Different colors continue to represent vehicles assigned to different zones. This representation is superior for evaluating actual travel distances, travel paths, and aisle congestion, since they consider actual routes from the origin to the destination using user-defined aisles. Additional graphs (e.g., Figure 3, Appendix) and numerical output reports captured key performance metrics. For example, Figure 3 summarized tugger utilization by plant zone (west, east, or LRS). At this stage of the project, vehicle travel time performance metrics are not yet subdivided into travel time carrying parts versus "returning empty."

From the client's viewpoint, the three major revelations of this simulation study were:

- Due to the large numbers of parts (and their high variety) stored in the dock and the central market area (CMA), actually a centralized storage area, congestion in both areas is severe and obtrusively significant.
- The workload is well balanced on the dock areas (80-85%). However, the stamping fork trucks' traveling time was unduly high compared with the time that they spend loading and unloading, due to the distances between the stamping presses, CMA and the secondary storage areas (95%).
- With respect to the tuggers from both dock areas that served the lines, analysis (using the straight flow study) of the material flows from the respective dock area to the consumption point (Using LOCation, abbreviated "ULOC") identified the parts "guilty of" requiring the tuggers to travel long distances; these parts were stored in a conspicuously inappropriate area.

Accordingly, two recommendations were made to the client:

After identifying some of the parts that were making the tuggers travel long distances from the origin to the using locations (#1 above), the consultants recommended that the client transfer storage of eight specific parts from the west dock location to the east dock location, and one specific part from the east dock location to the west dock location. The client implemented this change, causing utilization of the vehicles assigned to the west zone to fall from 73.1% utilization to 66.4% utilization.

As a follow-up to the success of recommendation #1, the client was advised to reduce the total number of vehicles assigned to the east area from nine to seven, and in the west area from five to four. After this removal of three vehicles at first seemed excessive (reducing the total number of vehicles from fourteen to eleven), the vehicles were not over-utilized. After the client made this second change (hence saving significant labor and operations costs) vehicles assigned to the east area were utilized 87.5% and in the west area 83.1%, while still meeting delivery demands. Furthermore, for small lots, three vehicles were originally assigned to three continuous routes. After analysis of consumption patterns for these small lots within the ULOC, which was their typical destination for consumption, the consultant engineers created various scenarios involving only two routes, not three. Experimentation with the model, again using FlowPlanner®, revealed that the three routes could be profitably coalesced into two routes, using only two vehicles. The software readily recalculated the utilization of the two tuggers using these two new routes, based on the volume of parts being delivered to their respective ULOCs from their respective Dock

LOCations, (DLOC) and the pickup of empty containers then being returned to their Empty container LOCation (ELOC). Figure 4 in the Appendix shows this spatial analysis from the vantage point of the client. In this figure, the yellow circle delimits the workspace of the first tugger handling small lots. The two green circles delimit the delivery operations of the second tugger handling small lots; this tugger typically serves each of the two delimited areas alternately. The client also made this recommended change, and – as the model predicted – delivery demand for these small parts was still met, with new tugger utilizations as shown in Figure 5 (Appendix). As is to be expected, the first of these tuggers (serving the two areas delimited in green) has a higher percentage of load-&-unload time, a higher percentage of travel time, and hence a lower percentage of idle time, all relative to the second tugger serving only one area (delimited in yellow). This recommendation, the culmination of studying several proposed scenarios for using two instead of three tuggers, came gratifyingly close to equalizing the utilizations of the two remaining tuggers.

VI. Planned and Anticipated Future Analyses

Aside from the quantitative financial benefits of this study, a significant qualitative benefit is the new understanding and appreciation, among the client engineers and managers, of the power of simulation. Since the enterprise is highly volatile, ongoing studies are very likely, and will be further refined. For example performance metrics on vehicles will be expanded to obtain travel distances and times "traveling empty" versus "traveling loaded," plus statistics on average, maximum, and minimum loads carried, both in aggregate and subdivided by part type. The model as currently implemented contains no provision for downtime of the material-handling equipment. Future work will include adding plausible downtimes to assist in the development of various contingency plans. Further, the graphical aids to client understanding (as exemplified by Figures 1, 2, and 4 in this paper) can be upgraded to two- or three-dimensional real-time animations.

Acknowledgments

The authors most gratefully acknowledge help, advice, and support graciously provided by consultant colleagues, client engineers and managers, and support personnel at Proplanner, the vendor of the Flow Planner® software. Furthermore, criticisms from anonymous referees have helped the authors greatly improve the organization and clarity of the paper.

References

[1] S. Miller and D. Pegden, "Introduction to manufacturing simulation," Proceedings of the 2000 Winter Simulation Conference, Volume 1, eds. J. A. Joines, R. R. Barton, K. Kang, and P. A. Fishwick, 63-66, 2000.

[2] B. Mathew and M. K. Nambiar, "A tutorial on modelling call centres using discrete event simulation," in Proceedings of the 27th European Conference on Modelling and Simulation, eds. W. Rekdalsbakken, R. T. Bye, and H. Zhang, 315-321, 2013.

[3] Z. S-Y. Wong, A. C-H. Lit, and S-Y. Leung, "A discrete-event simulation study for emergency room capacity management in a Hong Kong hospital," Proceedings of the 2016 Winter Simulation Conference, eds. T. M. K. Roeder, P. I. Frazier, R. Szechtman, E. Zhou, T. Huschka, and S. E. Chick, 1970-1981, 2016.

[4] A. E. Azab and A. B. Eltawil, "A simulation based study of the effect of truck arrival patterns on truck turn time in container terminals," Proceedings of the 30th European Conference on Modelling and Simulation, eds. T. Claus, F. Herrmann, M. Manitz, and O. Rose, 80-66, 2016.

[5] J. W. Gruber, R. Smiddy, J. M. Watson, and E. J. Williams, "Simulation helps local grocery store compete effectively against large chains," Fifth International Conference on Industrial Engineering and Operations Management 2421-2424, 2015.

[6] I. Garcia, G. Gutiérrez, and R. Moreno, "Simulation model for the redesign of the Spanish combined rail transport network," Proceedings of the 13th European Simulation Symposium, eds. N. Giambiasi and C. Frydman, 402-404, 2001.

[7] S. Takakuwa, "Efficient module-based modeling for a large-scale AS/RS-AGV system," Proceedings of the 1996 Winter Simulation Conference, eds. J. M. Charnes, D. J. Morrice, D. T. Brunner, and J. J. Swain, 1141-1148, 1996.

[8] I. García, Gil Gutiérrez, and Raúl Moreno, "Simulation of an Intermodal Rail Freight Terminal," Proceedings of the 13th European Simulation Symposium, eds. N. Giambiasi and C. Frydman, 399-401, 2001.

[9] G. Wickstrom and T. Bendix, "The 'Hawthorne Effect'--what did the original Hawthorne studies actually show?," Scandinavian Journal of Work, Environment & Health (26,4), 363–367, 2000.

[10] M. A. Centeno, "An introduction to simulation modeling," Proceedings of the 1996 Winter Simulation Conference, eds. J. M. Charnes, D. J. Morrice, D. T. Brunner, and J. J. Swain, 15-22, 1996.

[11] L. M. S Dias, A. A. C. Vieira, G. A. B. Pereira, and J. A. Oliviera, "Discrete simulation software ranking – a top list of the worldwide most popular and used tools," Proceedings of the 2016 Winter Simulation Conference, eds. T. M. K. Roeder, P. I. Frazier, R. Szechtman, E. Zhou, T. Huschka, and S. E. Chick, 1060-1071, 2016.

[12] D. P. Sly, "Plant design for efficiency using AutoCAD and FactoryFLOW," Proceedings of the 1995 Winter Simulation Conference, eds. C. Alexopoulos, K. Kang, W. R. Lilegdon, and D. Goldsman, 437-444, 1995.

[13] D. P. Sly, "Handling material problems as they arise," Cutting Tool Engineering (63,3):30, 2011.

[14] S. C. Albright, "VBA for modelers: Developing decision support systems with Microsoft Office Excel, 5th edition. Boston, Massachusetts: Cengage Learning, 2015.

[15] R. G. Sargent, " Verification, validation, and acccreditation of simulation models," Proceedings of the 2000 Winter Simulation Conference, vol. 1, 50-59, 2000.

APPENDIX

TABLE I: SUBSET OF PARTS-ROUTING DATA AS INPUT INTO MODEL FROM MICROSOFT EXCEL®.

*ROUTINGS (	User Defined	Part	Flow%	From	Method	Container	Containers/Trip	Parts/Container	To
1	Dolly Prep to ULOC	20827437	100	Dolly Prep-WEST	Tugger-WEST	AHB55997	2	100	11AD050
1	ULOC to Dolly Prep	20827437	100	11AD050	Tugger-WEST	AHB55997	2	100	Dolly Prep-WEST
2	Dolly Prep to ULOC	20827436	100	Dolly Prep-WEST	Tugger-WEST	AHB55999	2	62	11BH008
2	ULOC to Dolly Prep	20827436	100	11BH008	Tugger-WEST	AHB55999	2	62	Dolly Prep-WEST
3	Dolly Prep to ULOC	20936339	100	Dolly Prep-WEST	Tugger-WEST	28850	2	50	11BP010L
3	ULOC to Dolly Prep	20936339	100	11BP010L	Tugger-WEST	28850	2	50	Dolly Prep-WEST
4	Dolly Prep to ULOC	23458873	100	Dolly Prep-WEST	Tugger-WEST	AHB61142	2	24	11BP010L
4	ULOC to Dolly Prep	23458873	100	11BP010L	Tugger-WEST	AHB61142	2	24	Dolly Prep-WEST
5	Dolly Prep to ULOC	20936340	100	Dolly Prep-WEST	Tugger-WEST	28850	2	50	11BP010R
5	ULOC to Dolly Prep	20936340	100	11BP010R	Tugger-WEST	28850	2	50	Dolly Prep-WEST
6	Dolly Prep to ULOC	23458872	100	Dolly Prep-WEST	Tugger-WEST	AHB61142	2	24	11BP010R
6	ULOC to Dolly Prep	23458872	100	11BP010R	Tugger-WEST	AHB61142	2	24	Dolly Prep-WEST
7	Dolly Prep to ULOC	25854019	100	Dolly Prep-WEST	Tugger-WEST	AHB55998	2	31	11CM010
7	ULOC to Dolly Prep	25854019	100	11CM010	Tugger-WEST	AHB55998	2	31	Dolly Prep-WEST
8	Dolly Prep to ULOC	20934412	100	Dolly Prep-WEST	Tugger-WEST	28850	2	250	11FA005L
8	ULOC to Dolly Prep	20934412	100	11FA005L	Tugger-WEST	28850	2	250	Dolly Prep-WEST
9	Dolly Prep to ULOC	20934414	100	Dolly Prep-WEST	Tugger-WEST	28850	2	250	11FA005L
9	ULOC to Dolly Prep	20934414	100	11FA005L	Tugger-WEST	28850	2	250	Dolly Prep-WEST
10	Dolly Prep to ULOC	20934416	100	Dolly Prep-WEST	Tugger-WEST	28850	2	500	11FA005L
10	ULOC to Dolly Prep	20934416	100	11FA005L	Tugger-WEST	28850	2	500	Dolly Prep-WEST
11	Dolly Prep to ULOC	20934413	100	Dolly Prep-WEST	Tugger-WEST	28850	2	250	11FA005R
11	ULOC to Dolly Prep	20934413	100	11FA005R	Tugger-WEST	28850	2	250	Dolly Prep-WEST
12	Dolly Prep to ULOC	20934415	100	Dolly Prep-WEST	Tugger-WEST	28850	2	250	11FA005R
12	ULOC to Dolly Prep	20934415	100	11FA005R	Tugger-WEST	28850	2	250	Dolly Prep-WEST

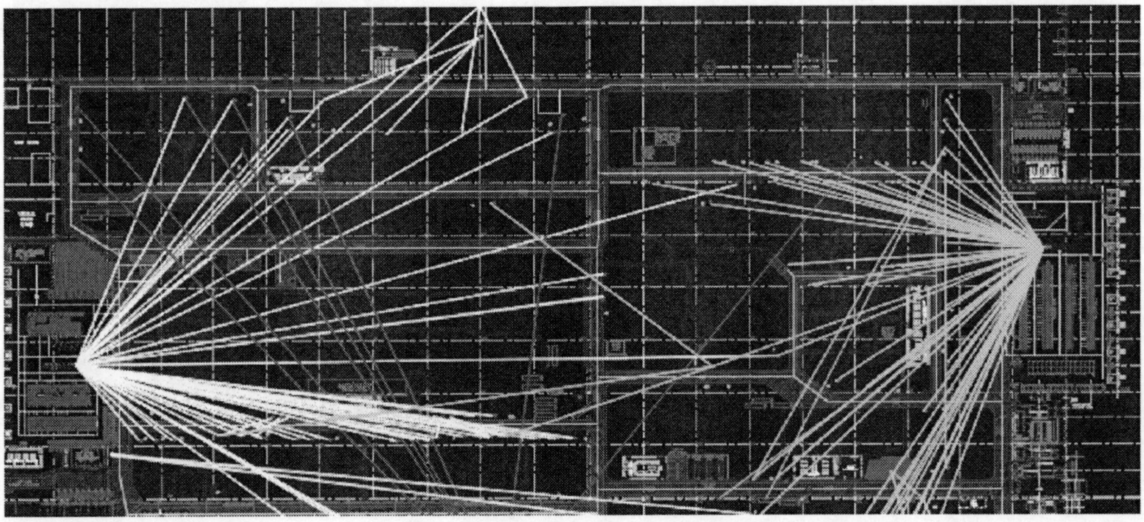

Figure 1. Straight Flow Point-to-Point Study.

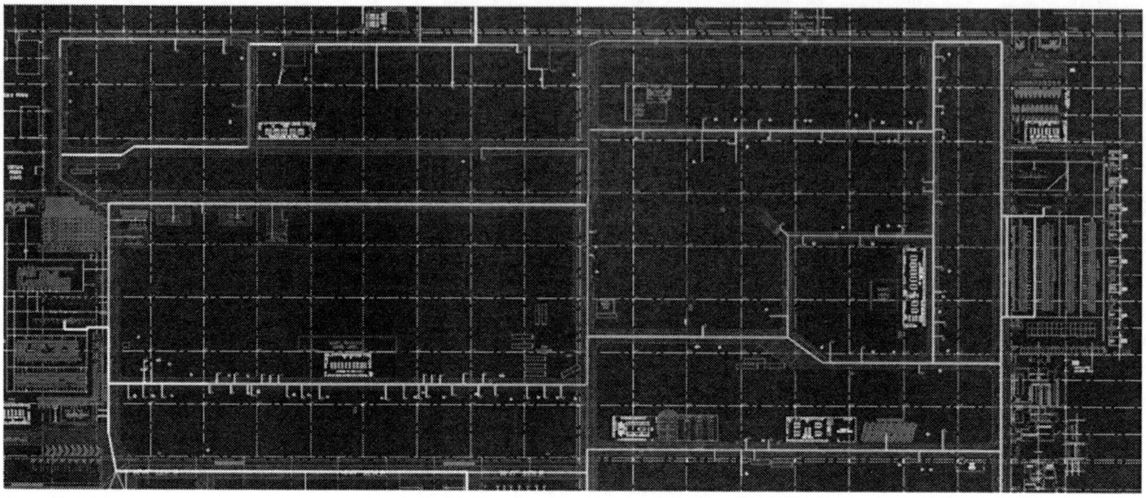

Figure 2. Vehicle Travel along Aisles.

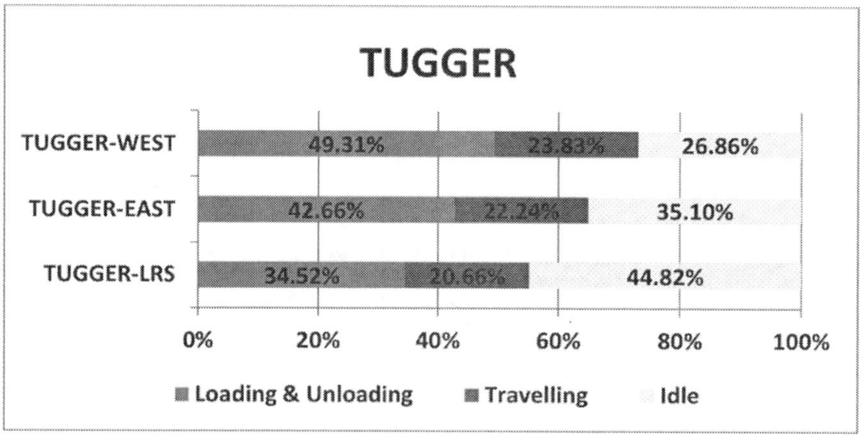

Figure 3. Tugger Utilization by Plant Zone.

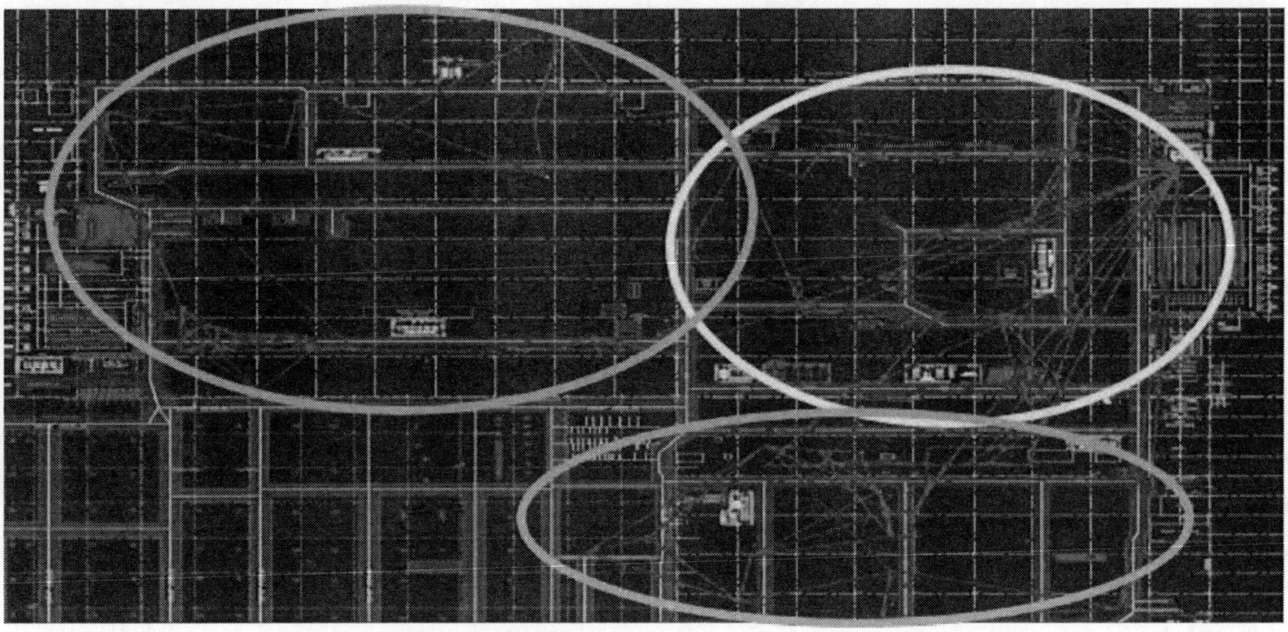

Figure 4. Scope of Operations of the "Coalesced" Small-Lot Tuggers

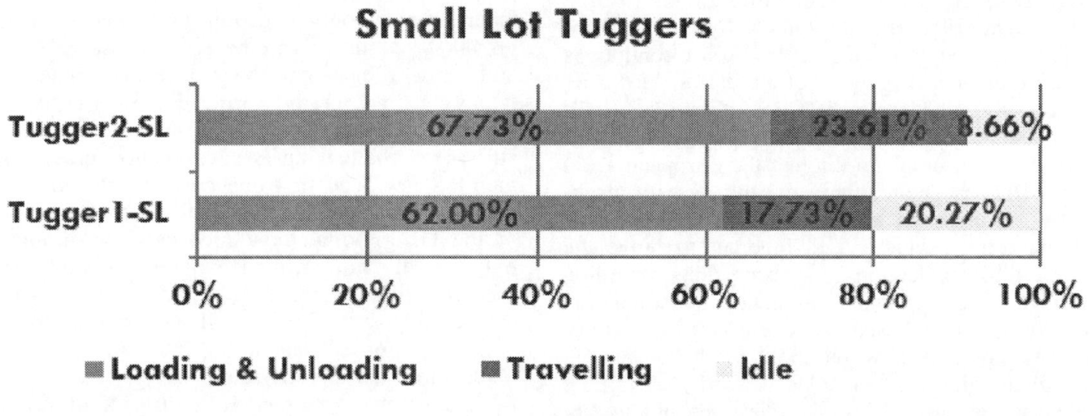

Figure 5. Small Tugger Utilization

Enhancing Formal Proofs of Network Protocols for Transport Systems using Discrete Event Simulation

Emna Chebbi
Université
du Littoral Cote d'Opale
Email: chebbi@univ-littoral.fr

Patrick Sondi
Université
du Littoral Cote d'Opale
Email: sondi@univ-littoral.fr

Eric Ramat
Université
du Littoral Cote d'Opale
Email: ramat@univ-littoral.fr

***Abstract*—This work proposes a methodology to increase the amount of proven properties of an intelligent transportation system component. A formal tool based on Event-B is used to build a first model of the component and to generate automatically the theorems. Then the model, the theorems and the residual proof obligations (RPO) are incorporated in a discrete event simulation in order to solve interactively some RPO based on simulation results. This paper describes the idea and the challenging issues.**

Keywords–Formal Modeling, Simulation, Routing Protocol, Security, Intelligent Transportation Systems.

I. INTRODUCTION

WIRELESS communications technologies are one of the key factors in the development of Intelligent Transportation Systems (ITS). Early deployed in the European Rail Traffic Management System (ERTMS), the Global System for Mobile communications Railway (GSM-R) allows a continuous location and movement management of the trains. However, before GSM-R was adopted in ERTMS, it had to fulfill several specific requirements regarding notably the control-command processes, materialized through the European Train Control System (ETCS) applications, and the security mechanisms, achieved through the Euroradio protocol. While formal methods have been widely used in order to prove the correctness of ETCS applications, the evaluations regarding the GSM-R have been performed essentially by simulation [1] and real-world testing based on key performance indicators. The same trend is now observed in the evaluation of wireless technologies for vehicular networks (VANET), where the evaluations regarding the wireless technology are mostly conducted through simulation and testings, considering mainly performance issues instead of proven properties. The convergence of the main network architectures to the all-IP (Internet Protocol) is pushing both railway operators and car manufacturers to evolve from dedicated infrastructures to a global network connecting all the communicating objects in the smart city. The Internet protocols, initially designed for best-effort applications, are now confronted to the requirements of application domains that are traditionally more sensitive such as tactical units, e-health, and intelligent transport systems. Given the variety of the requirements that could be imposed by such applications, rapid and efficient tools for validating and evaluating custom domain-specific protocols are suitable at the earliest stages of their design. Based on the formal models of the custom protocols designed on top of IP for managing the communications, the research work announced in this paper aims at developing a methodology for obtaining through simulation, not only performance indicators, but also additional formal proofs of some properties attached to both the designed protocols and the entire transport system itself, despite the impairments of the wireless technology.

II. RELATED WORK

The design of communication protocols usually relies on a functional model constructed according to the needs of the system. In ITS, the functionalities mainly studied include self-organizing and routing [2], safety and reliability, quality of service, and security. Regarding vehicular networks, several studies have focused on security issues [3]. The increasing number of cyber-attacks over vehicular networks, mainly exploiting protocols weaknesses, have emphasized the need of having robust communications protocols with guaranteed and proven properties regarding security. Several formal models and methodologies have been developed to address that issue, notably in [4] for the verification of security properties of VANET routing protocols. Despite these efforts, there are still some challenging issues, notably the two following, to mention few. The first one concerns the joint evaluation of the components modeled formally with the other components of the ITS. Formal tools such as Event-B allow evaluating only formal model, while simulation tools offer the possibility of connecting heterogeneous models and devices in a single evaluation process. The second one concerns completeness and scalability: formal tools allow animating a limited number of objects in order to verify the behavior of a system in presence of interactions. However, it is difficult to verify large-scale and timed systems. To address this problem, Yacoub and al [5] proposed an approach in order to integrate discrete-event simulation in formal methods. They improved existing model-checking tools by combining them with DEVS simulation in order to allow them detecting the errors that were not previously spotted, especially on timed systems. Though it is a significant step in the resolution of the second issue mentioned previously, it does not address the first.

III. RESEARCH IDEA AND PRELIMINARY WORK

Multi-modeling is a paradigm that allows connecting heterogeneous models, individually based on a different formalism, in a single simulation. DEVS-based multi-modeling has been applied successfully in several simulation based analysis of complex system. Instead of introducing DEVS simulation mechanisms in a formal tool as done in [5], the research idea

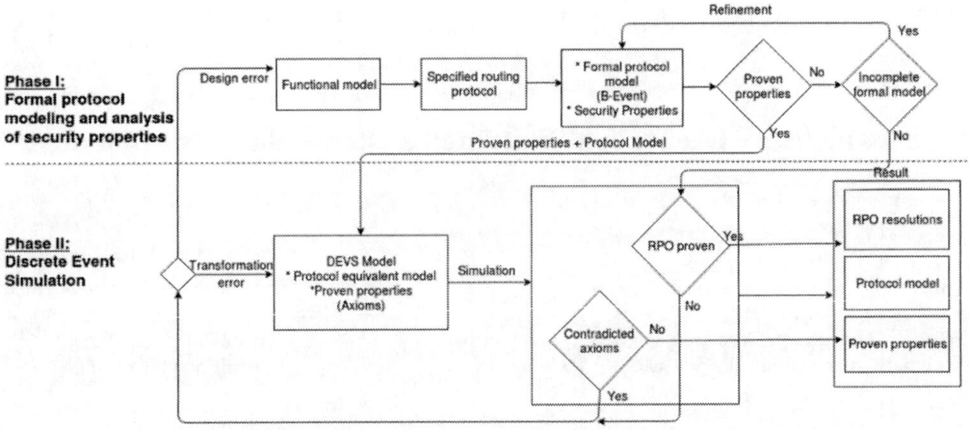

Figure 1. Main steps of a methodology for enhancing the proofs on the properties of an ITS component using Event-B and DEVS

proposed in this work aim at introducing formal models in a multi-modeling development process. In this way, both the components that are modeled with formal methods and the others will be connected in a single simulation of the entire ITS by the mean of multi-modeling. Though this approach would solve the two main issues mentioned in the previous section, it implies three main problems that we propose to solve in our research work:

- problem 1: how the components modeled with a formal tool will be integrated in a ITS multi-modeling?
- problem 2: formal tools include an automatic prover, how multi-modeling approach can manage this?
- problem 3: how multi-modeling simulation could enhance the proofs of the ITS components properties?

Figure 1 describes two major phases of the proposed approach when applied using a formal modeling tool, namely Event-B, and a multi-modeling simulation environment based on DEVS. An ad hoc routing protocol [2], CBL (Chain-Branch-Leaf) designed for vehicular networks is used for illustrating the methodology. The overall operation is to formally model CBL with an Event-B tool in order to prove some of its properties related to security. The automatic prover of the Event-B tool is used in order to build this first set of proven properties, which would solve the problem 2. The next step is to build a DEVS model of CBL that can be guaranteed as rigorously equivalent to the its formal model in the Event-B too. For example, it can be stated that no other assumptions than those used as axioms and those proven as theorem in the formal model can be added in the simulation model. The contributions at this step could solve the problem 1. One key–point is to specify how the proven properties could be taken into account in the simulation model (assumptions, choices, constraints, or parameters ?). With formal modeling through a formalism like Event-B, processes can be executed on the models in order to obtain a list of proven properties that will be guaranteed all the time, and another list containing residual proof obligations (RPO). A former work analyzing a routing protocol with Event-B [6] suggested to discharge the proof obligations interactively. The idea is to find a way to represent each residual proof obligation as a list of queries in DEVS simulation and that could be satisfied using simulation results. Instead of a human agent, the simulation plays the role of the expert. Provided that no other automatic proof is needed between all the different queries related to a residual proof obligation and that all of them are satisfied by the simulation results, the RPO could become a theorem. This could be an answer to the question posed in problem 3. Currently, we are developing a formal model of CBL with Event-B. Specific mechanisms related to security are being introduced in order to verify formally the properties related to mutual authentication between the cluster heads (branch nodes) and their cluster members (leaf nodes). An equivalent model is being developed in a DEVS multi-modeling framework in order to evaluate the efficiency of the first theoretic developments concerning the transfer of Event-B model and theorems of a component to a DEVS simulation multi-modeling of an entire ITS.

IV. Conclusion

This paper presented the first steps of a research idea where formal models are added to a multi-modeling simulation which results are used to solve interactively the residual proof obligations that the formal tool could not automatically demonstrate. The goal is to automatize that interactive resolution.

Acknowledgment

The authors acknowledge the Hauts de France Region.

References

[1] P. Sondi, M. Berbineau, M. Kassab, and G. Mariano, Generating Test Scenarios Based on Real-World Traces for ERTMS Telecommunication Subsystem Evaluation. Springer Berlin Heidelberg, 2013, pp. 223–231.

[2] L. Rivoirard, W. Martine, P. Sondi, M. Berbineau, and G. Dominique, "Cbl : a clustering scheme for vanets," in The 6th Int. Conference on Advances in Vehicular Systems, Technologies and Applications, 2017.

[3] F. Sakiz and S. Sen, "A survey of attacks and detection mechanisms on intelligent transportation systems: Vanets and iov," Ad Hoc Networks, vol. 61, 2017, pp. 33–50.

[4] L. Gyesik, "How to formally model features of network security protocols," International Journal of Security and Its Applications, vol. 8, no. 1, 2014, pp. 423–432.

[5] A. Yacoub, C. Frydman et al., "Using dev-promela for modelling and verification of software," in Proceedings of the 2016 annual ACM Conference on SIGSIM Principles of Advanced Discrete Simulation. ACM, 2016, pp. 245–253.

[6] D. Méry and N. K. Singh, "Analysis of dsr protocol in event-b," in Symposium on Self-Stabilizing Systems. Springer, 2011, pp. 401–415.

Seeking Rare Events in a Simulated System using Risk Distances

Volker Gollücke
Institute for Information Technology
OFFIS e.V.
Oldenburg, Germany
email: volker.gollueckeoffis.de

Axel Hahn
Department of Computing Science
Carl von Ossietzky Universität Oldenburg
Oldenburg, Germany
email: hahn@wi-ol.de

***Abstract*— The identification and avoidance of potential risks is an important task in any system design process. The probability of underestimating a risk depends strongly on the complexity of the system under consideration. It is helpful to know the ways and means, which help reviewing the suspected risks. Current safety regulations, for example in the domain of offshore operations, require a description of all the risks involved. In order to create this description, a system including a behavioral specification modeled by a system expert is analyzed. Within this system, risks have to be searched and reasons for their occurrence have to be analyzed. The approach presented in this work describes a method to calculate the distance to a risk using a simulative analysis. The approach uses concepts from the field of Rare Event Simulations, which are used to accelerate the simulative reach of a risky situation. During the simulation runs data is collected about the way, which was taken to reach the avoidable situation. These data can be further used in a manual risk analysis and for matching rules and processes in terms of safety. The presented work describes how distance functions are created and used to assess system states in terms of their proximity to risky situations. In addition, the question of how the results of the distance functions can be used to guide co-simulations to the examined risky situations is answered.**

Keywords-System Analysis; Risk Analysis; Simulation, Distance Metrics.

I. INTRODUCTION

Many products and technologies for risk assessment are only suitable for specific application areas. An important need for action can be seen in the time consuming process of describing functions to assess a risk or measure the proximity to a risk situation. It was noticeable that in the examined programs [1]–[5], either only certain predetermined risks could be assessed or general functions could be specified. In addition, the consideration of distributed simulators (especially external simulators) was not the focus of any software under consideration. A structured guide with regard to the creation of risk-distance functions was not available in the investigated methods and tools. In addition, the consideration of the support of black-box simulators and the use of simulation run overlapping information were little or not considered at all.

When using classical methods, such as fault tree analysis, there are questions about the completeness of the information, e.g. whether all the causes for the identified errors have been identified. In this context, the use of simulation as a method of investigation is suitable, which allows experiments to be carried out under various configurations of the modeled system and to collect information on the occurrence of risks.

The approach presented in this work describes a methodology that can be used to define and calculate the distance to a risk in a simulative analysis using a so-called risk-distance function. The distance does not describe a spatial distance, but the proximity of a system state to an avoidable system state - the risk situation.

In addition, the use of concepts from the field of rare event simulation, which are used to accelerate the simulative reach of a risk situation, is implemented. The approach supports a part of the Importance Splitting technique [6]–[8], which is used to guide black box simulations to risky situations. It is assumed that a simulated state closer to a danger reaches it faster than a more distant one. In this case, the risk distance function is used as an importance function, which is used to evaluate the simulation states in the importance splitting technique.

In order to comprehensively collect information about the course of the simulation run, simulation states achieved in the simulation runs can additionally be persisted in a database and enriched with meta information. These include the evaluation of the state using the risk distance function, how often the persistent state was reached, how often this state was explored and, in addition, the minimum risk distance, the states reached from this state from previous simulation runs. All this information can also be integrated into the control of the simulation with regard to a faster reaching of risky states In order to implement this approach, description methods are required for situations and similarity measures with which different situations can be described and compared with each other. In order to establish and apply these techniques, techniques from the domain of information retrieval are used, which can compare the two system states with regard to their similarity in an appropriate time [9]. This paper is structured as follows: in Section 1 an introduction to the topic is given, in Section 2 the methodology to create a risk distance function and the use of the risk distance functions in a co-simulation are presented, we move on with an evaluation experiment to show the applicability of risk distance functions in Section 3, and conclude in Section 4.

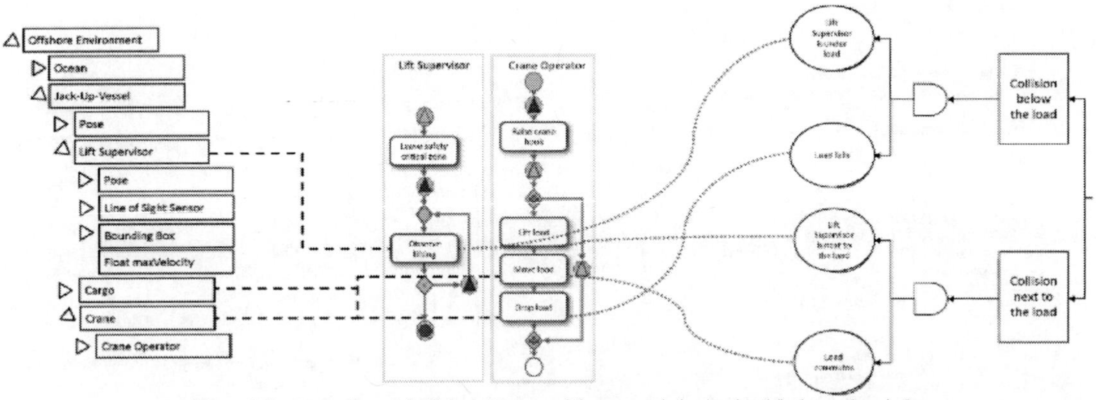

Figure 1. Representation of the linked elements of the system, behavioral and fault tree description.

II. METHODOLOGY

The methodology developed consists of three aspects and their predetermined order. The first aspect is the modeling of the system to be analyzed, which reveals a system, behavior and hazard description. The first aspect is achieved by the use of Droste's (cf. [10], [11]) and Pinkowski's (cf. [12], [13]) work and developed tools. The second aspect is the risk-distance description used to create the risk-distance functions. The last aspect is the simulative analysis, in which the previously ascertained descriptions enter in order to describe the simulation process.

A. *Modelling the system under test*

A model of the system to be analyzed is needed as starting point for the investigation. This consists of a system description including a behavior specification. A process model based on concepts of business process models and notation languages is used for the behavioral specification. The process describes actors, tasks and related interactions. This model type has been developed for use in the maritime domain, more specifically for offshore operations but can also be applied to other domains [10]. The graphical elements of the model describe task sequences and interactions. It is also possible to annotate these with associated hazards and their causes. A hazard describes a potential risk, such as the injury of a person or a machine damage. A cause describes a possible trigger for a hazard. When annotating the process model, a formal specification for hazards and causes is used [14]. Using a system model, the described physical objects and environmental conditions can be described. These are also useful to map actors from the process model to specific avatars (physical objects of the system) in the simulated environment. For example, a ship can be assigned to a ship resource of the simulated environment that has a position, maximum speed, and other attributes relevant to the simulation.

A well-known way to carry out a characterization of the risks involved are fault trees [15]. Fault trees provide an overview of the potential risks and the connection of their possible causes. In addition, fault trees split the risk in different events that presumably lead in their combination to the undesirable risk. For each annotated hazard to the behavior specification, a fault tree is created to logically structure the respective failures that may cause the hazard. Since each cause is related to an element of the process, the fault tree is also associated with this element. Conversely, each top event of a fault tree (root node) is associated with a hazard. For example, causes associated with a task item may be associated with multiple fault trees representing the hazards and associated causes graphically. In contrast to other methods for fault tree generation, which use UML diagrams as sources for generation (cf. [16], [17]), all necessary information is available in the presented process model. In order to avoid errors, the specific hazards and causes associated with the process have to be modeled by an experienced system expert [12]. Figure 1 shows an example of the three used models and their connection between each other. Basic Events are connected to specific tasks from the behavior description while tasks are linked to elements from the system model. The *Cargo* element from the system model is connected to the task *Observe lifting* from the behavioral specification and the basic event *Lift Supervisor is next to load.*

B. *Description of the risk distance*

This section presents the methodology used to determine the distance description to a risk. Figure 2 shows the construction of the risk-distance function with the new approach. Using the System Description, a Fault Tree is generated from which the structure of the risk distance function is derived. Hazards and faults, which are annotated at the behaviour specification by a system expert describe the sub-distance functions. The combination of the structure of the risk distance function and the sub-distance functions lead to the complete risk distance function. This process is described in more detail in the following sections.

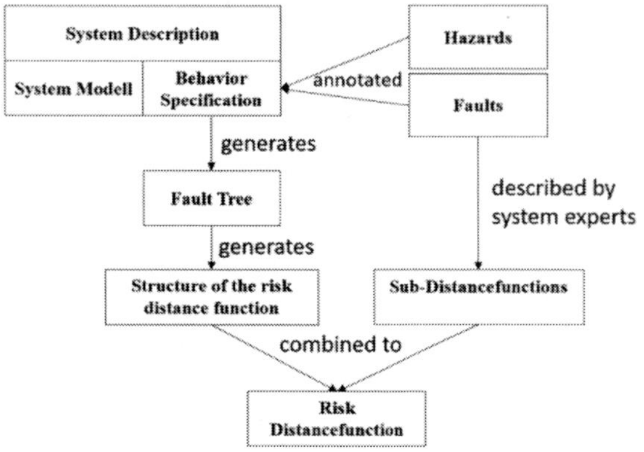

Figure 2. Overview of the creation of the risk distance function.

The process is based on the basis presented in the previous section for describing the system including the risks and causes expected by the system expert. The result of the distance description is a risk distance function, which represents a mathematical function that evaluates the proximity to an abstract risk situation to be investigated. The lower the distance to the risk, the lower the result of the risk distance function. The result of a risk distance function is always a value between 0 and 1, where 0 indicates that the risk situation has occurred, while 1 means that the currently checked situation has no relevant proximity to the risk situation under investigation.

1) Deriving the structure of the risk distance function

In order to obtain the structure of a risk-distance function, the logical links ("and" / "or" relationships) of the basic and intermediate Events (sub-elements of the top event, which are not leaf elements) of the fault tree are used. In Figure 3, the mapping between fault tree and the structure of the risk distance function is shown by an example. The top-level element sets the name for the created risk distance function (D_A). By "and" linked elements are calculated by multiplication. Since the calculation is not based on probabilities but on distances, the incoming, previously calculated distances are inverted, multiplied and inverted again to obtain a distance as a result. The equation, for elements linked by "and", is $D_A = 1 - ((1 - D_B) * (1 - D_C))$. Multiple elements associated with "or" are determined by the calculation of the minimum distance ($D_B = \min(D_D, D_E)$). The calculation of the leaf elements is done by the calculation of the products of the distances to the various properties of the causes, which are described in this work as sub-distance functions ($D_C = 1 - \prod_{i \in 1..n} (1 - d_{c_i})$).

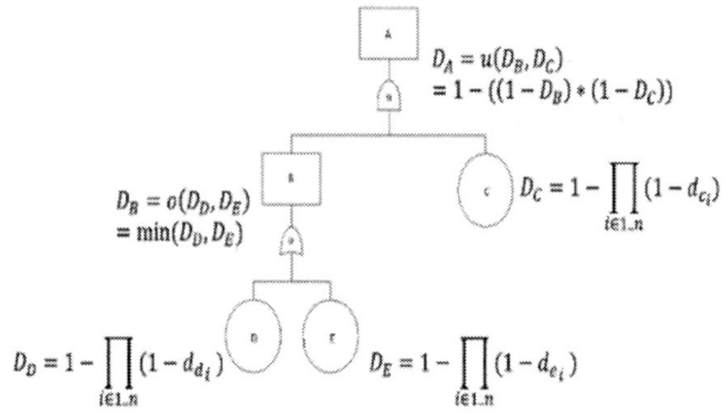

Figure 3. Relationship between fault tree and structure of the risk distance function.

The resulting structure of the risk distance function for the fault tree from Figure 3 can be seen in (1).
The sub distance functions, which are needed to complete the risk distance function, are derived in a subsequent step.

2) Deriving the sub distance function

Figure 4 shows the link between a fault tree basic event and the path to create the required sub distance functions.

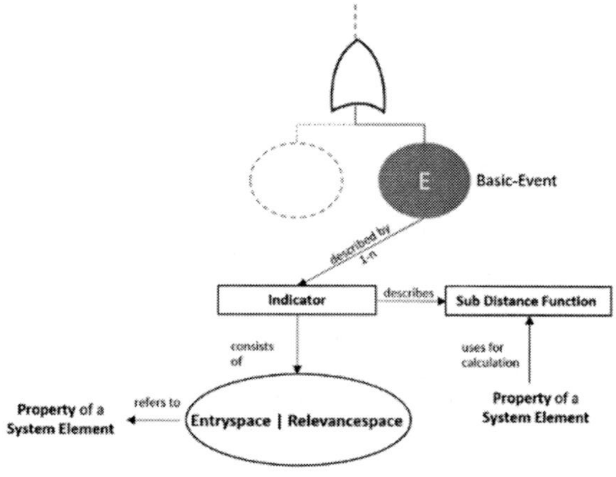

Figure 4. Description of the basic events for the risk distance function.

In the first step, the system experts determine so-called indicators, describing the space in which the cause described in the Basic Event is considered to have occurred.
For the basic event E of the fault tree in Figure 4 the equation 1-$\prod_{i \in 1..n}(1 - d_{E_i})$ was created to calculate the cause distance. The product is calculated because the different indicators are specified as joint events that must have occurred so that the cause specified in the basic event may be considered to have occurred. The combination of the indicators by mathematical operators is

therefore done in the same way as the elements in the fault tree linked by the logical "and".

d_{E_i} represents the sub distance function for the i-th indicator of the leaf node E. Each indicator refers to exactly one property of an element of the system with continuous values and is defined by an entry space (E_E) and relevance space (R_E). Starting from the considered indicator, the entry space and relevance space can be described by a lower $E_{E_{min}}/R_{E_{min}}$ and/or upper limit $E_{E_{max}}$ respective $R_{E_{max}}$.

The entry space describes the value range of the property that favors the cause described in the basic event.

$$D^A = 1 - \left(\left(1 - \min\left(1 - \prod_{i \in 1..n} 1 - d_{d_i}, 1 - \prod_{i \in 1..n} 1 - d_{e_i}\right)\right) * \left(1 - \left(1 - \prod_{i \in 1..n} 1 - d_{c_i}\right)\right)\right) \quad (1)$$

The relevance space describes the value range of the property, which is relevant for an approach to the risk under investigation, and from which value of the property there is no relevance for the risk under investigation.
A very simple example is the risk of a broken mobile device. Let us assume that the device is only prone to a too low (-20°C) or too high (40°C) temperature. Then, the entry space is defined by those two values. The relevance space is determined by two more temperature values, which define when the temperature of the device gets close to the risky temperatures.
Figure 5 shows an illustration for the entry and relevance spaces for this example.

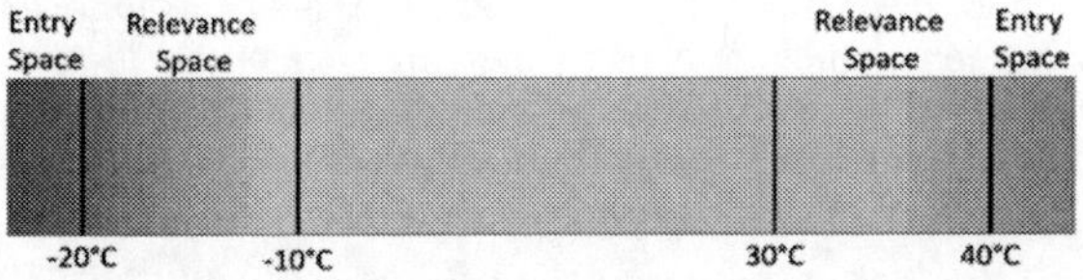

Figure 5. Illustration for the use of the entry and relevance spaces.

The entry and relevance spaces are given by the following equations (2), (3), (4) and (5), where A, B, C and D are constants to be determined by the system expert, with which an indicator is described. Y can represent a predefined value of the considered property of the system (e.g., the centre point of the bounding box of a container).

$$E_{min}(Y) = Y - A \quad (2)$$

$$E_{max}(Y) = Y + B \quad (3)$$

$$R_{min}(Y) = Y - C \quad (4)$$

$$R_{max}(Y) = Y + D \quad (5)$$

When the indicator is described by the entry and relevance space, the sub distance function is created for the respective indicator (6).
This consists of the determined limits of the entry and relevance space as well as the considered property X of the system.

$$d_{D_i} = \begin{cases} 0, if\ X \geq E_{D_{min}}(Y) \wedge X \leq E_{D_{max}}(Y) \\ 1, if\ X \leq R_{D_{min}}(Y) \vee X \geq R_{D_{max}}(Y) \\ \min\left(\frac{\left(X - E_{D_{min}}(Y)\right)}{\left(R_{D_{min}}(Y) - E_{D_{min}}(Y)\right)}, \frac{\left(X + E_{D_{max}}(Y)\right)}{\left(R_{D_{max}}(Y) - E_{D_{max}}(Y)\right)}\right), else \end{cases} \quad (6)$$

At first, it is checked whether the property under consideration is already in the entrance space. If this is the case, the result of the sub distance function is *0*. The next check refers to the relevance space. If the property is outside the relevance space, *1* is output as the result of the sub distance function. If neither assumption is true, the result of the sub distance function is determined by the distance of the system element property to the minimum and maximum entry space. These distances are then normalized over the distance between minimum or maximum event space and relevance space. The normalized values of the sub distance functions, which all describe a partial distance irrespective of the properties used, allow a comparability. The minimum is then selected from the normalized distances and output as the result of the sub distance function. If there is only a minimum or maximum limit of the entry space, the distance to it is the result.

C. *Simulative Analysis*

This section describes how the simulative analysis is carried out using the described system and the determined risk distance functions. In this context, the co-simulation environment used is discussed and the use of the distance functions for controlling the simulation with regard to a reduction of simulation runs is explained. To be able to use the importance splitting technique, the used simulators, must ensure a state control. This means that they must be able to store and load their current situation at the request of a co-simulation controller.

1) Integration of the risk distance functions

Figure 6 shows the integration of the values determined in the methodology, in the context of co-simulation. A system model instance is linked to the connected simulators and receives the values updated by the simulators. Through the system model instance, the components "Risk Distance Calculation" and "Situation Comparison" necessary for the integration of a distance description are informed about the values of a new simulation state. In this context, the risk distance measurement uses the risk distance function determined in the methodology in order to calculate the risk distance to an abstract risk (i.e., "collision with cargo") using the values of the system model instance.

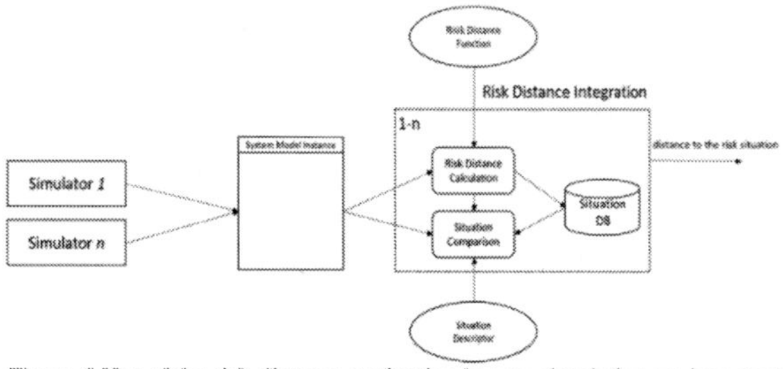

Figure 6 Use of the risk-distance evaluation in a co-simulation environment

The situation database is based on the information retrieval technique used to classify information. A descriptor is automatically defined by the underlying system model and its characteristic, the system model instance. It allows the request for the similarity to already reached situations. For this purpose, the comparative component uses a situation descriptor based on the elements of the system model and the data of the system model instance. The situation descriptor is a vector whose elements reflect the characteristics of the system elements. The order of the element properties in the vector is fixed, so that the comparison is not falsified. The size or the number of elements of the descriptor for a simulation scenario is defined by the structure of the system model. The comparison is made based on a distance measure. Static properties can be ignored for the calculation of the similarity. Properties with numeric values can be used directly while Boolean values are used as false (value 0) and true (value 1) and textual values in comparison over their equality or inequality. Within the developed framework, the use of the Euclidean distance (L2), the known universally applicable distance measure, was chosen.

Through the use of databases developed for the information retrieval technique (e.g., Apache Lucene), the similarity calculation can be performed within a reasonable time by the predetermined distance measure, despite invoking mathematical operations to calculate the distance.

If there is no similar situation in the database, the database is supplemented by this data set and enriched after a simulation run by the minimally achieved risk proximity. If a similar situation is persisted in the database, it is checked and updated how many simulation runs have already been carried out and how the maximum approach to the abstract risk situation was.

If not enough simulation runs explored to the same situation or the maximum approximation to the risk situation is promising, the results of the situation evaluation are output and can be used, e.g., to save the current situation or to abort the current simulation run.

2) *Exploration to the risk situation*

As described in the previous section, the inclusion of the risk distance measurement within the simulation can be used to react to the distance of the respective situation to the examined situation. An advantage that is derived from this is the description of a controlled co-simulation based on the calculated distances. As known from the previous section, the functionality of the risk distance calculation is achieved via a link to the system model instance. The current values stored in the system model instance are forwarded to the distance calculation, the calculation of the distance takes place and can be used for further processing in a simulation sequence logic. In this, all decisions regarding the simulation process are defined. It thus allows the distance calculations to be tested with respect to a threshold value and on this basis, the further course of the simulation can be determined.

In order to define the course of the simulation the control functions are used.

This means that the situation of the co-simulation, after the risk situation has been approached according to the calculation of the distance function, can be stored and further simulation runs can be started from this.

III. VALIDATION

In this section, the simulation guidance by risk distance functions is evaluated. For this purpose, a scenario was chosen with two vessels involved, which are in the opposite direction on an inland waterway. A collision between these two ships has to be observed, which, however, can only be achieved very rarely by the conditions set out in the following sections. In order to obtain a more frequent observation of a collision, the approaches and concepts presented in this work were used to control the simulation.

A. *Structure and procedure of the experiment*

In the experiment under consideration, two simulators were used, which control the two participating ships. Both ships have a high probability of reaching their destination and are only very unlikely to deviate from their direct course to their destination (Figure 7).

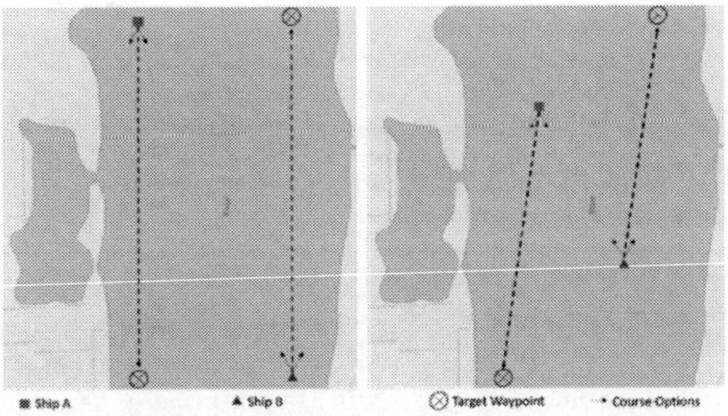

Figure 7. Evaluation scenario: The two ships involved try to reach their destination. With a very low probability, the ships depart to the left or right of their course.

As a termination condition for a simulation run, the arrival of the destination waypoints by both ships was determined. The event that was investigated in this evaluation was a collision between the two ships, which should be observed within this evaluation 100 times under the respective simulation settings. The simulation settings consisted of a naive and a guided simulation, in which there were three variants of how to determine the next splitting point (the next lower risk distance level). On the one hand, an adaptive method, which in each simulation step checks whether a lower risk distance evaluation has been achieved than before and, secondly, a method, which has applied the splitting points at predetermined intervals (0.01 and 0.05).
In all methods, except for the naive simulation, a new simulation run was started when a state with a new lower risk distance was reached in the case of the adaptive method or a new risk level in the case of the predefined intervals.
All simulation runs in which no collision occurred were counted as well as the real time measured up to the time of the occurrence of a collision. This operation was performed 100 times, with no parallel execution. The generated simple fault tree for the scenario consists of three basic events (close range, dangerous speed and a specific heading angle of the two ships) which have to occur together so that a high risk of a frontal ship collision exists (Figure 8).

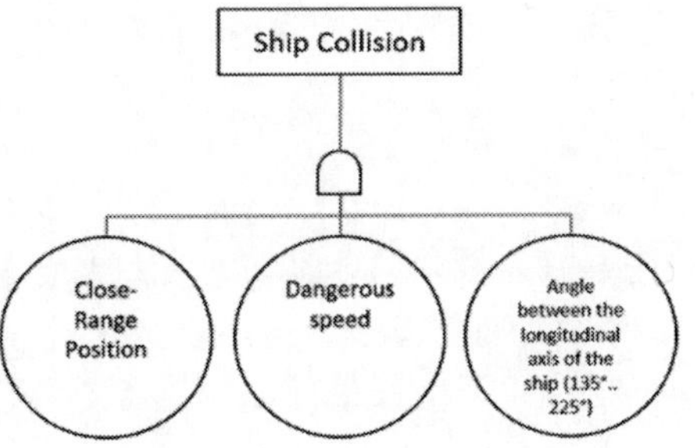

Figure 8. Simple Fault Tree for a frontal collision between two ships.

The following risk distance function was derived (s. equation (7)), which uses the proximity, speed and orientation of the two ships to determine the risk distance.
As a basis for the sub-distance functions values "Collisions and their Causes" [18] and "Managing Collision Avoidance at Sea: A Practical Guide" [19] where used.

$$D_K = 1 - \left(\left(1 - \begin{cases} 0, if\ distance = 0m \\ 1, if\ distance \geq 4980m \\ \frac{distance}{4980m}, else \end{cases} \right) \times \left(1 - \begin{cases} 0, if\ speed \geq 12{,}5kn \\ 1, if\ speed \leq 10kn \\ \frac{(speed - 12{,}5kn)}{(10kn - 12{,}5kn)}, \quad else \end{cases} \right) \times \left(1 - \begin{cases} 0, if\ angle \geq 135° \wedge angle \leq 225° \\ 1, if\ angle \leq 100° \vee angle \geq 250° \\ \min\left(\frac{(angle - 135°)}{(100° - 135°)}, \frac{(angle + 225°)}{(250° - 225°)} \right), else \end{cases} \right) \right) \quad (7)$$

During the experiment, the two ships had a 99.9% probability to drive towards their target waypoint, while they changed their course to the left or right with a probability of 0.1%. The decision to change the course was recalculated by the two ships in each simulation step.

B. *Evaluation of the experiments*

The results of the experiment showed that the naive simulation took about 152 minutes to observe 100 collisions, while the simulation runs, which were guided by means of a risk distance function, produced 100 collisions after approx. 3 seconds (distance 0.05) ,95 milliseconds (distance 0.01) and 92 milliseconds (adaptive). While in the naive simulation 44,076,619 simulation runs were required before 100 collisions could be observed, the number of simulation runs for the distance of the splitting points from 0.05 was 5.374.930 runs, for the distance of the splitting points from 0.01 59.551 runs and for the adjusted distance 53.150 runs.
In the case of this experiment, the method with the adaptive distance was the best, with regard to the sum of the simulation runs as well as the measured real time, until 100 independent collisions were observed.

IV. CONCLUSION

The approach developed in this work, consisting of a methodology for describing risk assessment and the use of this in co-simulations, differs in some aspects from current programs and concepts in science and technology. In particular, the approach to assess a risk is revisited in using a system-, process and fault tree model, which gives the possibility for non-information technicians to create risk distance functions. Additionally, it is described how the specific risk distance functions are used to reach risky situations faster by using approaches from the rare event simulation and the information retrieval field also when using black-box simulators. A situation database helps to store simulation run spanning information about the achieved simulation states and to use them for the further control of the co-simulation.

ACKNOWLEDGMENT

The work presented in this paper is supported by the Center for Critical System Engineering for Sociotechnical Systems at the University of Oldenburg, OFFIS and DLR. The center is funded by the Federal State of Lower Saxony, Germany under grant numbers VWZN3237 and VWZN3270.

REFERENCES

[1] EMSO, "EMSO Environment for Modelling, Simulation, and Optimization," *EMSO Environment for Modelling, Simulation, and Optimization*, 2004. [Online]. Available: http://www.vrtech.com.br/rps/emso.html. [Accessed: 14-Jun-2015].

[2] Plant Simulation, "Plant Simulation," *Simulation mit Plant Simulation*, 2015. [Online]. Available: http://www.plant-simulation.de/?gclid=Cj0KEQjwzPSrBRC_oOXfxPWP6t0BEiQARqav2OQQo8_Xb5B-iBS-zLZQ0TyqNfXTt7NH0KGFPEggQI8aAm-58P8HAQ. [Accessed: 14-Jun-2015].

[3] K. W. Ross and J. Wang, "Implementation of Monte Carlo integration for the analysis of product-form queueing networks," *Perform. Eval.*, vol. 29, no. 4, pp. 273–292, 1997.

[4] S. Shyam and V. Bertacco, "Distance-guided hybrid verification with GUIDO," in *Proceedings of the conference on Design, automation and test in Europe: Proceedings*, 2006, pp. 1211–1216.

[5] The OptQuest Engine, "The OptQuest Engine," *OptQuest | OptTek Systems, Inc.*, 2011. [Online]. Available: http://www.opttek.com/OptQuest. [Accessed: 14-Jun-2015].

[6] C. Jegourel, A. Legay, and S. Sedwards, "Importance splitting for statistical model checking rare properties," in *Computer Aided Verification*, 2013, pp. 576–591.

[7] S. Juneja and P. Shahabuddin, "Rare-event simulation techniques: an introduction and recent advances," *Handb. Oper. Res. Manag. Sci.*, vol. 13, pp. 291–350, 2006.

[8] J. Morio, R. Pastel, and F. Le Gland, "An overview of importance splitting for rare event simulation," *Eur. J. Phys.*, vol. 31, no. 5, pp. 1295–1303, Sep. 2010.

[9] S. Büttcher, C. Clarke, and G. V. Cormack, *Information Retrieval: Implementing and Evaluating Search Engines*. The MIT Press, 2010.

[10] R. Droste, "Modellbasierte Planung und Analyse von Offshore-Operationen (unveröffentlicht)," Dissertation, Carl-von-Ossietzky Universität Oldenburg, Oldenburg, 2016.

[11] C. Läsche, J. Pinkowski, S. Gerwinn, R. Droste, and A. Hahn, "Model-Based Risk Assessment of Offshore Operations," in *ASME 2014 33rd International Conference on Ocean, Offshore and Arctic Engineering*, 2014, p. V01BT01A010–V01BT01A010.

[12] J. Pinkowski, "Prozessgetriebene Risikoanalyse zur Bewertung maritimer Operationen," Dissertation, Carl-von-Ossietzky Universität Oldenburg, Oldenburg, 2015.

[13] V. Gollücke, J. Pinkowski, C. Läsche, S. Gerwinn, and A. Hahn, "Simulation-based Completeness Analysis and Adaption of Fault Trees," in *SIMUL 2014, The Sixth International Conference on Advances in System Simulation*, Nice, France, 2014, p. 228 to 235.

[14] C. Läsche, E. Böde, and T. Peikenkamp, "A method for guided hazard identification and risk mitigation for offshore operations," in *Computer Safety, Reliability, and Security*, Springer, 2012, pp. 37–48.

[15] W. Vesely, J. Dugan, J. Fragola, Minarick, and J. Railsback, "Fault Tree Handbook with Aerospace Applications," National Aeronautics and Space Administration, Washington, DC, Handbook, 2002.

[16] C. Lauer, R. German, and J. Pollmer, "Fault tree synthesis from UML models for reliability analysis at early design stages," *ACM SIGSOFT Softw. Eng. Notes*, vol. 36, no. 1, pp. 1–8, 2011.

[17] G. J. Pai and J. B. Dugan, "Automatic synthesis of dynamic fault trees from UML system models," in *Software Reliability Engineering, 2002. ISSRE 2003. Proceedings. 13th International Symposium on*, 2002, pp. 243–254.

[18] R. A. Cahill and N. I. (Great Britain), *Collisions and Their Causes*. Nautical Institute, 2002.

[19] G. W. U. Lee and J. Parker, *Managing Collision Avoidance at Sea: A Practical Guide*. Nautical Institute, 2007.

Derivation of a New Method for Derivative Estimation by Linear Combinations

Simon Genser

VIRTUAL VEHICLE Research Center
Inffeldgasse 21a, 8010 Graz, Austria
Telephone: +43/316/873-9600
Email: Simon.Genser@v2c2.at

Martin Benedikt

VIRTUAL VEHICLE Research Center
Inffeldgasse 21a, 8010 Graz, Austria
Telephone: +43/316/873-9048
Email: Martin.Benedikt@v2c2.at

***Abstract*—This paper introduces a new method to estimate derivatives of a noiseless time-domain signal, the so called Derivative Estimation by Linear Combinations method. This method can be considered as a generalization of the Finite Difference Method, for the case of backward differentiation. The advantages in computational effort and accuracy of the proposed method compared, to widely known methods of derivation approximation, are demonstrated based on an analytical reference solution. Especially the output-input sensitivity of systems can be determined more robust, with significant fields of application in control, simulation and sensitivity analysis. It is shown that the method is well-suited for real-time applications due to the low computational effort and low time-delay.**

Keywords*–derivative estimation; generalized finite difference method; sensitivity analysis; numerical derivation.

I. Introduction

Many algorithms which are used in control engineering [1], signal processing [2] or numerical simulations need derivatives of differentiable time signals. As computer-implemented algorithms are processing discrete quantities by nature, the computation of derivatives is based on these samples exclusively. Furthermore, for ensuring a proper working of the related and derivative utilizing algorithms, a high approximation of the derivatives is crucial and has a significant impact on the overall performance. Commonly used to compute such derivatives are Finite Difference Methods (FDM) [3], [4], the Complex-Step method [5] or the algebraic method (AM) [6]. Typical drawbacks of those methods are in accuracy, especially for AM, in the computational effort and in time-delay.

The aim of this paper is to introduce a new method to compute derivatives of a discrete signal, using only linear combinations of samples. This proposed method is called Derivative Estimation by Linear Combinations (DELC). The requirements for the newly introduced DELC method are a high accuracy, a low computational effort and a small time delay.

The first target is to compute derivatives of the signal by exclusively using past time samples, which makes the method applicable for real-time applications, as therefore a causal method is strictly mandatory. The second focus on the derivation of the DELC method is that, the computation time is sufficiently low, so it is usable for real-time applications.

The usage of the DELC Method is pointed out by an output-input sensitivity analysis of a control system, so one is intrested in

$$\frac{dy(t)}{du(t)}.$$

From the control system are only the input $u(t)$ and output $y(t)$ known, there is no information about the structure or the dynamics of the system, it is a so called black box.

The key idea of the method is to use linear combinations consisting of the past discrete-time samples y_k

$$y_k^{(j)} = \sum_{i=0}^{N} \hat{c}_{i_j} y_{k-i}, \qquad (1)$$

whereby $y_k^{(j)}$ denotes the j-th derivative of the signal $y(t)$ at the actual time instant k, N stands for the number of used samples and $\hat{c}_{i_j}$ represents the appropriate scalars depending on the order of the derivative j. Instead of interpreting (1) as a linear combination of one dimensional vectors, it is possible to identify it as a weighted sum.
To reduce the computational effort it is advantageous, if the scalars $\hat{c}_{i_j}$ are fixed and time invariant. It will be shown that, this is the case if the step size is chosen constant over the whole computation, as it is typically the case in real-time applications. It will also be pointed out that the accuracy depends on the number of samples, which makes it possible to improve accuracy by increasing the number of used samples N. The proposed method is designed for differentiable signals, excluding status signals, discontinuities and events.

The paper is organized as follows: in Section II, the DELC method is derived from two different points of view, first by a Taylor series and then by an approach which is based on the first derivation. It also contains important properties of the method, especially regarding the computational effort, an error estimation and the time delay. The advantages of the DELC method compared to the FDM and the AM and the fulfilment of the requirements will be shown by various examples.

II. Derivation of the DELC method

This section establishes the method to approximate the derivatives of a differentiable time signal based on discrete samples, i.e., discrete time signal. The following notation is used:
y_k stands for the evaluation of a function $y(t): \mathbb{R} \to \mathbb{R}$ at the sample time t_k. For simplicity, we consider only constant step size h, this means

$$t_{k+1} = t_k + h. \tag{2}$$

The general statement of the problem, in detail, is that

$$\boldsymbol{y} = \{y_r : r = 1, \ldots, k\}$$

is given, thereby stands k for the index of t_k, so data points at sample times $t_r \leq t_k$ are known. The aim is to compute the j-th derivatives of y at t_k:

$$y_k^{(j)} \quad \forall j = 1, \ldots, N.$$

This states the fact, that the method is causal.

A. Derivation from Taylor-Series

The origin of the derivation is the Taylor series expansion of the function $y(t)$

$$y(t) \approx \sum_{i=0}^{N} \frac{y^{(i)}(t_0)}{i!}(t - t_0)^i, \tag{3}$$

where N denotes the order of the approximation and t_0 the center of the series. It should be mentioned that the order of the approximation N is equivalent to the highest computable derivative.
Note: The idea is to set $t_0 = t_k$ and evaluate the series expansion (3) at $t = t_{k-i}$ for $i = 1, \ldots, N$. This leads to

$$y_{k-1} = \sum_{i=0}^{N} \frac{y_k^{(i)}}{i!}(t_{k-1} - t_k)^i,$$
$$y_{k-2} = \sum_{i=0}^{N} \frac{y_k^{(i)}}{i!}(t_{k-2} - t_k)^i,$$
$$\vdots$$
$$y_{k-N} = \sum_{i=0}^{N} \frac{y_k^{(i)}}{i!}(t_{k-N} - t_k)^i.$$

Considering, the assumption that the step size h is constant, which is outlined in (2), it follows

$$y_{k-l} = \sum_{i=0}^{N} \frac{y_k^{(i)}}{i!}(-lh)^i \quad \forall l = 1, \ldots, N,$$

leading to

$$y_{k-l} - y_k = \sum_{i=1}^{N} \frac{y_k^{(i)}}{i!}(-lh)^i \quad \forall l = 1, \ldots, N.$$

After rewriting, in matrix vector representation, it results in

$$\hat{A}\boldsymbol{y} = \boldsymbol{b}, \tag{4}$$

whereby

$$\hat{A}[l, i] := (-1)^i \frac{(lh)^i}{i!},$$
$$\boldsymbol{y}[i] := y_k^{(i)},$$
$$\boldsymbol{b}[l] := y_{k-l} - y_k$$

for $l, i = 0, \ldots, N$. This linear system of equations should be solved symbolically, because the formular should be able to handle arbitrary but constant step size h.

For $N = 2$ the computation of (4) results in the following calculation formulas, for the first and second derivative:

$$y_k^{(1)} = \frac{1}{h}\left[1.5 y_k - 2 y_{k-1} + 0.5 y_{k-2}\right] \tag{5}$$
$$y_k^{(2)} = \frac{1}{h^2}\left[1 y_k - 2 y_{k-1} + 1 y_{k-2}\right] \tag{6}$$

B. Derivation from an approach

The formulas (5) and (6) suggest the approach

$$y_k^{(j)} = \frac{1}{h^j} \sum_{i=0}^{N} c_{i_j} y_{k-i}, \tag{7}$$

where $c_{i_j} \in \mathbb{R}$ are constants which have to be determined. The key idea is, to demand that the derivatives has to be exact for

$$p(t) = \sum_{i=0}^{N+1-j} a_i t^i,$$

whereby $a_i \in \mathbb{R}$. So p stands for polynomials up to degree $N + 1 - j$. The j-th derivative of p at t_k is

$$p_k^{(j)} = \sum_{i=j}^{N+1-j} a_i \frac{i!}{(i-j)!} t_k^{i-j}.$$

Using the approach from (7) with respect to (2) leads to

$$\sum_{i=j}^{N+1-j} a_i \frac{i!}{(i-j)!}(kh)^{i-j} = \frac{1}{h^j} \sum_{l=0}^{N} c_{l_j} \sum_{i=0}^{N+1-j} a_i((k-l)h)^i$$

Using the method of equating the coefficients for h^i leads to

$$a_i \frac{i!}{(i-j)!} k^{i-j} = \sum_{l=0}^{N} c_{l_j} a_i (k-l)^i \quad \forall i = 0, \ldots, N+1-j,$$

under the assumption that,

$$\frac{i!}{(i-j)!} = 0 \quad \text{for } i - j < 0.$$

In matrix and vector representation, the system of equations results in

$$A\boldsymbol{c} = \boldsymbol{b} \tag{8}$$

whereby

$$A[i, l] := (k - l)^i, \tag{9}$$
$$\boldsymbol{c}[l] := c_{l_j},$$
$$\boldsymbol{b}[i] := \frac{i!}{(i-j)!} k^{i-j}$$

for $i, l = 0, \dots, N$ and for $\frac{i!}{(i-j)!} = 0$ for $i - j < 0$. It should be mentioned that $k \in \mathbb{N}$ is arbitrary and it is possible to set

$$k = 0,$$

because the solution of the system is independent of the choice of k.

To calculate the constants for the linear combination via the system resulting from the derivation with the approach is easier because, the system in (8) is independent from h and so can be solved numerically more efficient, instead of the system (4). But the derivation due to the Taylor-series is fundamental to get the correct approach (7), whereas both ways are important.

C. Properties of the DELC method

The following section discusses important properties of the DELC method, including implementation aspects.

1) Computational Effort: For the computation of the derivative of a signal

$$y_k^{(j)} = \frac{1}{h^j} \sum_{i=0}^{N} c_{i_j} y_{k-i}, \tag{10}$$

has to be evaluated, which is a linear combination of known samples. For the taken assumption that the step size h is arbitrary but constant, the c_{i_j} are constant for the whole computation, so the determination of the c_{i_j} has not to be done in every time step. It is convenient to store them in a map and use the appropriate constants in the algorithm. It does not matter which system (4) or (8) is solved, the solution is equal, it might only make a difference for numerical issues. The remaining computation in every time step is represented by (10), which needs $(N+1)+1$ multiplications and $N+1$ additions. The calculation is non-iterative and therefore the method is applicable for real-time applications.

2) Generalization of the FDM: When choosing $j = 1, N = 1$ and have a close look on (7), or just compute the constants, it follows

$$c_0 = 1,$$
$$c_1 = -1$$

and (7) turns into

$$y_k^{(1)} = \frac{y_k - y_{k-1}}{h},$$

which matches exactly with backward difference quotient. Therefore the DELC method can be interpreted as an generalization of the FDM.

3) Error Estimation: An error estimation of the method can be derived from the Taylor-series expansion (3) of y, whereby y needs to be sufficiently smooth. It holds

$$y(t) = \sum_{i=0}^{\infty} \frac{y^{(i)}(t_0)}{i!}(t - t_0)^i \tag{11}$$
$$\tilde{y}_N(t) = \sum_{i=0}^{N} \frac{y^{(i)}(t_0)}{i!}(t - t_0)^i,$$

whereby $\tilde{y}_N$ is an approximation of y from degree N, leading to

$$|y - \tilde{y}_N| = \left| \sum_{i=N+1}^{\infty} \frac{y^{(i)}(t_0)}{i!}(t - t_0)^i \right|.$$

As outlined in the derivation of the method, the center of the series t_0 is set to t_k and y is evaluated in the discrete points $t = t_{k-i}$ for $i = 1, \dots, N$. For simplicity, the assumption of constant step size h is here also applied. This results in

$$|y - \tilde{y}_N| \leq ch^{N+1}$$

where $c > 0$ represents an appropriate constant. This error estimation, which is only valid for y and not its derivatives, has to be generalized for derivatives up to degree N. From (11) follows

$$y^{(j)} = \sum_{i=j}^{\infty} \tilde{c}_i y^{(i)}(t_0)(t - t_0)^{i-j}$$
$$\tilde{y}_N^{(j)} = \sum_{i=j}^{N} \tilde{c}_i y^{(i)}(t_0)(t - t_0)^{i-j},$$

for appropriate $\tilde{c}_i$ and $j = 1, \dots, N$. Again $t_0 = t_k$ and y is evaluated in $t = t_{k-i}$ for $i = 1, \dots, N$ and this leads to

$$\left| y^{(j)} - \tilde{y}_N^{(j)} \right| = \left| \sum_{i=N+1}^{\infty} \tilde{c}_i y_k^{(i)} h^{i-j} \right|.$$

That results in the error estimation

$$\left| y^{(j)} - \tilde{y}_N^{(j)} \right| \leq ch^{N-j+1}, \tag{12}$$

for $c \in \mathbb{R}^+$, $j = 0, \dots, N$ and $N \in \mathbb{N}$.

4) Preconditioning: It should be mentioned that the condition-number of the matrix (9) depends on the size of the matrix N, and for high order approximation ($N \geq 11$), a preconditioning strategy should be implemented because the matrix nearly gets singular, for more details on preconditioning see [7]–[10].

5) Time-Delay: Typically methods like the FDM or the AM underlie the problem of the so called time-delay t_{delay}, as the phase shift in Figure 1 shows. Especially for control systems applications time-delays represents significant limitations of performance.

To analyze the introduced time-delay of the different methods, the following example is chosen

$$y(t) = sin(t),$$

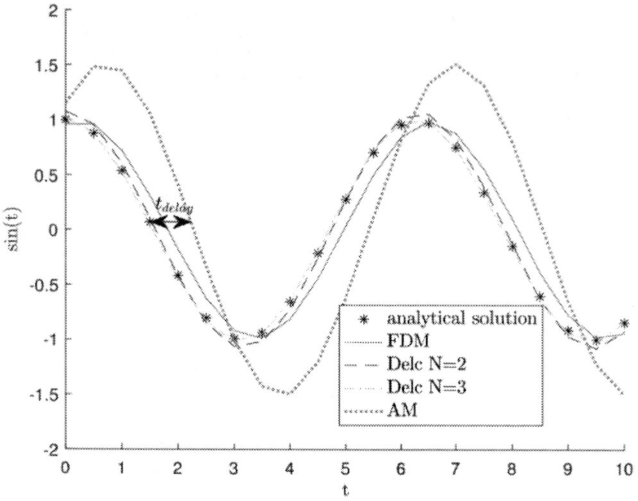

Figure 1. Time delay of the derivative estimation of $y(t) = sin(t)$ by the DELC method, the FDM and AM, parameters for the AM are $N = 2, v = 1, M = 10$, notation based on [6], the chosen step size is $h = 0.5$.

TABLE I. TIME DELAY OF THE DERIVATIVE ESTIMATION OF $y(t) = sin(t)$ BY THE DELC METHOD FOR AN DEGREE OF APPROXIMATION OF $N = 2, \dots, 16$ AND A CHOSEN STEP SIZE $h = 0.5$.

N	t_{delay}	N	t_{delay}	N	t_{delay}
2	0.0280198	7	-0.0000147	12	-0.0000058
3	-0.0250456	8	-0.0003928	13	-0.0000076
4	-0.0090735	9	-0.0000819	14	-0.0000005
5	0.0024091	10	0.0000607	15	0.0000015
6	0.0020479	11	0.0000301	16	0.0000005

sampled with a step size $h = 0.5$. For the FDM and the AM the following time delay is determined

$$t_{delay,AM} = 0.7030257,$$
$$t_{delay,FDM} = 0.2467885.$$

Table I shows, that the time delay of the DELC method gets quick smaller by increasing the degree of the approximation N. So this feature of the DELC method represents a significant benefit compared to the FDM or the AM.

III. EXAMPLES

In this section, the advantage of the DELC method compared to the FDM and the AM is demonstrated. Error measures are defined as

$$e = \frac{1}{M} \sum_{i=1}^{M} |\boldsymbol{y}[i] - \tilde{\boldsymbol{y}}[i]|,$$

where $|a|$ stands for the absolute value of $a \in \mathbb{R}$ and M denotes the size of the vector of the analytical solution $\boldsymbol{y}$ and of the vector of the approximation $\tilde{\boldsymbol{y}}$.

A. Differentiable Time Signal

For analysis purpose a time-domain signal, a differentiable function, is defined as follows

$$y(t) := sin(t)exp(t)$$

TABLE II. ERRORS AND NUMBER OF OPERATIONS OF THE DELC METHOD, FOR A DIFFERENTIABLE SIGNAL, FOR AN APPROXIMATION ORDER $N = 1, \dots, 12$ AND FOR THE STEP SIZE $h = 0.1$.

N	e	# operations
1	$4.2703 \cdot 10^{-1}$	5
2	$4.6332 \cdot 10^{-2}$	7
3	$3.7491 \cdot 10^{-3}$	9
4	$2.7147 \cdot 10^{-4}$	11
5	$4.3495 \cdot 10^{-5}$	13
6	$6.5061 \cdot 10^{-6}$	15
7	$6.8851 \cdot 10^{-7}$	17
8	$5.0015 \cdot 10^{-8}$	19
9	$7.7212 \cdot 10^{-9}$	21
10	$1.3139 \cdot 10^{-9}$	23
11	$1.6258 \cdot 10^{-10}$	25
12	$1.4103 \cdot 10^{-11}$	27

and discretized using a constant step size h. The theoretical results are proved by comparison to the analytical derivative

$$y'(t) = (cos(t) + sin(t))exp(t).$$

The first example approximates the first derivative of $y(t)$, compares the different methods and points out the performance of the DELC method by varying the order of the approximation, i.e., increasing the number of used samples (7). For this example the following parameters are chosen

$$t \in [0, 3], \quad h = 0.1.$$

For the FDM or the AM the errors are

$$e_{FDM} = 0.4270308, \quad e_{AM} = 0.4270573,$$

the parameters for the AM are $N = 2, v = 1, M = 10$ whereby the notation is based on [6]. In Table II the errors from the DELC method are given, there the error estimation (12) is clearly valid. It is worthy to point out that the errors of the introduced DELC method are much smaller, for $N > 1$. For $N = 1$ the error coincides with e_{FDM}, this shows the mentioned fact of section II.C.2. It is also obvious that the computational effort, also for high order approximations, is low, so the computation of derivatives can be made nearly instantly. In Figure 2, the errors depending on the order of the approximation N are depicted.

To check the error estimation (12) for decreasing step size and different orders of approximations, the same function and parameters are chosen. In Table III, the order of convergence is shown, if the absolute error gets small, about 10^{-12}, the convergence stops, that comes from numerical errors - this can be neglected. Table III shows that (12) is satisfied, concluding with a match of theory and practice.

To verify the error estimation (12) the function and the parameters are the same as above but the step size and the degree of the derivative is varied. For this purpose the order of the approximation with $N = 6$ is fixed. Table IV shows that the error estimation is satisfied, also for high order derivatives.

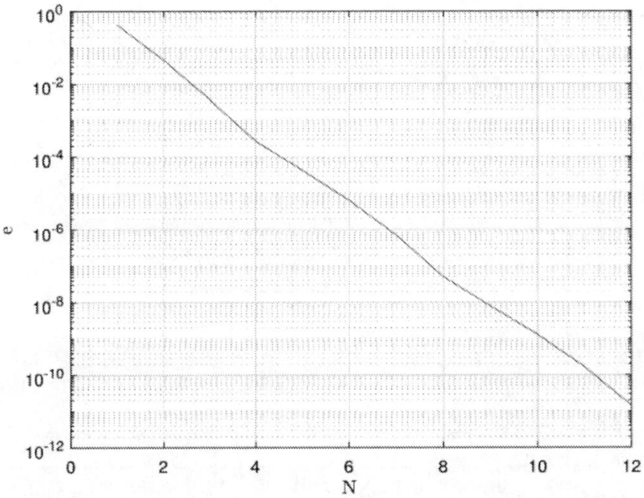

Figure 2. Plot of the errors from Table II, depending on the approximation order N.

TABLE III. ORDER OF CONVERGENCE OF THE DELC METHOD, FOR A DIFFERENTIABLE SIGNAL, FOR THE FIRST DERIVATIVE AND AN APPROXIMATION ORDER $N = 1, \ldots, 6$.

h	N=1	N=2	N=3	N=4	N=5	N=6
1/2	0.93	1.65	2.41	3.54	3.80	3.36
1/4	1.00	1.82	2.75	3.63	3.99	4.83
1/8	1.00	1.90	2.89	3.71	4.50	5.49
1/16	1.00	1.95	2.95	3.85	4.75	5.76
1/32	1.00	1.98	2.98	3.92	4.88	5.89
1/64	1.00	1.99	2.99	3.96	4.94	5.95
1/128	1.00	2.00	2.99	3.98	4.97	5.93
1/256	1.00	2.00	3.00	3.99	4.94	1.03
1/512	1.00	2.00	3.00	4.00	1.98	-0.95

TABLE IV. ORDER OF CONVERGENCE OF DELC METHOD, FOR A DIFFERENTIABLE SIGNAL, FOR AN APPROXIMATION ORDER 6 AND FOR AN ORDER OF DERIVATIVE $j = 1, \ldots, 6$.

h	j=1	j=2	j=3	j=4	j=5	j=6
1/2	3.36	2.55	1.80	1.13	0.50	0.26
1/4	4.82	3.88	2.95	2.06	1.22	0.51
1/8	5.49	4.50	3.52	2.56	1.62	0.75
1/16	5.76	4.77	3.78	2.79	1.82	0.87
1/32	5.89	4.89	3.89	2.90	1.91	0.94
1/64	5.95	4.95	3.95	2.95	1.96	0.97
1/128	5.93	5.10	3.87	2.95	1.99	0.99

B. Black Box System

The task is to compute the output-input sensitivity of a black box system. Using $u(t)$ the input and $y(u(t))$ the output of the system, the chain role leads to

$$\frac{dy}{dt} = \frac{dy}{du}\frac{du}{dt}$$

which is equivalent to

$$\frac{dy}{du} = \frac{dy}{dt} / \frac{du}{dt}.$$

By computing dy/dt and du/dt the output-input sensitivity dy/du can be determined. This has to be performed by using the discrete signals of u and y exclusively.
To simulate the black box the following linear, time invariant system is used

$$\dot{\boldsymbol{x}} = A\boldsymbol{x} + \boldsymbol{b}u$$
$$\boldsymbol{y} = \boldsymbol{c}^T\boldsymbol{x}$$

whereby $u(t) := cos(t)$ and

$$A = \begin{bmatrix} -0.1 & 0 \\ 1 & -1 \end{bmatrix}, \boldsymbol{b} = \begin{bmatrix} 1 \\ 1 \end{bmatrix}, \boldsymbol{c} = \begin{bmatrix} 2 \\ 1 \end{bmatrix},$$
$$\boldsymbol{x} = \begin{bmatrix} x_1 \\ x_2 \end{bmatrix}, \boldsymbol{y} = \begin{bmatrix} y_1 \\ y_2 \end{bmatrix}, \boldsymbol{x}(0) = \begin{bmatrix} 0 \\ 1 \end{bmatrix}.$$

Note: The simple linear system is chosen for the derivation of the analytical solution for comparison purpose. For the calculation of dy/dt and du/dt it does not matter if the system is linear, non-linear or high-dimensional in general, unless the signal is differentiable, the computation exclusively depends on the discrete input and output signals.

To compute dy/du three different methods are applied, the FDM, the AM and the DELC. The chosen parameters of the simulation are

$$t \in [5, 10], \quad h = 0.1,$$

leading to following errors

$$e_{FDM} = 10.039617, \quad e_{AM} = 15.289524.$$

The errors of the DELC method are stated in Table V. As pointed out in Figure 3, there are two singularities in the derivative, especially in their vicinity the solution from the FDM and the AM is poor. To prove that, this is not the only reason why the DELC method is outperforming, the time interval for a second simulation is changed to

$$t \in [7, 9],$$

the solutions in this case are depicted in Figure 4. For this the errors are

$$e_{FDM} = 0.2657728 \quad e_{AM} = 0.4568813.$$

So the errors, in case of no singularity, are much smaller, but still huge compared to the DELC method. Also the errors of the DELC decreases a lot, comparing to the cases with and without singularities, see Table V.

IV. CONCLUSION AND FUTURE WORK

A. Conclusion

The DELC method has some major advantages in accuracy, computational effort and time-delay compared to the FDM or the AM, the examples show that the approximation works well. Especially the low computational effort, the high accuracy and the small time delay, makes the introduced DELC method attractive and well suited for control systems and real-time applications.

TABLE V. ERRORS OF THE DELC METHOD, FOR THE BLACK BOX EXAMPLE, FOR AN APPROXIMATION ORDER $N = 1, \dots, 12$, FOR DIFFERENT TIME INTERVALS AND FOR STEP SIZE $h = 0.1$.

N	e for $t \in [5, 10]$	e for $t \in [7, 9]$
2	$8.7236 \cdot 10^{-2}$	$1.3019 \cdot 10^{-3}$
3	$8.5957 \cdot 10^{-2}$	$1.3543 \cdot 10^{-3}$
4	$1.1549 \cdot 10^{-3}$	$1.7732 \cdot 10^{-5}$
5	$5.6694 \cdot 10^{-4}$	$8.8775 \cdot 10^{-6}$
6	$1.2895 \cdot 10^{-5}$	$1.9959 \cdot 10^{-7}$
7	$4.1388 \cdot 10^{-6}$	$6.4848 \cdot 10^{-8}$
8	$1.3604 \cdot 10^{-7}$	$2.1108 \cdot 10^{-9}$
9	$3.1904 \cdot 10^{-8}$	$4.9962 \cdot 10^{-10}$
10	$1.4402 \cdot 10^{-9}$	$2.1866 \cdot 10^{-11}$
11	$1.5474 \cdot 10^{-10}$	$3.7318 \cdot 10^{-12}$
12	$1.8636 \cdot 10^{-10}$	$2.9004 \cdot 10^{-12}$

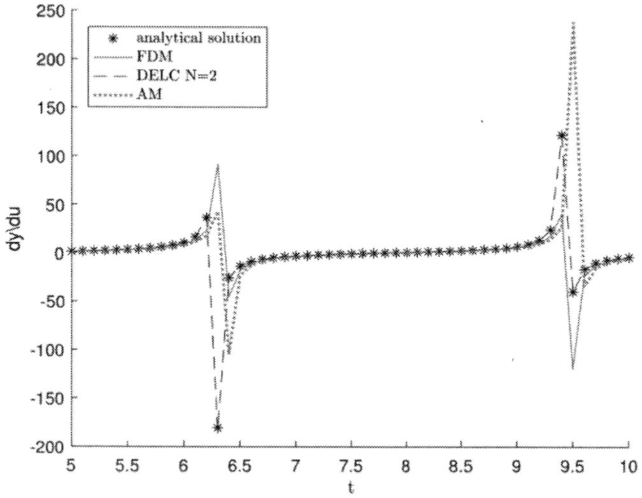

Figure 3. dy/du for $t \in [5, 10]$, with two singularities at $t_1 = 6.3$ and $t_2 = 9.4$, parameters for the AM are $N = 2, v = 1, M = 20$, notation based on [6].

B. Future Work

Future work will focus on implementation aspects like:

1) adaptive step size: The assumption that the step size is constant might represent a significant restriction for industrial applications, so the method has to be generalized for completely arbitrary step size. Only then the method will be completely applicable for simulations in the industrial context, where typically the step size is chosen in an adaptive manner.

2) noise handling: The DELC method presented in this paper is developed and tested for noiseless signals, which is fine e.g., simulations. In case of noisy signals the proposed method has to be improved due to the fact that polynomial interpolation, see Section II.B, is not useful for noisy signals.

3) solvability of the matrix equation: From a theoretical point of view, the solvability of the matrix equations should be proofed. It would also be interesting to verify if the coefficients are the optimal choice and how big the influence of round off errors for the computation is.

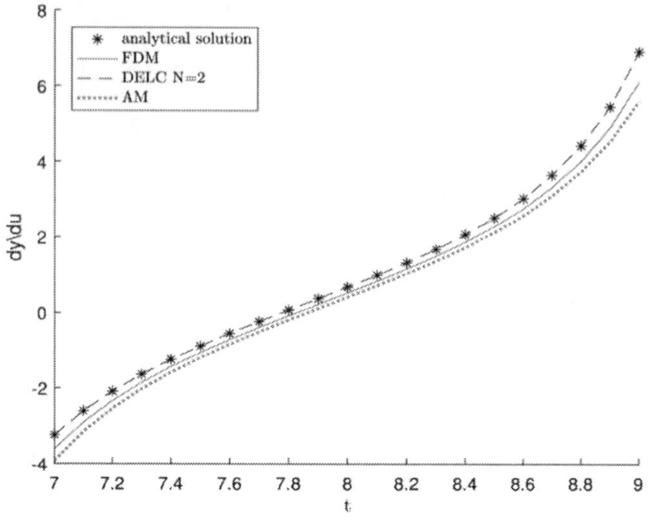

Figure 4. dy/du for $t \in [7, 9]$, without a singularity, parameters for the AM are $N = 2, v = 1, M = 20$, notation based on [6].

ACKNOWLEDGMENT

This work was accomplished at the VIRTUAL VEHICLE Research Center in Graz, Austria. The authors would like to acknowledge the financial support of the COMET K2 - Competence Centers for Excellent Technologies Programme of the Austrian Federal Ministry for Transport, Innovation and Technology (bmvit), the Austrian Federal Ministry of Science, Research and Economy (bmwfw), the Austrian Research Promotion Agency (FFG), the Province of Styria and the Styrian Business Promotion Agency (SFG).

REFERENCES

[1] S. P. Banks, Ed., *Control systems engineering: modelling and simulation, control theory and microprocessor implementation.* Prentice-Hall, 1986.

[2] P. Sircar, Ed., *Mathematical aspects of signal processing.* Cambridge University Press, 2016.

[3] A. Kaw and E. Kalu, "A stable finite difference ansatz for higher order differentation of non exact data," *Bull.Austral. Math. Soc.*, vol. 58, pp. 223–232, 1998.

[4] J. W. Thomas, Ed., *Finite difference methods.* Springer, 1995.

[5] D. De Pauw and P. Vanrolleghem, "Using the complex-step derivative approximation method to calculate local sensitivity functions of highly nonlinear bioprocess models."

[6] J. Zehetner, J. Reger, and M. Horn, "Realtime implementation of an algebraic derivative estimation scheme," *Oldenbourg Wissenschaftsverlag*, pp. 553–560, 11/2007.

[7] A. Owe, Ed., *Iterative Solution Methods.* Cambridge University Press, 1994.

[8] M. Benzi, "Preconditioning techniques for large linear systems: A survey," *Mathematics and Computer Science Department, Emory University, Atlanta, Georgia*, 2002.

[9] A. J. Wathen, "Preconditioning," *Cambridge University Press*, vol. 48, pp. 329 – 376, 2015.

[10] K. Chen, Ed., *Matrix Preconditioning Techniques and Applications.* Cambridge University Press, 2005, vol. 1.

Using VIRL to Improve the Scale-out of Large Virtual Network Testbeds in Higher Education

Sven Reißmann*, Sebastian Rieger†, Christian Pape†
*Datacenter
Fulda University of Applied Sciences, Fulda, Germany
Email: sven.reissmann@rz.hs-fulda.de
†Department of Applied Computer Science
Fulda University of Applied Sciences, Fulda, Germany
Email: {sebastian.rieger, christian.pape}@cs.hs-fulda.de

Abstract—**To build laboratory setups for courses and research projects in higher education dealing with computer networks, virtualized network environments have been continuously gaining momentum over the last years. Depending on the desired practical or theoretical orientation, they can be implemented using different hardware or software solutions. A high practical relevance and functional realism can be achieved using network emulation. However, the emulation requires more resources compared to network simulators, due to the complexity of realistic network functions. To offer emulated virtual network environments, e.g., for a large number of participants in higher education courses, scalable virtualization backends and cluster solutions are necessary. This paper describes the solutions used for network emulation and simulation in the network laboratory (NetLab) of Fulda University of Applied Sciences and discusses possibilities to evaluate and improve their scalability and performance.**

Keywords–Emulation; Simulation; Network Virtualization; Higher Education; VIRL.

I. Introduction

In research and higher education, especially in the area of computer networks, experimental testbeds are a typical requirement. To provide such environments, various approaches are possible, depending on the intended focus on theoretical or practical relevance. Figure 1 gives an overview of corresponding gradations of possible approaches, including references to some of the tools available. While the implementation of testbeds in real-world networks, e.g., campus networks of organizations and universities as shown at the left end of the figure, would provide the most realistic testbed, the risk of interference with regular operation and availability of the production network forbids this option in most cases. To overcome this problem, a separate physical testbed can be created apart from the production network. However, bootstrapping such a testbed with realistic characteristics is complex and expensive, hence making fast adaption to varying requirements and ever-changing network environments far from realistic. Virtual testbeds can reduce the setup cost immensely, but besides the additional effort and complexity introduced by the virtualization, still a lot of manual work is required for providing the required networking components and interfaces, setting up virtual networks and so on.

Theoretical models, as shown on the right of Figure 1, take a completely different approach by abstracting complex network topologies and protocols in the model. This is specifically useful when designing experimental protocols, but the implementation of such formal specifications - or even the transfer of the insights learned - in the real world can be quite challenging due to missing practical orientation. Simulations, though also based on an abstract model of the network and protocols, improve the practical relevance by trying to replicate real-world characteristics. One of the big advantages of simulations is the capability of exact modeling of real-world behavior, such as timing or transmission quality. Another advantage of deterministic simulation is the option of changing the simulation speed. However, only an abstract network is modeled by a simulation, which does not fully reflect the characteristics of a real network.

To resolve these issues, emulation is recommended in [1] as the means of choice to implement virtual network testbeds. The authors come to this conclusion by evaluating the goals and advantages of emulation using the following criteria: *Functional Realism*, *Timing Realism*, *Traffic Realism*, *Topology Flexibility*, *Easy Replication*, and *Low Cost*. In their research, they show that emulation only lacks in the area of *Timing Realism* while fulfilling all other evaluation criteria. Therefore, emulation provides a flexible foundation for experimental network testbeds being positioned in the middle between practical implementations with high relevance for real-world environments and accurate but typically rather abstract theoretical models. Besides the evaluation in [1], the advantages perceived by using emulation for virtual network testbeds with a high practical relevance is also described in [2], [3] and [4]. Hence, this approach is currently primarily used for higher education courses in the NetLab providing similar advantages that will be discussed in this paper.

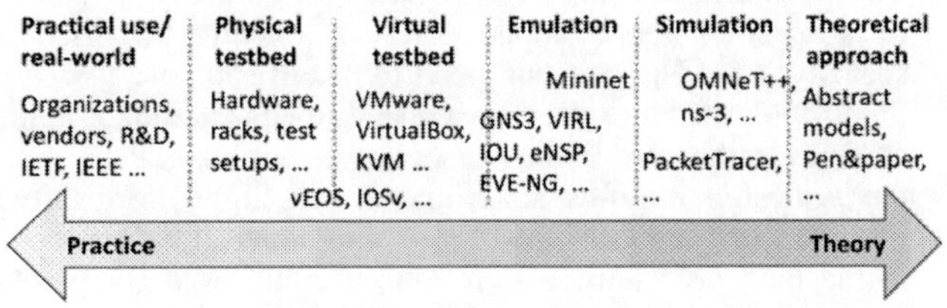

Figure 1. Classification of experimental scientific networking testbeds.

Nevertheless, the emulation of scalable virtual network testbeds results in high resource requirements due to the number of virtual machines needed, especially for large research projects or higher education courses. In this paper, we present an analysis of these resource requirements of virtual network testbeds based on experiences from providing such an environment in the networking laboratory (NetLab) in the Applied Computer Science department of Fulda University of Applied Sciences. Solutions that were evaluated and used in the NetLab, are shown in Figure 1 (e.g., GNS3, EVE-NG, VIRL). Primarily, currently Cisco's Virtual Internet Routing Lab (VIRL) is used. Advantages of this solution will be presented in this paper. Further, we discuss options to improve the scalability of such an environment.

The remaining part of this paper is laid out as follows. Section II introduces software products available for experimental networking testbeds based on the classification and examples shown in Figure 1. The following Section III discusses related work in this area. Based on our experiences during the implementation of these solutions, in Section IV we present our selection of tools for creating a scalable platform for virtual networking testbeds. Section V gives examples for emulated network topologies used in higher education courses in the NetLab including a description of the implementation. Next, an evaluation of the scalability and performance of the environment is presented in Section VI. Finally, a conclusion and future work can be found in Section VII.

II. Virtual Environments for Network Testbeds

Emulation can be seen as a compromise between theory and practice, especially when it is used to implement virtual network testbeds. It allows to deploy real-world operating systems (i.e., GNU/Linux servers, Windows clients) and utilize typical network management tools, like Wireshark or iperf. In the NetLab *physical and virtual testbeds*, as well as *emulation* and *simulation* have been used over the past years to support higher education courses and research projects. In accordance with the results discussed in [1], emulation has proven to be a particularly flexible solution. Physical testbeds are provided in the lab in form of pre-packed experimental racks to allow realistic student projects and Cisco certifications (i.e., CCNA, CCNP) [5]. However, due to the complex and time-intense preparation of the environment, these physical testbeds are not suitable for short-term exercises and lab sessions in which students should carry out experiments, e.g., to see the practical use of theoretical concepts presented in a corresponding lecture.

Yet, the realization of *virtual testbeds* (i.e., using a distributed approach with VMware Workstation or a central approach with VMware vSphere ESXi) doesn't require less effort, as the preparation and maintenance of the virtual machines and networks is time consuming. For this reason, in the NetLab *virtual testbeds* are mostly used for practical relevant client-server applications and experiments in the IT security area. The constant need to install software updates in the virtual machines used for these testbeds and adapt them to changes in the surrounding laboratory environment throughout the semester, requires additional effort. Simulation software like ns-3 [6] or OMNeT++ [7] is mentioned in some lectures in master's programs, but are not currently used for practical relevant experiments in the lab.

Practical training for the previously mentioned CCNA certification includes the use of Cisco Packet Tracer [8]. However, in some lecture exercises students criticized the missing practical relevance. For example, network clients (i.e., PCs) in Packet Tracer are simulated and do not provide feature-complete implementations of common network tools, such as arp, ping or traceroute. Another drawback of the simulation is, that there are peculiarities that only appear in the simulation and need to be specifically explained to students. One example of such behavior is that in case of an ICMP PING, the first packet will be dropped at the router in the destination network until the destinations MAC address has been determined using ARP. While this behavior is correct, it typically can't be observed in a real network, where almost any client starts to send packets to the router immediately after booting the operating system, hence its MAC address is already in the routers ARP table, when sending ICMP PING packets. Besides this lack in *Traffic Realism* and the stated lack in *Functional Realism*, e.g., due to missing common tools in the simulated clients and network components, there is also no *Timing Realism* achieved within Packet Tracer, which is an even bigger problem for research projects.

The software Mininet [9], mentioned in [10] and [1], is also provided in our NetLab, where it is mainly used for experiments in the SDN area. While the resource requirements of Mininet are low, due to a container-based approach, individual topologies require decent knowledge of the underlying Python-API, which again is time-consuming in short-term courses. Further, it is not possible to use or connect arbitrary real-world network components in Mininet topologies.

III. Related Work

Services in today's cloud-driven infrastructures are based on sophisticated network topologies that interconnect various network and server components. The simulation and emulation of such network topologies for teaching higher education classes is subject of current research. In [3], a virtual environment based on VIRL is compared to physical setups using CCNA pods and network simulation software like Cisco Packet Tracer. Furthermore, the cost, setup requirements and limitations are estimated and reviewed. The use of VIRL in the area of research and education is also discussed in [4]. An extensible and scalable emulation/simulation framework based on a declarative XML-based language (as also used in VIRL) for modeling and evaluation of large network topologies is explained in [11]. This open-source toolset is also compared to other well-known simulation and emulation environments like ns-3 or PlanetLab. A brief introduction to model and simulate interconnected autonomous systems using the Boson Network Simulator is described in [12]. An open-source tool for simulating protocol behavior in congested networks by throttling network links and controlling delay and packet loss is described in [13]. This software is widespread and used in other emulation products to alter link transmission properties in network topologies. The didactics-oriented software called Netkit to model and emulate a wide-range of real-world devices is outlined in [2]. The goal of this emulation environment software is to setup networking experiments at low cost and with little effort. A framework for reproducible container-based emulation of networking experiments is presented in [1].

IV. Rationale for the Selection of VIRL

Over the last years, eNSP [14], GNS3 [15], EVE-NG [16] (formerly UNetLab) and VIRL [17] have been deployed and evaluated as a solution for realistic emulation of networking environments in the NetLab. Currently, VIRL is the most promising option used in the several courses. The advantages of VIRL are related to the findings in [1] and [4]. The functional realism of VIRL is extended compared to the other alternatives as it allows to use official network operating system images of Cisco components, like IOS or NX-OS, while at the same time, images from other vendors (i.e., Arista vEOS, HP VSR, Juniper vSRX/vMX, Cumulus VX) are supported as well. However, the most important advantage over the other alternatives is the underlying scale-out architecture (based on OpenStack). This allows a central and scalable installation and enables the users to access the emulated network topologies location-independent (i.e., from within the NetLab or from at home using private PCs and laptops, which is specifically important for students). Multiple VIRL hosts in the NetLab enable a scale-out of the testbed, which allows to emulate much bigger topologies than possible on a single PC in the laboratory or on a student notebook. In addition, the open architecture of OpenStack, as well as the open components used by VIRL (i.e., Ubuntu 14.04, LXC, linux-bridge, VXLAN) make it possible to extend the environment with in-house developed components to build specially tailored testbeds for the use in research and education. Improvements in terms of scalability (i.e., the size and amount of emulated testbeds), performance (i.e., the time to bootstrap a complete emulated topology) and usability (i.e., initial configuration) of VIRL in the area of research and education will be discussed in the following sections of the paper.

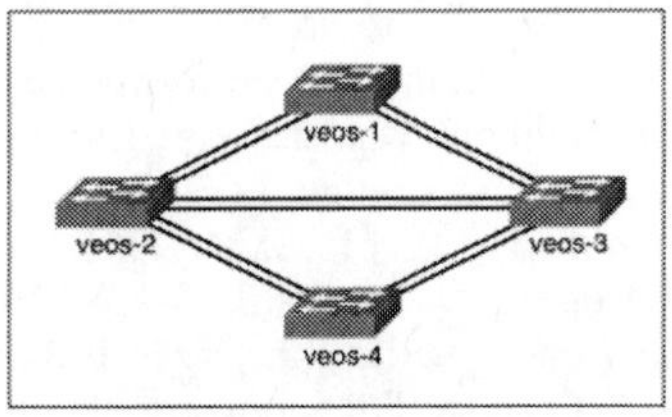

(a) 4-node Arista vEOS MLAG

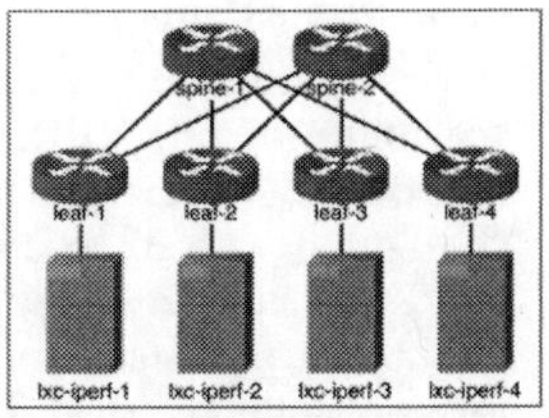

(b) Leaf-Spine BGP Fabric

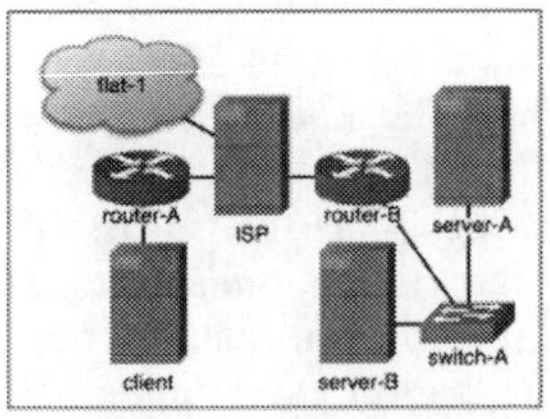

(c) Simple Toubleshooting

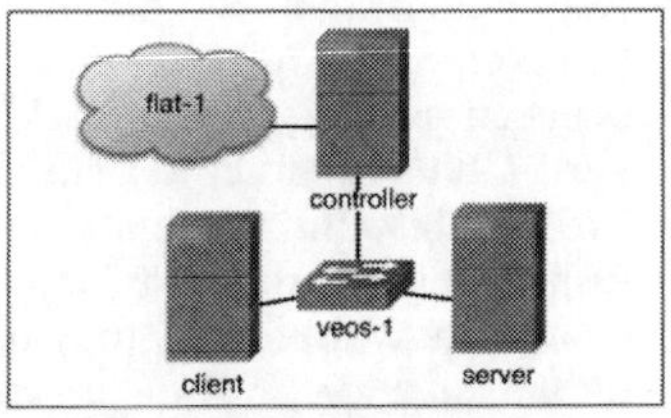

(d) vEOS/OpenDaylight SDN topology

Figure 2. Examples of emulated network topologies for student exercises.

V. Examples for Emulated Network Topologies in our Networking Laboratory (NetLab)

Refer to Figure 2 for VIRL-based network topologies used in our NetLab environment for student laboratory exercises. Figure 2a shows a topology consisting of four Arista vEOS (4.16.9) nodes with redundant links between them. The topology is one out of many used by master's students to understand and troubleshoot real-world networks. In this specific case, students team up to investigate the impact of the Spanning Tree Protocol (STP) in various data center scenarios using technologies like MSTP, LACP and MLAG. Based on similar exercises, the master's students also work on Leaf-Spine-based topologies including BGP fabrics, which are widely used in web-scale data centers by companies like Facebook or Microsoft (Figure 2b). Here, the endpoint nodes are based on Ubuntu 14.04 GNU/Linux Containers (LXC), while the Spine and Leaf switches are driven by Cisco IOSv (15.6(2)T). In the past we also realized similar topologies using vEOS (BGP) and NX-OSv (FabricPath). A great advantage of this setup is the flexibility we provide for the students. LXC containers can be managed using standard Linux commands via SSH, nodes can be started and stopped in the middle of a running emulation, network links can be connected or disconnected, and it is also possible to configure various QoS parameters like delay, jitter or packet loss on the links. Beyond that, traffic entering or leaving a specific interface can be collected and investigated using Wireshark. SDN-based scenarios including the OpenFlow controller *OpenDaylight* and OpenFlow 1.3 capable *Arista vEOS* switches, can be explored using the topology shown in Figure 2d. Since vEOS behaves identical compared to the EOS-based Arista hardware switches, by choosing VIRL over the previously used Mininet, students can test OpenFlow deployment in a near real-world environment.

An example of a much simpler network topology is shown in Figure 2c. Students in the bachelor program troubleshoot network misconfiguration (i.e., ARP, routing, delay, packet loss, port status) and discover the underlying network topology by using tools like ping, traceroute/mtr and Wireshark, before they establish connections to an Apache web server running on node Server-B. Again, all server and client nodes are based on Ubuntu 14.04 LXC, while switches in this scenarios are based on IOSvL2 (15.2(4.0.55)E). For realistic WAN emulation we use the standard Linux network emulation *netem* on the ISP node to inject delay and add packet loss. The node named ISP acts as a default gateway for the emulated topology, which is connected to the physical local area network for NetLab projects (flat-1). Thus, the invocation of commands like ping or traceroute targeting hosts on the Internet (i.e., google.com) is possible from inside the emulated environment. Furthermore, from within the NetLab, students can connect to their nodes in the emulated network using OpenVPN, for instance to configure the web server.

All examples mentioned in this section are managed using Git and can be downloaded from [18]. For the operation of VIRL in our environment, a few extensions were implemented, including customizations to the Arista vEOS and CumulusVX operating system images for our university's environment and for deployment in VIRL [19]. For example, to allow the operation of MLAG, it was necessary to modify the *base_mac* in order to prevent clashes of MAC address generated by vEOS with locally generated KVM MAC addresses [19].

VI. Performance and Scalability Evaluation

Thanks to using virtual networks for the exercises shown in Figure 2, students can especially benefit from the advantages of the emulation as discussed in Section I. However, for complex topologies and a large number of students in the class, the benefits of the emulation places enormous demands on the virtual infrastructure it is running on. Even for smaller topologies it can take more than 5 minutes to start the emulations. Hence, in the following sections, we describe a way to benchmark and optimize the waiting time until the emulations are ready to be used by the students in our laboratory.

A. *Implementation of a VIRL benchmarking environment*

The hardware we use for evaluating the performance and scalability of our VIRL environment was described in detail in [20]. All VIRL hosts are based on Ubuntu 14.04 VMs, each configured with 32 vCPUs and 64 GB of RAM. These VMs build a nested virtualization environment inside our VMware vSphere 6.5 cluster in which each of the four VMs is bound to a separate physical ESXi host by DRS constraints. Each underlying ESXi host is equipped with two 8-core Intel(R) Xeon(R) E5-2650v2 2.60 GHz CPUs, 256 GB RAM and uses two NetApp E2700 over a redundant 16 Gbit/s Fibre Channel connection as a storage back end. The nodes are connected via 1 Gbit/s Ethernet to a Cisco Catalyst 3850 switch and with two 10 Gbit/s links to an Arista 7150S-24 and Arista 7050S-52, respectively. As discussed in [1], the *Timing Realism* regarding emulation with regard to virtualization particularly depends on the isolation level of the virtualization environment. When strict isolation is not guaranteed, concurrently running VMs can have a negative performance impact. Therefore, we defined a separate resource pool with static resource allocation for our VIRL environment. All benchmarking scenarios were performed at night in the semester break to ensure minimum load on the ESXi cluster. By monitoring the overall performance and capacity of our VMware vSphere cluster, we were able to verify that VMs related to the VIRL benchmark were the only systems that produced considerable load in our VMware environment during the tests. The topology shown in Figure 2a was used to evaluate the performance and scalability of our environment. Due to its small size and node count, it can be scaled fine-grained up to the full capacity of our cluster. For the evaluation of the scalability of virtual testbeds and their application in higher education courses with a large number of participants, the following four metrics are of special interest:

- *Start Time*, the time until the start of all submitted topologies is processed by VIRL's REST API
- *Active Time*, the time until all VMs start to boot
- *Usable Time*, the time until booting has finished and the virtual console of all vEOS nodes is accessible
- *Console delay*, the latency of the virtual console

To measure these metrics and in order to minimize outliers, we developed a script to run our performance tests in a reliable and reproducible manner. Each test run first starts up the network topologies using VIRL's REST API and measures the time until the start is confirmed (*Start Time*) and all nodes become active (*Active Time*). In our terminology, *Active Time* means that the VM is deployed by the OpenStack Nova scheduler on a VIRL host system, all virtual networks and ports are up and accessible, the vEOS image is provided and the boot sequence starts. Next, we measure the time until the VM really becomes responsive by connecting to the virtual console (*Usable Time*) and finally measure the interaction delay of keyboard inputs (*Console delay*). For this purpose, a Python script was developed that establishes WebSocket connections to the serial consoles of the nodes running on the VIRL hosts.

A schematic representation of the VIRL environment is depicted in Figure 3. At first, we performed all tests on only a single VIRL node, meaning that the node not only executes the VMs needed for the emulated topology, but also acts as control node, which provides the OpenStack and VIRL environment.

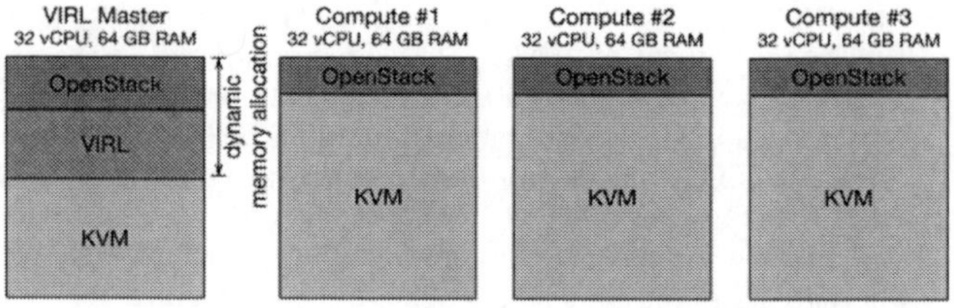

Figure 3. Schematic view of the environment's memory usage.

In Section VI-B we will share some negative observations we made, when including the control node in VM execution. Each individual test run for an increasing number of simultaneously emulated network topologies was executed ten times in a row. We started with only one topology and scaled in steps of five, until the VIRL host was working to capacity. Next, all tests were repeated on a 2-node and finally on a 4-node VIRL cluster to draw conclusions concerning scalability of the environment. The benchmark script and related toolset is available at [21].

B. *Scalability Evaluation*

The results from our previously explained test case are illustrated in Table I and Figure 4. When using a single VIRL host, the maximum number of simultaneously emulated network topologies is mainly limited by the resources (primarily the amount of main memory) available to the host. Each vEOS node uses 1 vCPU and 2 GB of RAM. Therefore, a test run with ten concurrently emulated network topologies requires 80 GB of main memory (10 * 4 vEOS nodes * 2 GB RAM) to be available, which is more than a single VIRL host in our test system can provide (Figure 3). Hence, a stable execution was not possible with a single host, even with memory over-provisioning enabled (Figure 4a).

TABLE I. RELATIVE CHANGE IN *Start Time*, *Active Time* AND *Usable Time* DEPENDENT ON THE NUMBER OF TOPOLOGIES.

Number of Topologies			*Start Time*	*Active Time*	*Usable Time*
1	→	5	5.0617	2.5242	1.7440
5	→	10	2.0378	1.8517	1.6705
10	→	15	1.5105	1.4693	1.4686
15	→	20	1.3597	1.4548	1.4420
20	→	25	1.2334	1.2797	1.2793
25	→	30	1.2081	1.2304	1.2349

Looking at the effects of the number of parallel topologies in respect of performance, Figure 4b clearly depicts our expectation of a linear increase of the *Start Time*, while with an increasing number of topologies the *Active Time* and *Usable Time* ascends non-linear. The effect can best be observed when performing the test on a cluster with four or more nodes (Figure 4c). Up to a number of 10 simultaneously started topologies, the difference between *Active Time* and *Usable Time* gets smaller. This can be explained by the overhead the OpenStack-based resource scheduling and management introduces, which decreases with the number of simultaneously started topologies. For higher numbers of concurrent simulations, the system load generated from setting up virtual networks and interfaces causes and increase the difference between *Active Time* and *Usable Time*. The curve for *Usable Time* has a larger slope as expected, as for an increasing number of virtual nodes, the time until all nodes are usable increases due to the limited resources.

Alongside with the overhead introduced by the scheduling, the comparatively large difference between *Start Time* and

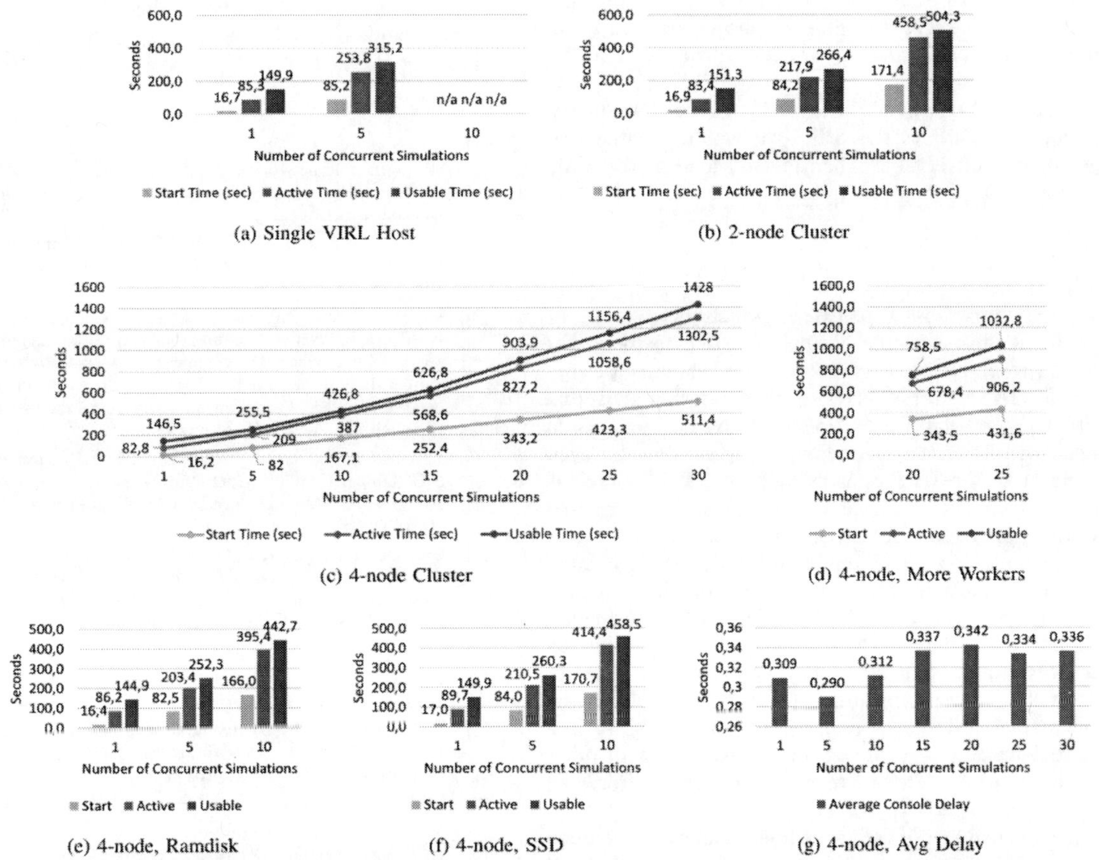

Figure 4. Results from measuring the time it takes to start multiple instances of the topology shown in Figure 2a.

Active Time results from the expensive process of creating all required virtual networks for connecting the devices. All links of the topology (Figure 2a) are redundant, which requires the creation of two VXLAN segments and its associated ports per pair of devices on the GNU/Linux bridge interface of the OpenStack nodes. The overhead of this was clearly visible by the CPU load produced by the Neutron process on the OpenStack controller node. The main limitation here is the fact, that neutron-server and nova-conductor are single-threaded in VIRL's OpenStack Kilo setup, which limits the maximum performance of virtual network creation to a single CPU core. In most of our test-cases, the CPU core neutron-server was executed on, was working to capacity. To overcome this limitation, we increased the number of neutron-server, nova-api and nova-conductor worker processes to ten. However, due to the fact that memory gets reserved on the VIRL master for these processes, the additional resource requirements resulted in a decrease of the maximum number of simultaneously started topologies to only 25 (Figure 3). Even more problematic was the observation, that some of the vEOS nodes were not successfully started at the end of the test run, which is most likely explained by the dynamic memory allocation. When starting all topologies nearly at the same time, nova-scheduler is not able to determine the truly remaining amount of main memory and schedules too many VMs to the control node. At the same time, Figure 4d depicts that the *Usable Time* of the 20 topologies decreased by 16% and *Active Time* by 18%. While we assume room for improvement by carefully optimizing the OpenStack and KVM configuration, our recommendation is rather the use of a dedicated VIRL master node, which is currently not possible in VIRL, but can be manually achieved by deactivating nova-compute on the controller. The average console delay of the emulated vEOS nodes stays nearly constant with a growing number of simultaneously active topologies, as shown in Figure 4g. As a result, even if the time to start the concurrent simulations increases, a smooth use of the individually usable emulations is guaranteed despite the increased CPU load of the hypervisors. Limiting factors regarding our benchmark are more related to the amount of main memory and I/O performance, rather than the CPU load. What accounts for the latter is primarily the OpenStack und VIRL management processes, as well as the boot process of the vEOS instances, which utilizes the assigned vCPU to capacity for about 60 seconds in case of our test setup. As a performance improvement, Cisco recommends the use of a ramdisk for running Nova VMs, as well as a SSD for the VIRL hosts. We implemented both recommendations in our test environment to compare the impact on performance. First, a ramdisk was created, which is only supported on the controller in VIRL, hence we needed to manually configure it on the compute nodes. Figure 4e depicts the measurement results, clearly showing only a minor performance improvement, which is obviously attributable to the small amount of required ephemeral storage of only about 213 MB for a vEOS image.

Second, we added two local solid state drives (Samsung 850 PRO) to each of the servers. Figure 4f shows no significant improvement of the performance, which is attributable to the previously used storage back end (NetApp E2700) already offering about 650 MB/s read/write performance. Due to the higher number of IOPS of the SSD, we would assume that an improvement is observable when the I/O load of the VMs increases as a result of more complex topologies.

VII. Conclusion and Future Work

Cisco VIRL provides a platform, which is capable of creating realistic and scalable virtual network testbeds for education and research projects. In comparison with alternatives, such as GNS3 or EVE-NG, a clear advantage is that it offers to use original Cisco operating system images in conformance with license requirements. Beyond that, an even more important feature is the foundation of VIRL, which is based on the open source project OpenStack. This enabled us to modify and extend the environment as shown in this paper, and to build a well-scaling multi-node VIRL cluster, which supports a sufficiently large number of simultaneous emulations for application in education. Further, by allowing the utilization of standard network management applications (i.e., ping, traceroute) and operating systems (i.e., Ubuntu VMs) inside the emulated network testbeds, as well as the connection to real physical networks, a great flexibility and functional realism can be achieved in comparison with other simulation approaches. The increased start time introduced by the emulation, especially for complex topologies, can be compensated by using a VIRL scheduler that we developed to specifically address the requirements of our NetLab. It offers to pre-load topologies based on a schedule, e.g., in advance of an upcoming seminar, hence minimizing delays for the students. Additionally, we are actively developing a management application for VIRL labs. When finished, it will provide a self-service system enabling students to subscribe to courses and to start working on topologies and reserving virtual lab time. To increase performance even further, the most promising approaches are given by increasing the number of cluster nodes and optimizing to the OpenStack resources management, as well as the underlying network infrastructure.

By the time of writing, new major versions of the previously mentioned software projects GNS3 and EVE-NG were released, both with valuable new features. As an example, EVE-NG added support for multiple simultaneous users who can work on the same topology, which is a requirement to qualify for educational use. Still, both projects do not provide a way to use Cisco operating system images in conformance with the license requirements, however, other network operating systems like Arista vEOS are available. In the future, we will setup a new lab environment with these software projects to evaluate the suitability and scalability for our use-cases. Since Cisco seems to have changed the strategy for VIRL and tries to move universities to the expensive Cisco Modeling Lab, the new version of GNS3 could become an interesting alternate candidate for our environment. We are currently looking into the possibility to develop appropriate extensions to GNS3 or EVE-NG to fix the current lack in cluster-based load balancing and centralized management and real-time collaboration options on running simulations compared to VIRL.

Acknowledgment

We thank Cisco for providing us with a research license within the context of the Cisco dev/innovate research program.

References

[1] N. Handigol, B. Heller, V. Jeyakumar, B. Lantz, and N. McKeown, "Reproducible network experiments using container-based emulation," in Proceedings of the 8th international conference on Emerging networking experiments and technologies. ACM, 2012, pp. 253–264.

[2] M. Pizzonia and M. Rimondini, "Netkit: network emulation for education," Software: Practice and Experience, vol. 46, no. 2, Feb. 2016, pp. 133–165.

[3] S. V. Tagliacane, P. W. C. Prasad, G. Zajko, A. Elchouemi, and A. K. Singh, "Network simulations and future technologies in teaching networking courses: Development of a laboratory model with Cisco Virtual Internet Routing Lab (Virl)," in 2016 International Conference on Wireless Communications, Signal Processing and Networking (WiSPNET). IEEE, 2016, pp. 644–649.

[4] J. Obstfeld et al., "VIRL: The Virtual Internet Routing Lab," SIGCOMM Comput. Commun. Rev., vol. 44, no. 4, Aug. 2014, pp. 577–578. [Online]. Available: http://doi.acm.org/10.1145/2740070.2631463

[5] C. Pape and C. Seifert, "Adaption and improvement of an industry-developed IP Telephony curriculum," in 7th Annual International Conference on Computer Science and Education in Computer Science, Sofia/Dobrinishte, Jul. 2011, pp. 199–210.

[6] ns-3. URL: https://www.nsnam.org, 2017.06.07. (2017)

[7] OMNeT++ Discrete Event Simulator. URL: https://omnetpp.org, 2017.06.07. (2017)

[8] Packet Tracer - A free network simulation and visualization tool for the IoT era. URL: https://www.netacad.com/about-networking-academy/packet-tracer, 2017.06.07. (2017)

[9] Mininet - An Instant Virtual Network on your Laptop (or other PC). URL: http://mininet.org, 2017.06.07. (2017)

[10] B. Lantz, B. Heller, and N. McKeown, "A network in a laptop: rapid prototyping for software-defined networks," in Proceedings of the 9th ACM SIGCOMM Workshop on Hot Topics in Networks. ACM, 2010, p. 19.

[11] B. Momeni and M. Kharrazi, "Partov - a network simulation and emulation tool." J. Simulation, vol. 10, no. 4, 2016, pp. 237–250.

[12] M. A. Qadeer, P. Varshney, and N. H. Khan, "Design and Simulation of Interconnected Autonomous Systems," in 2009 International Conference on Computer Engineering and Technology (ICCET). IEEE, 2009, pp. 270–275.

[13] S. Hemminger, "Network emulation with NetEm," in Linux conf au, 2005, pp. 18–23.

[14] eNSP - Enterprise Network Simulator. URL: http://support.huawei.com/enterprise/en/network-management/ensp-pid-9017384, 2017.06.07. (2017)

[15] GNS3 - The software that empowers network professionals. URL: https://www.gns3.com, 2017.06.07. (2017)

[16] Emulated Virtual Environment Next Generation (EVE-NG) / Unified Networking Lab (UNL). URL: http://www.unetlab.com, 2017.06.07. (2017)

[17] VIRL - Virtual Internet Routing Lab. URL: http://virl.cisco.com, 2017.06.07. (2017)

[18] HS-Fulda NetLab VIRL Topologien. URL: https://gogs.informatik.hs-fulda.de/srieger/git-virl-hs-fulda, 2017.06.07. (2017)

[19] S. Rieger. Arista vEOS image on VIRL. URL: https://learningnetwork.cisco.com/thread/99040, 2017.06.07. (2017)

[20] K. Spindler et al., "AEQUO: Enhancing the energy efficiency in private clouds using compute and network power management functions," International Journal on Advances in Internet Technology Volume 8, Number 1 & 2, 2015, vol. 8, no. 1 & 2, 2015, pp. 13–28.

[21] HS-Fulda NetLab VIRL Utilities. URL: https://gogs.informatik.hs-fulda.de/srieger/virl-utils-hs-fulda, 2017.06.07. (2017)

A Framework for Simulation Validation & Verification Method Selection

Bill Roungas
Alexander Verbraeck

Department of Multi Actor Systems
Delft University of Technology
Delft, The Netherlands
Email: v.roungas@tudelft.nl,
a.verbraeck@tudelft.nl

Sebastiaan Meijer

Department of Health Systems Engineering
KTH Royal Institute of Technology
Huddinge, Sweden
Email: sebastiaan.meijer@sth.kth.se

***Abstract*—Thirty years of research on validation and verification (V&V) has returned a plethora of methods, statistical techniques, and reported case studies. It is that abundance of methods that poses a major challenge. Because of overlap between methods and time and budget constraints, it is impossible to apply all the available methods in a single study, so a careful selection of methods has to be made. This paper builds on two assumptions: a) that both simulations and V&V methods can be defined on the basis of different characteristics and b) that certain V&V methods are more suitable than others for different kinds of simulations. The present study aims at identifying the specific characteristics that make a V&V method more effective and more efficient than others, when confronting these with the simulations' different characteristics. The conclusion will advance a methodology for choosing the most appropriate method or methods for validating and/or verifying a simulation.**

Keywords–simulation; validation; verification; method selection.

I. INTRODUCTION

Back in 1972, based on Forrester's work [1], Meadows et al. [2], [3] introduced World 3, a simulation of the world for the years 1900-2100. The purpose of the simulation model was to project the dynamic behavior of population, capital, food, non-renewable resources, and pollution. The model's forecast was that the world would experience a major industrial collapse, which would be followed by a significant decrease in human population. The model became very popular especially because of the increasing interest in environmental degradation due to human activities [4]. Even though the model gained support for being "of some use to decision makers" [3] and generated the spark for many later global models, it had several shortcomings, for which it received a lot of criticism as well [5]. In turn, this criticism raised the question of whether, and to what extent, such simulation models are validated and verified. This is just one example of the notion that V&V is a fundamental part of a simulation study [6].

The term V&V is used to characterize two relatively different approaches, which almost always go hand in hand, validation and verification. Validation is this phase of a study that ensures that the simulation imitates the underline system, to a greater or lesser extent, and in any case to a satisfactory degree [7], or in layman terms validation address the question: did we build the "right" model [8]. On the other hand, verification is the phase of the study that ensures that the model and its implementation are correct [9], or in layman terms verification addresses the question: did we build the model "right" [8]. V&V has become a well-researched field with a significant amount of produced literature and commercial case studies. The large number of methods and techniques created by this wide range of research, is the greatest impediment to the designing of a V&V study.

The predetermined budget of a simulation study usually limits the amount of time and resources that can be spent on V&V. Additionally, the nature and the diverse characteristics of simulations limit the number of V&V methods that are applicable for each simulation. In other words, not all V&V methods are suitable for every simulation. To the best of our knowledge, a taxonomy for characterizing V&V methods and, subsequently, matching them with different simulations does not exist.

This paper aims at identifying the majority of the available V&V methods in order to classify them on the basis of their different characteristics and on whether they can validate or verify a simulation, and eventually match them with characteristics of simulation models.

Section II starts with a literature analysis on V&V methods, simulation properties, and simulation study phases, and then proceeds with introducing a methodology towards developing a framework for simulation V&V method selection. In Section III, a case study is presented to illustrate how the proposed framework can be put in practice. Finally, in Section IV, the future potential extensions of the framework are presented and final remarks are made.

II. THE FRAMEWORK

This section starts with a 3-step literature analysis and then proceeds with proposing a methodology for selecting one or more methods for a V&V study.

A. The 3-step Literature Analysis

The initial hypothesis of this study is that simulations exhibit certain properties that influence the effectiveness of a V&V method. Therefore, the 3 steps of the literature analysis are the following:

Step 1: Identification of V&V methods.
Step 2: Identification of simulations' properties.
Step 3: Identification of the phases of a simulation study.

1) Step 1: V&V methods, as indicated by their definitions on Table I, are different in many aspects; some methods are strictly mathematical whereas others accommodate the more qualitative aspects of simulations, etc. Balci [10] identified more than 70 V&V methods, which he in turn categorized into four categories: informal, static, dynamic, and formal. Balci's [10] list is the most accurate representation of the body of work on V&V methods and, even to date, is considered as the most extensive one. This paper adopts the list in reference - but not the categorization - and goes as far as to propose a new classification of V&V methods. Further to the above, whilst the list is adopted in its entirety, some methods may occasionally appear to have been excluded. In effect, this occurs only when a particular method belongs to a group of methods, in which case if there are no significant differences between these methods, only the "parent" method is enlisted. Due to size restrictions, it is not possible to provide the definition of each method in this section. Nevertheless, references to detailed definitions can be found in Table I.

2) Step 2: Since simulations differ from one another in various ways, distinctions are made on whether they represent an existing system, or whether they simulate a system at a microscopic or macroscopic level, or whether they are intended for learning or decision making, and so forth. This is an indication that simulations can be characterized by various properties. Based on literature, this study has identified 10 properties of simulations. The rationale behind selecting those properties was to describe simulations with as much detail as possible. Hence, the properties span multiple levels. Not all identified properties necessarily influence the selection of V&V methods, therefore this step is not only about identifying the properties but also determining which are the ones that really influence the effectiveness of a method; in other words, this step serves as the rationale for choosing those properties of simulations that are applicable to specific V&V methods, and provides for the reasons behind this selection.

The 10 identified properties of simulations are the following:

1) Access to the source code of the simulation. Accessibility, or lack of it, influences the selection of a V&V method [11], since several methods require some sort of a check on the code level. Hence, this property is included in the analysis.
2) The simulation represents an existing real-system for which real data exist [12]. The existence of, or more importantly the lack of, real data heavily influences the selection process since several methods require real data and thus cannot be used when there are not any. Hence, this property is included in the analysis.
3) The formalism the simulation is based on, like Discrete Event System Specification (DEVS), Differential Equation Specified System (DESS), System Dynamics, etc. [13]. Several frameworks and methods have been proposed on how to verify and validate DEVS [14], [15], DESS [16], [17], or system dynamics models [18], [19], but they are either application specific or the same method can be used in more than one formalisms, making it independent of the actual formalism. Therefore, while formalisms are an important aspect of simulation modeling, their influence on the V&V method selection are minimal, ergo excluded from the analysis.
4) The simulation's worldviews: i) Process Interaction/Locality of Object, ii) Event Scheduling/Locality of Time, iii) Activity Scanning/Locality of State [20]. While worldviews allow for more concise model descriptions by allowing a model specifier to take advantage of contextual information, there is not any evidence from a literature point of view that they have an influence on the V&V method selection, hence, they are excluded from the analysis.
5) The fidelity level of the simulation (Low, Medium, High) [21]. While from a literature point of view there is no evidence to support the influence of the level of fidelity on the V&V method selection, common sense dictates that there must be some. Indeed, in order to characterize a simulation as of high fidelity, it must imitates an existing system and real-world data must exist, thus making the comparison and the final characterization possible. Therefore, as discussed in the second property and is shown in Table I, since the existence of data of the real system influences the V&V method selection, so does the level of fidelity, but since the correlation between real data and high fidelity is almost 1-to-1, the fidelity level is excluded from the analysis for reasons of simplification.
6) The type of the simulation (Constructive, Virtual, Live) [22]. This classification, which is adopted by the U.S. Department of Defense [23], should be seen more as a continuum rather than a discrete characterization. Once a simulation moves towards the Virtual or the Live side of the continuum, it can also be referred to as 'a game'. A game has the distinct characteristic that the game session is succeeded by debriefing, whereby the participants reflect upon the game session to link the content presented during the session with reality [24]. It has been demonstrated that debriefing can in general facilitate validation [25], [26], but except for two methods, i.e., *User Interface Analysis* and *User Interface Testing*, there is no evidence in literature on whether the type of simulation affects the V&V method selection. Hence, this classification is excluded from the analysis.
7) The purpose the simulation was built for (learning, decision making, etc.). Several case studies on V&V of simulations for different purposes have been reported; in training [27], [28], in decision making [29], in concept testing [30], etc., but there are no reports of specific V&V methods being more effective for a certain purpose. Hence, this property is excluded from the analysis.
8) The simulation imitates a strictly technical, a socio technical system (STS), or a complex adaptive system (CAS) with multiple agents. There are several studies on modeling and validating simulations for STS [31] and CAS with multiple agents [32], [33] but there are no indications that certain V&V methods are more effective for an STS or a CAS. Therefore, this property is excluded from the analysis.
9) The application domain of the simulation (logistics, business, physics, etc.). Although the application domain of the simulation plays a significant role in the modeling process, since different approaches are required (Newtonian physics for object movement, Navier–Stokes equations for fluid behavior, etc.) for modeling different systems [34], literature, or more precisely the lack of it, suggests that the V&V process

and thus the V&V method selection is not affected by the application domain. Hence, this property is excluded from the analysis.

10) The functional (hard goals) and non-functional (soft goals) requirements of the simulation [35]. Validating the simulation's requirements is indeed an important part of the V&V process [36], since validation is always relative to the intended use [37], in other words the use defined in the requirements. Hence, making a distinction between the hard and soft goals is paramount and as such this property is included in the analysis.

3) Step 3: According to Sargent [38], there are 4 distinct phases of V&V: *Data Validation*, *Conceptual Model Validation*, *Model Verification*, and *Operational Validation*. *Data Validation* is concerned with the accuracy of the raw data, as well as the accuracy of any transformation performed on this data. *Conceptual Model Validation* determines whether the theories and assumptions underlying the conceptual model are correct, and whether the model's structure, logic, and mathematical and causal relationships are "reasonable" for the intended purpose of the model. *Model Verification* ensures that the implementation of the conceptual model is correct. Finally, *Operational Validation* is concerned with determining that the model behaves accurately based on its intended purpose. This study adopts Sargent's [38] characterization and aims at using it to classify the methods, in addition to the simulations' properties.

4) Conclusion of the Literature Review: It is evident that selecting one method over another for a V&V study depends on several characteristics from both sides, i.e., the simulation and the methods, as well as the phase of the simulation study. In Section II-B, a methodology that combines all three steps aiming at the development of a framework for V&V method selection is proposed.

B. Methodology

As discussed in Section II-A2, dimensions 3, 4, 5, 6, 7, 8, and 9 are perceived to have little influence on the method selection, hence, there are excluded from the analysis. On the other hand, the purpose of the method selection, discussed in Section II-A3, seems to be crucial; in other words, it is important to differentiate on whether the selected method will be used for data validation, conceptual model validation, model verification, or operational validation. Therefore, the list of the dimensions is refined, and is expressed in questions, as follows:

1) Does the V&V method require access to the simulation model's source code?
Possible answers: Yes or No. A positive answer to this question means that this method can only be used when the person or persons performing the V&V have access to the simulation's source code, whereas a negative answer means that it can be used in any occasion regardless of the accessibility to the simulation model's source code. It should be noted that the current study - and consequently this dimension - is not concerned with the specific programming language the simulation is built on (Assembly, C++, NetLogo, etc.), but solely with whether the application of a V&V method depends upon having access to the source code.

2) Does the V&V method require data from the real system?
Possible answers: Yes or No. A positive answer to this question means that this method can only be used when data from the real system are available, whereas a negative answer means that it can be used in any occasion regardless of the availability of data from the real system. It should be noted that the current study - and consequently this dimension - is not concerned with the nature of the data in general (qualitative or quantitative), but solely with their existence and

TABLE I. LIST OF V&V METHODS & PROPERTIES OF SIMULATIONS.

Method	1	2	3	4	Source
Acceptance Testing	No	No	Both	O. Val.	[39]
Alpha Testing	No	No	Both	O. Val.	[40]
Assertion Checking	Yes	No	Hard	M. Ver.	[41]
Audit	Yes	No	Soft	M. Ver.	[42]
Beta Testing	No	No	Both	O. Val.	[43]
Bottom-Up Testing	Yes	No	Both	M. Ver.	[44]
Boundary Value Testing	Yes	No	Both	M. Ver.	[45]
Cause-Effect Graphing	Yes	No	Hard	M. Ver.	[45]
Comparison Testing	No	No	Both	C.M. Val.	[46]
Compliance Testing	No	No	Soft	O. Val.	[42]
Control Analysis	Yes	No	Hard	M. Ver.	[47]
Data Analysis Techniques	Yes	No	Hard	D. Val. & M. Ver.	[42]
Data Interface Testing	No	No	Soft	D. Val.	[43]
Debugging	Yes	No	Both	M. Ver.	[48]
Desk Checking	Yes	No	Both	M. Ver.	[49]
Documentation Checking	Yes	No	Both	C.M. Val.	[10]
Equivalence Partitioning Testing	No	No	Hard	O. Val.	[50]
Execution Testing	No	No	Hard	C.M. Val.	[51]
Extreme Input Testing	No	No	Hard	O. Val.	[46]
Face Validation	No	Yes	Both	O. Val.	[52]
Fault/Failure Analysis	No	No	Hard	C.M. Val.	[43]
Fault/Failure Insertion Testing	No	No	Hard	C.M. Val.	[10]
Field Testing	No	Yes	Both	O. Val.	[53]
Functional (Black-Box) Testing	No	Yes	Hard	C.M. Val.	[45]
Graphical Comparisons	No	Yes	Both	O. Val.	[54]
Induction	No	No	Both	C.M. Val.	[55]
Inference	No	No	Both	C.M. Val.	[56]
Inspections	No	No	Both	C.M. Val.	[57]
Invalid Input Testing	No	No	Hard	O. Val.	[10]
Lambda Calculus	Yes	No	Hard	M. Ver.	[58]
Logical Deduction	No	No	Both	All	[51]
Model Interface Analysis	No	No	Soft	C.M. Val.	[10]
Model Interface Testing	No	No	Soft	C.M. Val.	[44]
Object-Flow Testing	No	No	Hard	O. Val.	[59]
Partition Testing	Yes	No	Hard	C.M. Val.	[60]
Predicate Calculus	Yes	No	Hard	M. Ver.	[61]
Predicate Transformations	No	Yes	Hard	M. Ver.	[62]
Predictive Validation	No	Yes	Hard	O. Val.	[63]
Product Testing	No	No	Both	O. Val.	[39]
Proof of Correctness	Yes	No	Hard	C.M. Val. & M. Ver.	[61]
Real-Time Input Testing	No	Yes	Hard	O. Val.	[10]
Regression Testing	Yes	No	Hard	M. Ver.	[51]
Reviews	No	No	Both	C.M. Val.	[42]
Self-Driven Input Testing	No	No	Hard	O. Val.	[64]
Semantic Analysis	Yes	No	Both	M. Ver.	[51]
Sensitivity Analysis	No	No	Hard	O. Val.	[65]
Stress Testing	No	No	Hard	O. Val.	[66]
Structural (White-box) Testing	Yes	No	Both	C.M. Val.	[40]
Structural Analysis	No	No	Hard	C.M. Val.	[51]
Submodel/Module Testing	No	No	Both	C.M. Val.	[67]
Symbolic Debugging	Yes	No	Hard	M. Ver.	[51]
Symbolic Evaluation	Yes	No	Hard	C.M. Val.	[68]
Syntax Analysis	Yes	No	Hard	M. Ver.	[40]
Top-Down Testing	Yes	No	Both	C.M. Val.	[44]
Trace-Driven Input Testing	Yes	Yes	Both	D. Val. & C.M. Val.	[10]
Traceability Assessment	Yes	Yes	Both	C.M. Val.	[43]
Turing Test	No	Yes	Both	O. Val.	[69]
User Interface Analysis	No	No	Soft	O. Val.	[10]
User Interface Testing	No	No	Soft	O. Val.	[70]
Visualization/Animation	No	Yes	Both	O. Val.	[38]
Walkthroughs	No	No	Both	C.M. Val.	[45]

availability.

3) For what type of requirements is the V&V method more suitable?
Possible answers: Hard (Functional), or Soft (Non-Functional), or Both. A method might be focused on either the functional part or the non-functional part of the model or on both.
4) For which type of study is the V&V method more suitable?
Possible answers: Data Validation (D. Val.), Conceptual Model Validation (C.M. Val.), Model Verification (M. Ver.), or Operational Validation (O. Val.). A method might be suitable for one or more of the available categories.

Table I summarizes the results of the analysis. The last column, i.e., *Source*, indicates the origin of each method but it is also a source that justifies the choices in columns 2-5.

C. Discussion

The intended use of Table I is to act as a filtering mechanism. Whenever an individual or a team wants to verify and/or validate a simulation model, they can utilize this table to narrow down the applicable V&V methods according to the different properties of the simulation at hand.

With regards to the first property, i.e., the accessibility to the source code, and in contrary to the second property, access to the source code does not imply that the methods categorized under "Yes" are stronger. Usually, access to the source code is associated with verification and in some cases conceptual model validation.

With regards to the second property, i.e., the availability of data from the real system, by all means, methods categorized under "No" can be used whether real data exist or not. Nevertheless, the methods categorized under "Yes" are more powerful in the sense that, if used appropriately, they provide evidence or a data trace of how the simulation should work. Hence, whenever real data are available, the methods categorized under "Yes" should be preferred, unless an alternative method is definitely more suitable.

With regards to the third and fourth property, i.e., the type of requirements being tested and the purpose of the V&V study respectively, the answers are more or less self-explanatory. Some methods are more suitable for testing one type of requirement. As an example, regression testing is more appropriate for functional requirements (hard goals). Other V&V methods are better suited for one purpose, such as Structural (White-box) Testing, which is more appropriate for conceptual model validation, while others are more suitable for testing both types of requirements (e.g., Graphical comparisons), or for more than one purpose (e.g., Trace-Driven Input Testing).

The novelty of the proposed framework does not lie in the content of Table I per se, but on the idea that the list of V&V methods can be narrowed down to a manageable level, thus making the V&V of a simulation better grounded, faster, more accurate, and more cost effective.

There is a threat towards the validity of the content on Table I. The line between whether data from the real system are needed, or whether access to the source code is needed, or whether a specific requirement is definitely functional or non-functional, or whether the purpose is to validate the data, the conceptual model, the operational ability of the model, or to just verify the model, is not always clear and well defined. In Section IV, future steps are proposed aiming at addressing and mitigating the above mentioned threat.

III. A Case Study

In this section, a case study illustrates how the framework, through the use of Table I, can be used. The case study is a computer simulation of a particular instantiation of the Dutch railway system. The authors were assigned to validate the simulation model with regards to punctuality; the precision of the delays of trains in the model.

The initial list, as it is shown on Table I, consists of 61 methods. Then with every step, the list is narrowed down. For this particular study, the selection process for each property was as follows:

1) Access to the source code was not available; *Answer: No*. Using this criteria reduces the available methods to 38.
2) There were available data from the real system; *Answer: Yes*. Using this criteria eliminates 27 more methods totaling in 9 available methods. Although, all 38 methods can be used in this particular case.
3) The main focus was on the punctuality, ergo functional (hard) requirements, but comments were also expected on the non-functional (soft) requirements; *Answer: Both (but main focus on hard)*. If on the previous criteria *Yes* was chosen as an option, choosing either *Both* or *Hard* on this criteria leaves the list intact (Total 9 methods). The same applies if on the previous criteria *All* was chosen as an option and *Both* is chosen as an option on this one. On the contrary, if on the previous criteria *All* was chosen as an option and on this criteria *Hard* is chosen as an option, the list is further reduced by 6 methods to a total of 32 available methods.
4) The study was mainly concerned with the operational validity of the simulation, but to a degree also with the conceptual model validity; *Answer: C.M. Val & O. Val.*. Using this criteria and based on the selections on the previous criteria, the final number of available methods was reduced to between 1 and 15 for the conceptual model validation and between 7 and 22 for the operational validation.

TABLE II. Refined List of V&V methods of the Case Study.

Method	1	2	3	4
Face Validation	No	Yes	Both	O. Val.
Field Testing	No	Yes	Both	O. Val.
Graphical Comparisons	No	Yes	Both	O. Val.
Predictive Validation	No	Yes	Hard	O. Val.
Real-Time Input Testing	No	Yes	Hard	O. Val.
Turing Test	No	Yes	Both	O. Val.
Visualization/Animation	No	Yes	Both	O. Val.

For the operational validation, which was the primary interest for the study, the final list of the seven methods is shown in Table II. From this list, in total four methods were used, namely the *Face Validation*, *Graphical Comparisons*, *Predictive Validation*, and *Turing Test*. *Predictive Validation* was first used to handle the initial datasets (simulation dataset & operational dataset) and to produce results for the different statistical tests. Then, a combination of the remaining three methods was used to ascertain the validity of the simulation.

In this section, the use of the proposed framework demonstrates clearly its effectiveness. As shown in Table II, the initial list of 61 methods was reduced in a matter of minutes to the manageable level of seven. By all means, the effectiveness of the framework is not only evident due to its time-saving nature but also due to the fact that it ensures that the chosen methods are appropriate for the simulation at hand and for the purpose of the V&V study.

IV. Conclusion & Future Work

In this paper, a framework for simulation validation and verification method selection was proposed. Various properties of simulations were taken into account and it was shown that indeed some of these properties, as well as the purpose of a V&V study, influence the method selection and thus, the result of the simulation study.

Moreover, the framework was applied on a case study, as a first step towards verifying its effectiveness. The case study showed that the framework is an effective time-saving tool, which also provides a safety net for choosing the method that best serves the intended purpose of the simulation and the V&V study.

With regards to future work, additional simulation properties may potentially influence the V&V method selection, or some of the discarded properties, identified in Section II-A2, might prove to be more influential than initially acknowledged. Moreover, there is a need to further verify the connection of each method to the simulation model's properties and the purpose for which they are more suitable; in other words, it should be verified that the answers on columns 2-5 in Table I are correct. Finally, more case studies, from the authors and more importantly from researchers unrelated to the authors, would further strengthen the validity and applicability of the framework.

Nevertheless, this paper paves the way for future research in the topic, and as discussed earlier, the main contribution of the framework does not lie in the results presented on Table I, but is related to the identification of the relationships between the V&V methods, and the simulation model's properties and purpose of the V&V study. Therefore, it is of utmost importance that any future research be focused on these relationships.

Acknowledgment

This research is funded through the Railway Gaming Suite 2 program, a joint project by ProRail and Delft University of Technology.

References

[1] J. W. Forrester, World dynamics. Wright-Allen Press, 1971.

[2] D. H. Meadows, D. L. Meadows, J. Randers, and W. W. Behrens III, The limits to growth. New York, U.S.A.: Universe Books, 1972.

[3] D. L. Meadows, W. W. Behrens III, D. H. Meadows, R. F. Naill, J. Randers, and E. Zahn, Dynamics of growth in a finite world. Cambridge, Massachusetts: Wright-Allen Press, 1974.

[4] M. Janssen and B. De Vries, "Global modelling: Managing uncertainty, complexity and incomplete information," in Validation of Simulation Models. SISWO, Amsterdam, The Netherlands, 1999, pp. 45–69.

[5] W. D. Nordhaus, "World dynamics: Measurement without data," The Economic Journal, vol. 83, no. 332, 1973, pp. 1156–1183.

[6] O. Balci, "Validation, verification, and testing techniques throughout the life cycle of a simulation study," Annals of Operations Research, vol. 53, no. 1, 1994, pp. 121–173.

[7] S. Schlesinger, R. E. Crosbie, R. E. Gagné, G. S. Innis, C. S. Lalwani, J. Loch, R. J. Sylvester, R. D. Wright, N. Kheir, and D. Bartos, "Terminology for model credibility," Simulation, vol. 32, no. 3, 1979, pp. 103–104.

[8] O. Balci, "Verification, validation, and certification of modeling and simulation applications," in Proceedings of the 35th Conference on Winter Simulation, S. Chick, P. J. Sánchez, D. Ferrin, and D. J. Morrice, Eds. New Orleans, Louisiana, USA: Winter Simulation Conference, 2003, pp. 150–158.

[9] R. G. Sargent, "Verification and validation of simulation models," in Proceedings of the 37th Conference on Winter Simulation, S. Chick, P. J. Sánchez, D. Ferrin, and D. J. Morrice, Eds. Orlando, Florida, USA: Winter Simulation Conference, 2005, pp. 130–143.

[10] O. Balci, "Verification, validation, and testing," in Handbook of Simulation, J. Banks, Ed. Engineering & Management Press, 1998, pp. 335–393.

[11] W. F. van Gunsteren and A. E. Mark, "Validation of molecular dynamics simulation," The Journal of Chemical Physics, vol. 108, no. 15, 1998, pp. 6109–6116.

[12] J. P. Kleijnen, "Verification and validation of simulation models," European Journal of Operational Research, vol. 82, no. 1, 1995, pp. 145–162.

[13] H. Vangheluwe, J. de Lara, and P. J. Mosterman, "An introduction to multi-paradigm modelling and simulation," in Proceedings of the AIS'2002 Conference (AI, Simulation and Planning in High Autonomy Systems), F. Barros and N. Giambiasi, Eds., Lisboa, Portugal, 2002, pp. 9–20.

[14] J. H. Byun, C. B. Choi, and T. G. Kim, "Verification of the DEVS model implementation using aspect embedded DEVS," in Proceedings of the 2009 Spring Simulation Multiconference. San Diego, CA, USA: Society for Computer Simulation International, 2009, p. 151.

[15] H. Saadawi and G. Wainer, "Verification of real-time DEVS models," in Proceedings of the 2009 Spring Simulation Multiconference. San Diego, CA, USA: Society for Computer Simulation International, 2009, p. 143.

[16] M. D. Di Benedetto, S. Di Gennaro, and A. D'Innocenzo, "Diagnosability verification for hybrid automata," in Hybrid Systems: Computation and Control, A. Bemporad, A. Bicchi, and G. Buttazzo, Eds. Springer, Berlin, Heidelberg, 2007, pp. 684–687.

[17] J. Jo, S. Yoon, J. Yoo, H. Y. Lee, and W.-T. Kim, "Case study: Verification of ECML model using SpaceEx," in Korea-Japan Joint Workshop on ICT, 2012, pp. 1–4.

[18] Y. Barlas, "Model validation in system dynamics," in Proceedings of the 1994 International System Dynamics Conference, Sterling, Scotland, 1994, pp. 1–10.

[19] J. W. Forrester and P. M. Senge, "Tests for building confidence in system dynamics models," in System Dynamics, TIMS Studies in Management Sciences, 14, 1980, pp. 209–228.

[20] M. C. Overstreet and R. E. Nance, Characterizations and relationships of world views, R. G. Ingalls, M. D. Rossetti, J. S. Smith, and B. A. Peters, Eds. Washington Hilton and Towers, Washington, D.C., U.S.A.: ACM, 2004.

[21] D. Liu, N. D. Macchiarella, and D. A. Vincenzi, "Simulation fidelity," in Human Factors in Simulation and Training, 2008.

[22] J. E. Morrison and L. L. Meliza, "Foundations of the after action review process," Alexandria, VA, p. 82, 1999.

[23] U.S. Department of Defense, "DoD Modeling and Simulation (M&S) Glossary," Tech. Rep., 1997.

[24] R. Fanning and D. Gaba, "The role of debriefing in simulation-based learning," Simulation in Healthcare, vol. 2, no. 2, 2007, pp. 115–125.

[25] J. van den Hoogen, J. Lo, and S. Meijer, "Debriefing in gaming simulation for research: Opening the black box of the non-trivial machine to assess validity and reliability," in Proceedings of the 2014 Winter Simulation Conference, A. Tolk, S. Y. Diallo, I. O. Ryzhov, L. Yilmaz, S. Buckley, and J. A. Miller, Eds. Savannah, Georgia, USA: IEEE Press, 2014, pp. 3505–3516.

[26] J. Lo, J. van den Hoogen, and S. Meijer, "Using gaming simulation experiments to test railway innovations: Implications for validity," in Proceedings of the 2013 Winter Simulation Conference, R. Pasupathy, S.-H. Kim, A. Tolk, R. Hill, and M. E. Kuhl, Eds. Washington, D.C., USA: IEEE Press, 2013, pp. 1766–1777.

[27] B. Zevin, J. S. Levy, R. M. Satava, and T. P. Grantcharov, "A Consensus-based framework for design, validation, and implementa-

tion of simulation-based training curricula in surgery," Journal of the American College of Surgeons, vol. 215, no. 4, 2012, pp. 580–586.

[28] P. J. Morgan, D. Cleave-Hogg, S. DeSousa, and J. Tarshis, "High-fidelity patient simulation: Validation of performance checklists," British Journal of Anaesthesia, vol. 92, no. 3, 2004, pp. 388–392.

[29] S. I. Gass, "Decision-aiding models: Validation, assessment, and related issues for policy analysis," Operations Research, vol. 31, no. 4, 1983, pp. 603–631.

[30] R. R. Nemani and S. W. Running, "Testing a theoretical climate-soil-leaf area hydrologic equilibrium of forests using satellite data and ecosystem simulation," Agricultural and Forest Meteorology, vol. 44, no. 3-4, 1989, pp. 245–260.

[31] A. Mavin and N. Maiden, "Determining socio-technical systems requirements: Experiences with generating and walking through scenarios," in Proceedings of the 11th IEEE International Conference on Requirements Engineering. IEEE Comput. Soc, 2003, pp. 213–222.

[32] F. Nilsson and V. Darley, "On complex adaptive systems and agent-based modelling for improving decision-making in manufacturing and logistics settings," International Journal of Operations & Production Management, vol. 26, no. 12, 2006, pp. 1351–1373.

[33] M. A. Louie and K. M. Carley, "Balancing the criticisms: Validating multi-agent models of social systems," Simulation Modelling Practice and Theory, vol. 16, no. 2, 2008, pp. 242–256.

[34] F. Landriscina, Simulation and learning. Springer, 2013.

[35] J. Mylopoulos, L. Chung, and E. Yu, "From object-oriented to goal-oriented requirements analysis," Communications of the ACM, vol. 42, no. 1, 1999, pp. 31–37.

[36] O. Balci, "Quality assessment, verification, and validation of modeling and simulation applications," in Proceedings of the 36th Conference on Winter simulation, R. G. Ingalls, M. D. Rossetti, J. S. Smith, and B. A. Peters, Eds. Washington, D.C., USA: Association for Computing Machinery, 2004, pp. 122–129.

[37] D. K. Pace, "Modeling and simulation verification and validation challenges," Johns Hopkins APL Technical Digest, vol. 25, no. 2, 2004, pp. 163–172.

[38] R. G. Sargent, "Verification, validation, and accreditation: Verification, validation, and accreditation of simulation models," in Proceedings of the 32nd Conference on Winter Simulation, J. A. Joines, R. R. Barton, K. Kang, and P. A. Fishwick, Eds. Orlando, Florida, USA: Society for Computer Simulation International, 2000, pp. 50–59.

[39] S. R. Schach, Classical and object-oriented software engineering (8th edition). McGraw-Hill, 2011.

[40] B. Beizer, Software testing techniques (2nd edition). Van Nostrand Reinhold Company Limited, 1990.

[41] L. G. Stucki, "New directions in automated tools for improving software quality," Current Trends in Programming Methodology, vol. 2, 1977, pp. 80–111.

[42] W. E. Perry, Effective methods for software testing. Wiley Publishing Inc., 2007.

[43] L. A. Miller, E. Groundwater, and S. M. Mirsky, "Survey and assessment of conventional software verification and validation methods," in No. NUREG/CR-6018; EPRI-TR-102106; SAIC-91/6660. Nuclear Regulatory Commission, Washington, DC (United States). Div. of Systems Research; Science Applications International Corp., Reston, VA (United States), 1993.

[44] I. Sommerville, Software engineering (9th edition). Addison-Wesley, Reading, MA, 2004.

[45] G. J. Myers, T. Badgett, T. M. Thomas, and C. Sandler, The art of software testing. John Wiley & Sons, Inc., 2011.

[46] N. Nayani and M. Mollaghasemi, "Validation and verification of the simulation model of a photolithography process in semiconductor manufacturing," in Proceedings of the 30th Conference on Winter Simulation, D. Medeiros, E. Watson, J. Carson, and M. Manivannan, Eds., vol. 2. Washington, D.C., USA: IEEE, 1998, pp. 1017–1022.

[47] M. C. Overstreet and R. E. Nance, "A specification language to assist in analysis of discrete event simulation models," Communications of the ACM, vol. 28, no. 2, 1985, pp. 190–201.

[48] G. A. Mihram, "Some practical aspects of the verification and validation of simulation models," Operational Research Quarterly (1970-1977), vol. 23, no. 1, 1972, pp. 17–29.

[49] P. Bunus and P. Fritzson, "Semi-automatic fault localization and behavior verification for physical system simulation models," in Proceedings of the 18th IEEE International Conference on Automated Software Engineering. IEEE Comput. Soc, 2003, pp. 253–258.

[50] N. Juristo, S. Vegas, M. Solari, and S. Abrahao, "Comparing the effectiveness of equivalence partitioning, branch testing and code reading by stepwise abstraction applied by subjects," in IEEE Fifth International Conference on Software Testing, Verification and Validation (ICST). IEEE, 2012, pp. 330–339.

[51] R. B. Whitner and O. Balci, "Guidelines for selecting and using simulation model verification techniques," in Proceedings of the 21st Conference on Winter Simulation, E. MacNair, K. Musselman, and P. Heidelberger, Eds. Washington, D.C., USA: ACM, 1989, pp. 559–568.

[52] C. F. Hermann, "Validation problems in games and simulations with special reference to models of international politics," Behavioral Science, vol. 12, no. 3, 1967, pp. 216–231.

[53] R. Shannon and J. D. Johannes, "Systems simulation: The art and science," IEEE Transactions on Systems, Man, and Cybernetics, vol. 6, no. 10, 1976, pp. 723–724.

[54] K. J. Cohen and R. M. Cyert, "Computer models in dynamic economics," The Quarterly Journal of Economics, vol. 75, no. 1, 1961, pp. 112–127.

[55] C. Reynolds and R. T. Yeh, "Induction as the basis for program verification," IEEE Transactions on Software Engineering, vol. SE-2, no. 4, 1976, pp. 244–252.

[56] L. G. Birta and F. N. Özmizrak, "A knowledge-based approach for the validation of simulation models: The foundation," ACM Transactions on Modeling and Computer Simulation, vol. 6, no. 1, 1996, pp. 76–98.

[57] F. A. Ackerman, P. J. Fowler, and R. G. Ebenau, "Software inspections and the industrial production of software," in Proceedings of a Symposium on Software Validation: Inspection-Testing-Verification-Alternatives. North-Holland, 1984, pp. 13–40.

[58] H. P. Barendregt, "The Lambda-calculus: Its syntax and semantics," Studies in Logic and The Foundations of Mathematics, 1984.

[59] J. R. Swisher, S. H. Jacobson, J. B. Jun, and O. Balci, "Modeling and analyzing a physician clinic environment using discrete-event (visual) simulation," Computers & Operations Research, vol. 28, no. 2, 2001, pp. 105–125.

[60] W. E. Howden, "Reliability of the path analysis testing strategy," IEEE Transactions on Software Engineering, vol. SE-2, no. 3, 9 1976, pp. 208–215.

[61] R. C. Backhouse, Program construction and verification. Prentice-Hall International, 1986.

[62] E. W. Dijkstra, "Guarded commands, non-determinacy and a calculus for the derivation of programs," in In: Bauer F.L. et al. (eds) Language Hierarchies and Interfaces. Lecture Notes in Computer Science, vol 46. Springer, Berlin, Heidelberg, 1976, pp. 111–124.

[63] J. R. Emshoff and R. L. Sisson, Design and use of computer simulation models. MacMillan, New York, 1970.

[64] A. M. Law and W. D. Kelton, Simulation modeling and analysis (3rd edition). McGraw-Hill, 1991.

[65] R. L. Van Horn, "Validation of simulation results," Management Science, vol. 17, no. 5, 1971, pp. 247–258.

[66] R. H. Dunn, "The quest for software reliability," in Handbook of Software Quality Assurance. New York: Van Nostrand Reinhold, 1987.

[67] O. Balci, "Guidelines for successful simulation studies (tutorial session)," in Proceedings of the 22nd Conference on Winter Simulations, O. Balci, Ed. New Orleans, Louisiana, USA: IEEE Press, 1990, pp. 25–32.

[68] C. V. Ramamoorthy, S.-B. F. Ho, and W.-T. Chen, "On the automated generation of program test data," IEEE Transactions on Software Engineering, vol. SE-2, no. 4, 1976, pp. 293–300.

[69] L. W. Schruben, "Establishing the credibility of simulations," Simulation, vol. 34, no. 3, 1980, pp. 101–105.

[70] R. S. Pressman, Software engineering: A practitioner's approach (8th edition). McGraw-Hill, New York, NY, 2015.

A New Approach to Modelling Fiber-Reinforced Plastics for Hydrocode Analysis

Experimental Model Validation of Composite Materials Under Ballistic Impact

Arash Ramezani and Hendrik Rothe
Chair of Measurement and Information Technology
University of the Federal Armed Forces
Hamburg, Germany
Email: ramezani@hsu-hh.de, rothe@hsu-hh.de

***Abstract*—In the security sector, the partly insufficient safety of people and equipment due to failure of industrial components is an ongoing problem that cause great concern. Since computers and software have spread into all fields of industry, extensive efforts are currently made in order to improve the safety by applying certain numerical solutions. A fiber-reinforced composite is a promising material for ballistic protection due to its high strength, stiffness and low density. The use of ultra-high molecular weight polyethylene (UHMW-PE) composite as part of the primary armour system in vehicles has the potential to provide significant weight savings or improved protection levels over traditional metallic materials. Although already used in vehicle armours, both as spall liners and within complex multi-element/multi-material packages, there is a limited understanding of the mechanisms driving ballistic performance. Existing analysis tools do not allow for a good approximation of performance, while existing numerical models are either incapable of accurately capturing the response of thick UHMW-PE composite to ballistic impact or are unsuited to model thick targets. In response, this paper aims to identify the key penetration and failure mechanisms of thick UHMW-PE composite under ballistic impact and develop analytical and numerical models that capture these mechanisms and allow accurate prediction of ballistic performance to optimize modern armor structures. An analysis methodology is proposed to model the behaviour of thick UHMW-PE composite panels under ballistic impact using inhomogeneities on the macroscale. A sub-laminate approach for discretisation of the target is proposed to overcome the problems of premature through-thickness failure in the material model. The methodology was extensively validated against existing experimental ballistic impact data and results for UHMW-PE targets. Finally, a numerical modelling methodology was developed for the analysis of thick UHMW-PE composite under ballistic impact.**

Keywords-solver technologies; simulation models; hydrocodes; fiber-reinforced plastics; optimization; armor systems; ballistic trials.

I. INTRODUCTION

This work will focus on fiber-reinforced plastics, more precisely composite armor structures consisting of several layers of ultra-high molecular weight polyethylene (UHMW-PE), a promising ballistic armor material due to its high specific strength and stiffness.

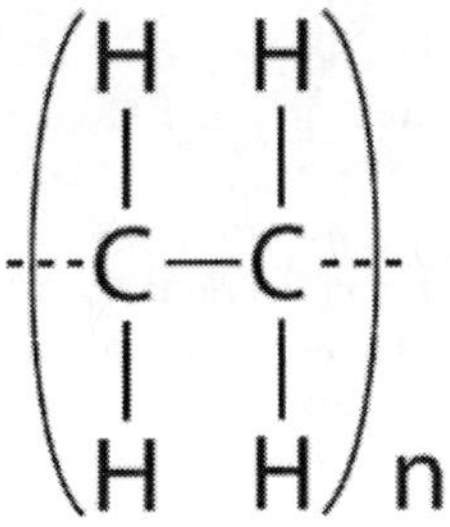

Figure 1. Polyethylene.

UHMW-PE is a thermoplastic polymer made from very long molecular chains of polyethylene. Figure 1 shows the chemical structure of polyethylene, where in UHMW-PE the number of repeated chains (n) is in the order of 10^5, giving rise to molecular weights in the order of 10^6 [1]. As a non-polar molecule, interaction between polyethylene molecules is by very weak Van der Waals forces.

However, due to the ultra-long polymer chain, significant strength can be derived through a gel spinning process that produces highly oriented and crystalline molecular structures aligned in the spinning direction. The gel spinning process firstly involves dissolving UHMW-PE in a solvent at high temperature. The solution is then pushed through a spinneret to form liquid filament that is then quenched in water to form gel-fibers. These fibers are then drawn in hot air at high strain rates of the order of 1 s^{-1} forming fibers with smooth circular cross-sections approximately 17 mm in diameter [2] with a molecular orientation greater than 95% and a crystallinity of up to 85% [1], see Figure 2.

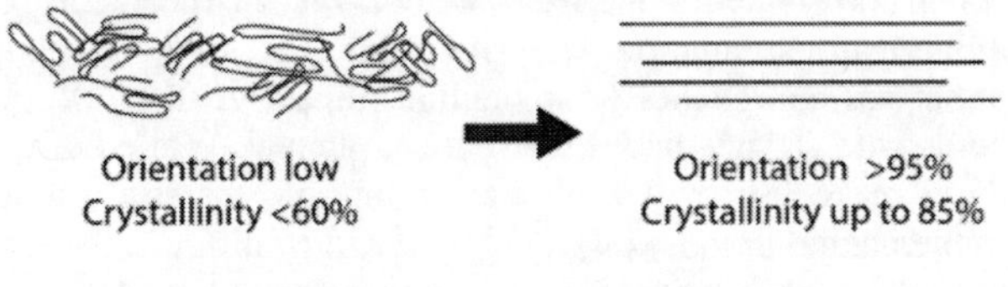

Figure 2. Increase in molecular orientation and crystallinity through gel spinning of UHMW-PE [3].

These fibers are composed of smaller macro-fibrils approximately 0.5 mm to 2 mm in diameter, which in turn are made of micro-fibrils, 20 nm in diameter (Berger et al., 2003). Commercial UHMW-PE fiber is manufactured by, amongst others, Dutch State Mines (DSM) and Honeywell under the trade names Dyneema® and Spectra®, respectively. The fibers are used in a variety of applications requiring high specific strength and low weight. This includes high strength ropes and nets, cut-resistant gloves, as well as blast and ballistic protection.

For ballistic protection applications, the fibers can be woven into fabrics to provide a soft and flexible material or coated in a matrix and aligned to form uni-directional plies, which are then stacked and pressed under temperature and pressure to form rigid laminates.

UHMW-PE composites and fabrics have been shown to be extremely effective against ballistic threats, particularly in weight-critical applications, e.g., personal protection vests and helmets for protection against small calibre threats [4]. The goal is to evaluate the ballistic efficiency of UHMW-PE composite with numerical simulations, promoting an effective development process.

Due to the fact that all engineering simulation is based on geometry to represent the design, the target and all its components are simulated as computer-aided design (CAD) models. The work will also provide a brief overview of ballistic tests to offer some basic knowledge of the subject, serving as a basis for the comparison of the simulation results. Details of ballistic trials on composite armor systems are presented. Instead of running expensive trials, numerical simulations should identify vulnerabilities of structures. Contrary to the experimental result, numerical methods allow easy and comprehensive studying of all mechanical parameters. Modeling will also help to understand how the transparent armor schemes behave during impact and how the failure processes can be controlled to our advantage. By progressively changing the composition of several layers and the material thickness, the composite armor will be optimized.

There is every reason to expect possible weight savings and a significant increase in protection, through the use of numerical techniques combined with a small number of physical experiments.

This work deals with numerical simulations of impact problems on fiber-based composite armor using the commercial finite-element-code ANSYS AUTODYN. Having presented some basic knowledge on the theory of numerical simulation in AUTODYN, two recently published approaches for modeling impact on the selected composite (Dyneema® HB26) are explained. While both of them make use of a nonlinear-orthotropic material model implemented in the AUTODYN-code, they differ in the way how the highly inhomogeneous microstructure of HB26 is represented geometrically. Lässig chooses a fully homogeneous description, whereas Nguyen discretizes the composite into sublaminates, which are kinematically joined at the surfaces and breakable when a certain contact-stress is reached. In order to validate the two approaches, the response of HB26-samples impacted by handgun-projectiles was determined experimentally and compared to the corresponding numerical results. Unfortunately, a poor agreement between experimental and numerical results was found, which gave rise to the development of an alternative modeling approach. In doing so, the composite was subdivided into alternating layers of two different types. While the first type of layers was modeled with open-literature properties of UHMW-PE-fibers, polymer-matrix-behavior was assigned to the second type. Having adjusted some of the parameters, good agreement between experiment and simulation was found with respect to residual velocity and depth of penetration for the considered impact situations.

After a brief introduction and description of the principles of simulation in Section II, state-of-the-art models of fiber-reinforced plastics are discussed in Section III. There is a short section on ballistic trials where the experimental set-up is depicted, followed by Section V describing the model validation. Section VI presents the analysis with numerical simulations and the results of this work. The paper ends with a concluding paragraph in Section VII and an outlook in Section VIII.

II. Principles of Simulation

To deal with problems involving the release of a large amount of energy over a very short period of time, e.g., explosions and impacts, there are three approaches: as the problems are highly non-linear and require information regarding material behavior at ultra-high loading rates which is generally not available, most of the work is *experimental* and thus may cause tremendous expenses. *Analytical* approaches are possible if the geometries involved are relatively simple and if the loading can be described through boundary conditions, initial conditions or a combination of the two. *Numerical* solutions are far more general in scope and remove any difficulties associated with geometry [5]. They apply an explicit method and use very small time steps for stable results.

For problems of dynamic fluid-structure interaction and impact, there typically is no single best numerical method which is applicable to all parts of a problem. Techniques to couple types of numerical solvers in a single simulation can allow the use of the most appropriate solver for each domain of the problem.

The goal of this paper is to evaluate a hydrocode, a computational tool for modeling the behavior of continuous media. In its purest sense, a hydrocode is a computer code for modeling fluid flow at all speeds [6]. For that reason, a structure will be split into a number of small elements. The elements are connected through their nodes (see Figure 3). The behavior (deflection) of the simple elements is well-known and may be calculated and analyzed using simple equations called shape functions [7].

Figure 3. Example grid.

By applying coupling conditions between the elements at their nodes, the overall stiffness of the structure may be built up and the deflection/distortion of any node – and subsequently of the whole structure – can be calculated approximately [8].

III. STATE-OF-THE-ART

The numerical modeling of composite materials under impact can be performed at a constituent level (i.e., explicit modeling of fiber and matrix elements, e.g. [9]), a meso-mechanical level (i.e., consolidated plies or fiber bundles, e.g. [10]), or macromechanically in which the composite laminate is represented as a continuum.

In [11–14] a non-linear orthotropic continuum material model was developed and implemented in a commercial hydrocode (i.e., ANSYS® AUTODYN®) for application with aramid and carbon fiber composites under hypervelocity impact. The non-linear orthotropic material model includes orthotropic coupling of the material volumetric and deviatoric responses, a non-linear equation of state (EoS), orthotropic hardening, combined stress failure criteria and orthotropic energy-based softening. For more detail refer to [15]. Lässig et al. [16] conducted extensive experimental characterization of Dyneema® HB26 UHMW-PE composite for application in the continuum non-linear orthotropic material model, and validated the derived material parameters through simulation of spherical projectile impacts at hypervelocity.

A number of researchers have applied the non-linear orthotropic model for UHMW-PE composites with varying levels of success (Hayhurst et al. [17], Herlaar et al. [18], Ong et al. [19], Heisserer and Van der Werff [20] and Lässig et al. [16]). Ong et al. [19] assumed material properties of UHMW-PE composite based on those of Kevlar® with some data from literature, which resulted in poor predictions of the penetration behaviour. Hayhurst et al. [17], Herlaar et al. [18] and Heisserer and Van der Werff [20] used material input parameters derived from a range of experiments, and reported better prediction, although the results cannot be independently verified because the material parameters are not provided.

Nguyen et al. [21] evaluated and refined the modeling approach and material model parameter set developed in [16] for the simulation of impact events from 400 m/s to 6600 m/s. Across this velocity range the sensitivity of the numerical output is driven by different aspects of the material model, e.g., the strength model in the ballistic regime and the equation of state (EoS) in the hypervelocity regime.

This paper will present an optimal solution of this problem with an enhanced model for ultra-high molecular weight polyethylene under impact loading. For the first time, composite armor structures consisting of several layers of fiber-reinforced plastics are simulated for all the current military threats.

IV. BALLISTIC TRIALS

Ballistics is an essential component for the evaluation of our results. Here, terminal ballistics is the most important sub-field. It describes the interaction of a projectile with its target. Terminal ballistics is relevant for both small and large caliber projectiles. The task is to analyze and evaluate the impact and its various modes of action. This will provide information on the effect of the projectile and the extinction risk.

Historically, impact events are classified according to the impact velocity. One such approach was proposed by Zukas et al. [22] who categorised impact problems based on impact velocity, where the material response and established strain rate characterised the impact problem. Figure 4 depicts the strain rate, the impact velocity required to achieve the strain rate and the material effects as proposed by Zukas et al. [22].

Under this classical approach, the ballistic regime could be considered to be within the strain rate range of 10^2 s^{-1} to 10^4 s^{-1} which corresponds to an impact velocity of between 50 m/s to 3000 m/s.

According to Zukas et al. [22], within this region the material strength is important in resisting penetration, and there is an onset of hydrodynamic effects. This approach to define the impact regime using the strain rate is insufficient when considering the impact behaviour for a diverse range of materials with different properties. For example, very low velocity impact of a hard object into a fluid can be described entirely using hydrodynamic theory, which under Figure 4 would be classified as both a low strain rate (low velocity) and high strain rate (hydrodynamic effects) problem.

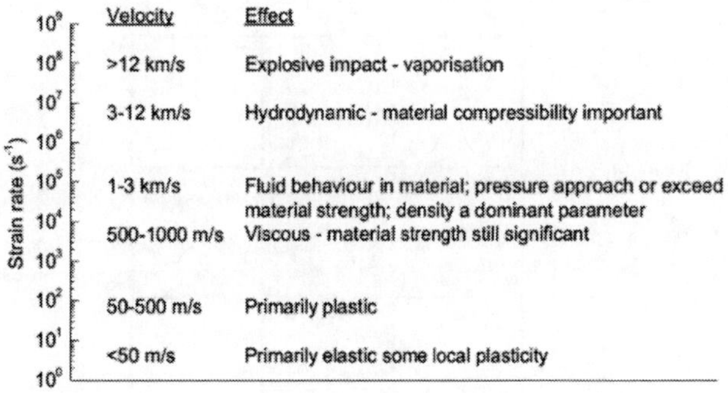

Figure 4. Impact response of high strength materials [22].

Wilbeck (in [23]) proposed classification by the ratio of the impact pressure (P) to the material strength (S).

$$P/S_p \text{ and } P/S_t \quad (1)$$

where subscripts p is the projectile and t is the target. The pressure, P, according to hydrodynamic theory is given by:

$$P \cong \rho V^2 \quad (2)$$

where ρ is material density and V is the impact velocity. From this, impact events can be classified in nine different regimes, depicted in matrix form in Figure 5.

The ballistic regime is considered to reside in regime 2, 4, 5, 6 and 8 according to Figure 5 where the impact pressure is close to the material strength of the target, projectile or both. For this paper, regime 5, 6 and 8 are of interest because at impact velocities typical of FSPs, the impact pressures are considered to be on the order of, or greater than the strength of UHMW-PE composite.

Given that a projectile strikes a target, compressive waves propagate into both the projectile and the target. Relief waves propagate inward from the lateral free surfaces of the penetrator, cross at the centerline, and generate a high tensile stress. If the impact was normal, we would have a two-dimensional stress state. If the impact was oblique, bending stresses will be generated in the penetrator. When the compressive wave reached the free surface of the target, it would rebound as a tensile wave. The target may fracture at this point. The projectile may change direction if it perforates (usually towards the normal of the target surface).

Because of the differences in target behavior based on the proximity of the distal surface, we must categorize targets into four broad groups. A semi-infinite target is one where there is no influence of distal boundary on penetration. A thick target is one in which the boundary influences penetration after the projectile is some distance into the target. An intermediate thickness target is a target where the boundaries exert influence throughout the impact. Finally, a thin target is one in which stress or deformation gradients are negligible throughout the thickness.

	$\frac{P}{S_t} \ll 1$	$\frac{P}{S_t} \sim 1$	$\frac{P}{S_t} \gg 1$
$\frac{P}{S_p} \ll 1$	1	2	3
$\frac{P}{S_p} \sim 1$	4	5	6
$\frac{P}{S_p} \gg 1$	7	8	9

Figure 5. Matrix of impact regime [23]. The ballistic regimes are shaded.

There are several methods by which a target will fail when subjected to an impact. The major variables are the target and penetrator material properties, the impact velocity, the projectile shape (especially the ogive), the geometry of the target supporting structure, and the dimensions of the projectile and target.

In order to develop a numerical model, a ballistic test program is necessary. The ballistic trials are thoroughly documented and analyzed – even fragments must be collected. They provide information about the used armor and the projectile behavior after fire, which must be consistent with the simulation results.

In order to create a data set for the numerical simulations, several experiments have to be performed. Ballistic tests are recorded with high-speed videos and analyzed afterwards. Testing was undertaken at an indoor ballistic testing facility. The target stand provides support behind the target on all four sides. Every ballistic test program includes several trials with different composites. The set-up has to remain unchanged.

The camera system is a PHANTOM v1611 that enables fast image rates up to 646,000 frames per second (fps) at full resolution of 1280 x 800 pixels. The use of a polarizer and a neutral density filter is advisable, so that waves of some polarizations can be blocked while the light of a specific polarization can be passed.

Several targets of different laminate configurations were tested to assess the ballistic limit (V_{50}). The ballistic limit is considered the velocity required for a particular projectile to reliably (at least 50% of the time) penetrate a particular piece of material [24]. After the impact, the projectile is examined regarding any kind of change it might have undergone.

V. Model Validation

Experimental characterisation of the ballistic performance of UHMW-PE composite can be prohibitively expensive, so it is highly desirable to establish computationally efficient numerical models that accurately predict the ballistic response of the material. First, existing models should be validated.

A. *Resources*

In [16], numerical simulations of 15 kg/m^2 Dyneema® HB26 panels impacted by 6 mm diameter aluminum spheres between 2052 m/s to 6591 m/s were shown to provide very good agreement with experimental measurements of the panel ballistic limit and residual velocities, see Figure 6. The modeling approach and material parameter set from [16] were applied to simulate impact experiments at velocities in the ballistic regime (here considered as < 1000 m/s). Lambert-Jonas parameters (a, p, Vbl) are provided in the legend.

In Figure 6, the results of modeling impact of 20 mm fragment simulating projectiles (FSPs) against 10 mm thick Dyneema® HB26 are shown. The model shows a significant under prediction of the ballistic limit, 236 m/s compared to 394 m/s.

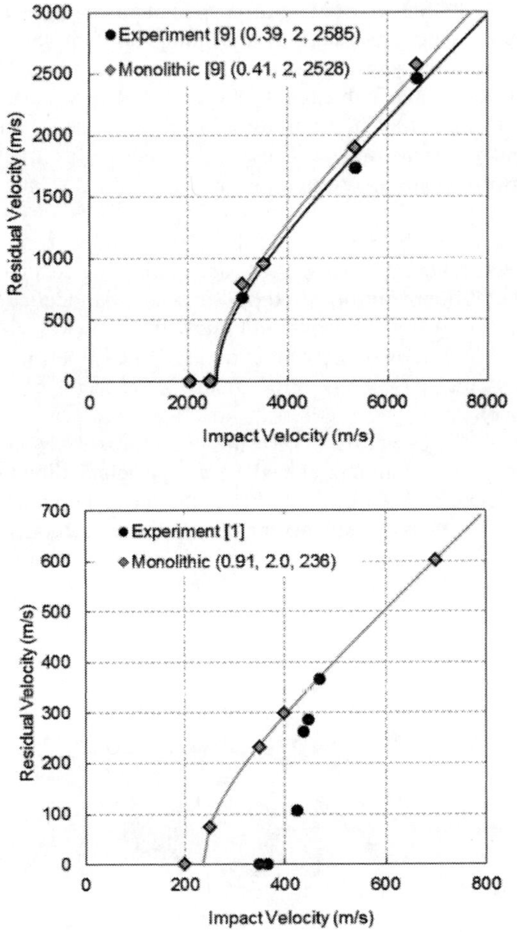

Figure 6. Experimental and numerical impact residual velocity results for impact of 6 mm diameter aluminum spheres against 15 kg/m^2 Dyneema® HB26 at normal incidence (left) and impact of 20 mm FSP against 10 mm thick HB26 at normal incidence (right).

B. Method

The FSP material was modelled as Steel S-7 from the AUTODYN® library described using a linear EoS and the Johnson-Cook strength model [25]. The aluminum sphere was modelled using AL1100-O from the AUTODYN® library that uses a shock EoS and the Steinburg Guinan strength model [26]. The master-slave contact algorithm was used to detect contact between the target and projectile.

The sub-laminate model with shock EoS was applied to the aluminum sphere hypervelocity impact series and 20 mm FSP ballistic impact series presented in Figure 6, the results of which are shown in Figure 7.

The sub-laminate model is shown to provide a significant improvement in predicting the experimental V_{50} of 394 m/s for the FSP ballistic impacts (377 m/s) compared to the monolithic model (236 m/s).

The ballistic limit and residual velocity predicted with the sub-laminate model for the hypervelocity impact case are shown to be comparable with the original monolithic model. For conditions closer to the ballistic limit, the sub-laminate model is shown to predict increased target resistance (i.e., lower residual velocity). For higher overmatch conditions, there is some small variance between the two approaches.

Now, regarding common handgun projectiles, the results look sobering. As the most widespread weapon in the world, the Kalashnikov rifle (AK-47) is a good example to compare ballistic trials and simulation results. A 7.62x39 mm full metal jacket (FMJ) projectile with a velocity of 700 m/s is used and the model is shown in Figure 3.

In Figure 8, a qualitative assessment of the bulge formation is made for the 11 mm panel. Prediction of bulge development is important as it is characteristic of the material wave speed and is also a key measure in defence applications, particularly in personnel protection (i.e., vests and helmets). In the ballistic experiments, the 11 mm target panel resists the 7.62x39 mm FMJ projectile. But in both models, material fails and the projectile penetrates the plate.

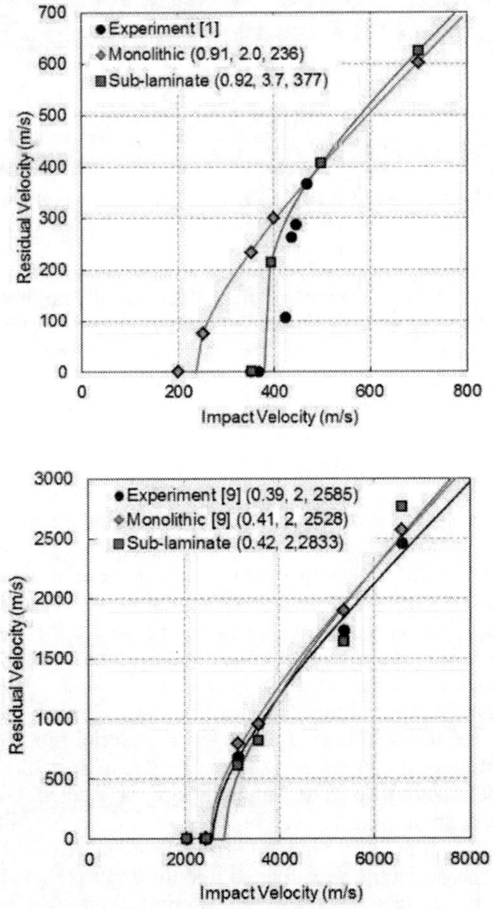

Figure 7. Comparison of the experimental results with the two numerical models for impact of 20 mm FSP against 10 mm thick Dyneema HB26® at normal incidence (left) , and impact of 6 mm diameter aluminium spheres against 15 kg/m^2 HB26 at normal incidence (right).

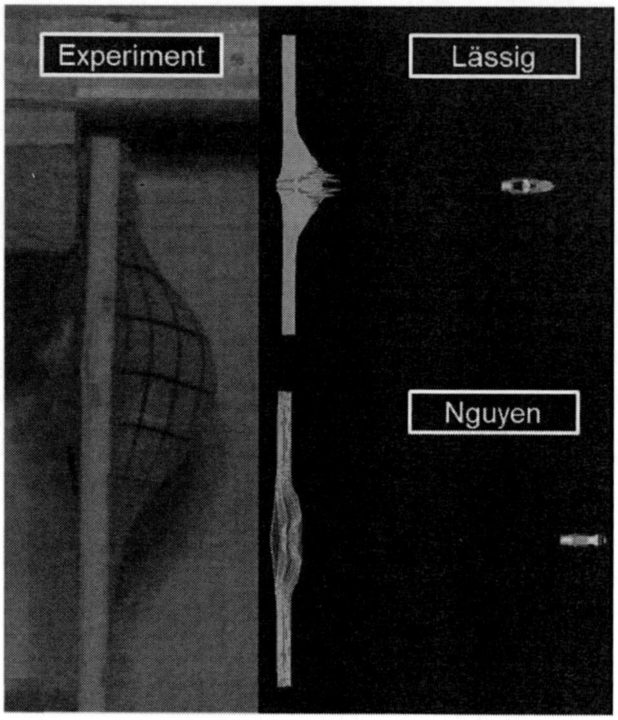

Figure 8. Bulge of a 11 mm target impact by a 7.62x39 mm FMJ projectile at 689 m/s (experiment) and the simulation results using both "state-of-the-art" models of Lässig and Nguyen700 m/s.

There is no accurate reproduction of the bulge. The problem is a neglect of micro-structures. Fraction and fragmentation between the laminate layers cannot be described by homogeneous continuum models. These disadvantages are addressed in a very new and more representative model.

VI. NUMERICAL SIMULATION

As mentioned before, the ballistic tests are followed by computational modeling of the experimental set-up. Then, the experiment is reproduced using numerical simulations. Figure 3 shows a cross-section of the projectile and a CAD model. The geometry and observed response of the laminate to ballistic impact is approximately symmetric to the axis through the bullet impact point.

Numerical simulation of modern armor structures requires the selection of appropriate material models for the constituent materials and the derivation of suitable material model input data. The laminate system studied here is an ultra-high molecular weight polyethylene composite. Lead and copper are also required for the projectiles.

The projectile was divided into different parts - the jacket and the base - which have different properties and even different meshes. These elements have quadratic shape functions and nodes between the element edges. In this way, the computational accuracy, as well as the quality of curved model shapes increases. Using the same mesh density, the application of parabolic elements leads to a higher accuracy compared to linear elements (1st order elements).

Modelling of fiber-reinforced composites under impact is challenging because of the complexity of the material composition and the many failure modes it exhibits at different scales (fibrillation, intra- and inter-laminar failure, etc.) and impact regimes. For this reason, numerical simulation of impact using hydrocodes was exclusively performed for isotropic materials up until the late 1990's. Since then, there have been many advances in modelling composites brought about by the introduction of more accurate constitutive models and modelling techniques. In general fiber-reinforced composites can be modelled at three different scales, as shown in Figure 9:

- Micro-scale, where the individual fiber, matrix and (in some cases) the fiber-matrix interface is explicitly modelled;
- Meso-scale, where the properties of the individual plies that are homogenised in the principal directions are modelled and stacked together to produce a laminate; and
- Macro-scale, where the laminate is modelled as a continuum and the properties of the laminate are homogenised in the principal directions.

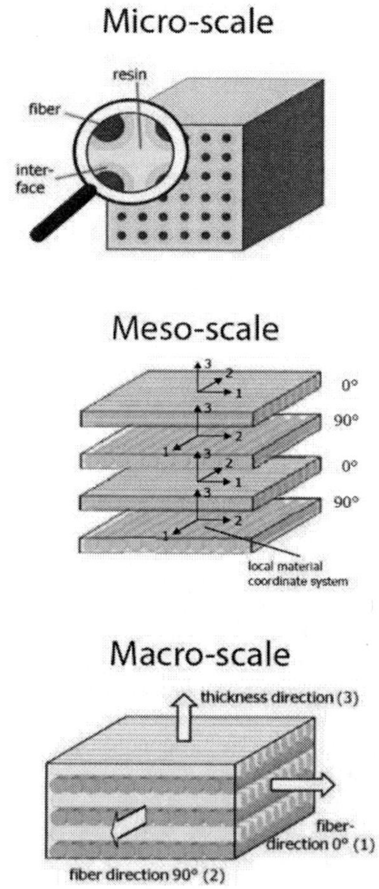

Figure 9. Micro, meso and macro mechanical model of fiber reinforced composites [27].

Modelling of fiber-reinforced composites at the micro-scale has several important advantages. This includes increased model fidelity, relatively simpler constitutive equations to describe the fiber, matrix and the interface, and characterisation tests that are relatively easy to perform. However, models at this scale require explicit modelling of every single fiber, matrix and the contact interface, which is extremely computationally expensive and not practical currently for typical engineering problems (see Figure 10).

While the meso-scale approach is far more computationally tractable compared to the micro-scale, models at this scale are still not practical for thick targets.

A. *Modelling*

Because of the discrepancies discussed in Section V, a new model was developed – a concept for the numerical simulation of fiber-reinforced plastics under impact loading. Here, the homogeneous continuum model is replaced. Alternating layers of fibers and matrix are used for the geometry. The layers are bonded and have different material models (see Figure 11).

The fiber layers apply anisotropic elasticity, no plasticity and anisotropic material failure (stress-dependent). The matrix layers use isotropic elasticity, von Mises plasticity and isotropic material failure (stress-dependent). To simulate the effect of delamination, principal stress failure is applied.

3D numerical simulations were performed of the full target and projectile, where both were meshed using 8-node hexahedral elements. The projectile was meshed with 9 elements across the diameter. The target is composed of sub-laminates that are one element thick, separated by a small gap to satisfy the master-slave contact algorithm (external gap in AUTODYN®) and bonded together as previously discussed. The mesh size of the target is approximately equal to the projectile at the impact site. The mesh was then graded towards the edge, increasing in coarseness to reduce the computational load of the model. Since UHMWPE composite has a very low coefficient of friction, force fit clamping provides little restraint. High speed video of ballistic impact tests typical showed clamp slippage upon impact. As such no boundary conditions were imposed on the target.

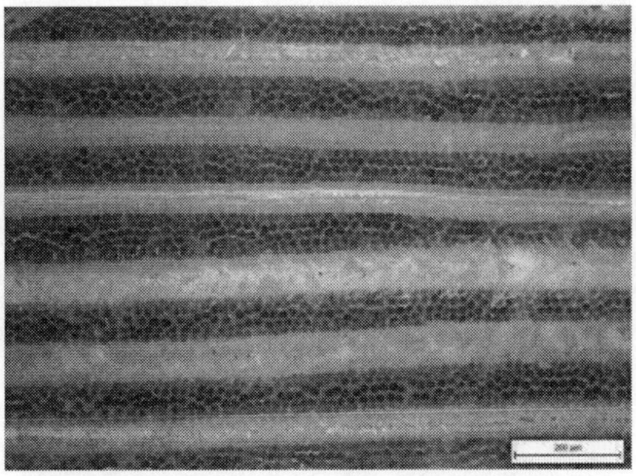

Figure 10. Cross section of a Dyneema® HB26 panel.

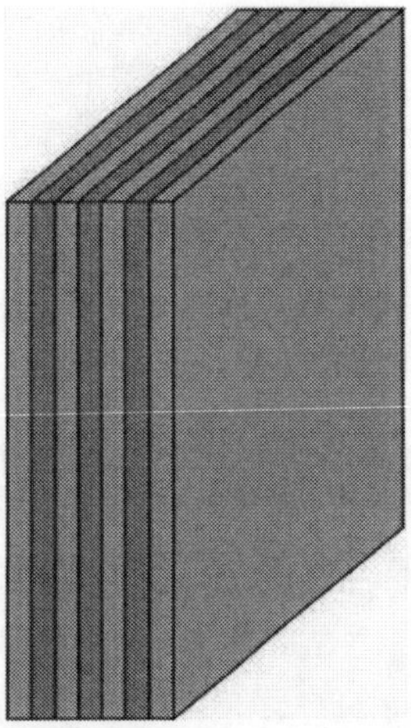

Figure 11. Geometry of a target plate: alternating layers of fibers and matrix are used in the computer model.

B. *Simulation Results*

The model developed in [16] was adjusted and the concept has been extended to different calibers and projectile velocities. Composite armor plates between 5.5 and 16.2 mm were tested in several ballistic trials and high-speed videos were used to analyze the characteristics of the projectile – before and after the impact. The simulation results with the modified model are shown in Figures 12 and 13.

The deformation of the projectile is in good agreement with the experimental observation. Both delamination and fragmentation can be seen in the numerical simulation. Compared to the homogeneous continuum model, fractures can be detected easily. Subsequently, the results of experiment and simulation in the case of perforation were compared with reference to the projectile residual velocity. Here, only minor differences were observed. The results are summarized in Table I.

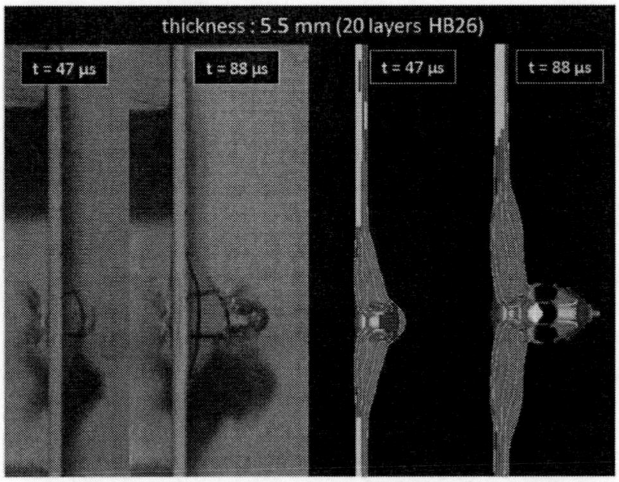

Figure 12. Effect of a 5.5 mm target impact by a 7.62×39 mm bullet at 686 m/s, 47 µs and 88 µs after the initial impact.

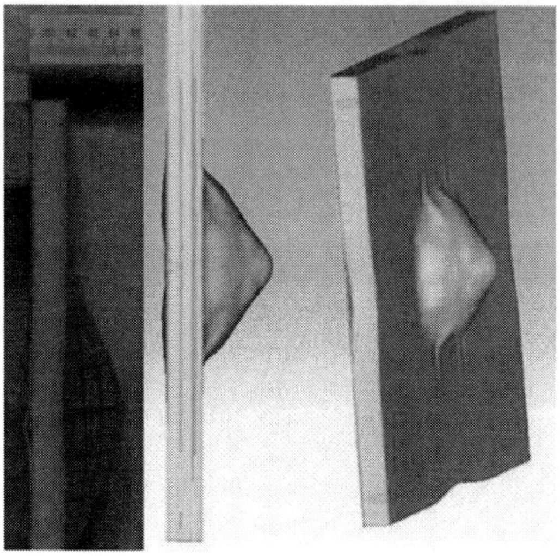

Figure 13. Effect of a 16.2 mm target impact by a 7.62×39 mm bullet at 679 m/s.

TABLE I. SUMMARY OF RESULTS

Target Thickness	5.5 mm Residual Velocity	11.0 mm Residual Thickness	16.2 mm Residual Thickness
Experiment	604 m/s	6 mm	11 mm
Simulation	587 m/s	4 mm	10 mm

The next step is to test the influence of meshing, based on Ramezani and Rothe [28]. The accuracy that can be obtained from any FEA model is directly related to the finite element mesh that is used. The finite element mesh is used to subdivide the CAD model into smaller domains called elements, over which a set of equations are solved. These equations approximately represent the governing equation of interest via a set of polynomial functions defined over each element. As these elements are made smaller and smaller, as the mesh is refined, the computed solution will approach the true solution. This process of mesh refinement is a key step in validating any finite element model and gaining confidence in the software, the model, and the results.

Early in the analysis process, it makes sense to start with a mesh that is as coarse as possible – a mesh with very large elements. A coarse mesh will require less computational resources to solve and, while it may give a very inaccurate solution, it can still be used as a rough verification and as a check on the applied loads and constraints.

After computing the solution on the coarse mesh, the process of mesh refinement begins. In its simplest form, mesh refinement is the process of resolving the model with successively finer and finer meshes, comparing the results between these different meshes. This comparison can be done by analyzing the fields at one or more points in the model or by evaluating the integral of a field over some domains or boundaries. Table II summarizes the four different mesh sizes. A Hewlett-Packard (HP) ProLiant DL380p G8 Server is used for all calculations.

TABLE II. COMPARISON OF THE CALCULATION TIME

Mesh Size	Number of Elements over Edge Lenght	Calculation Time [h]
Coarse	25	0.5
Medium	50	4
Fine	75	25
Very Fine	100	268

By comparing these scalar quantities, it is possible to judge the convergence of the solution with respect to mesh refinement. The results are shown in Figure 14.

It should be noted that an explicit modeling of the individual fibers is not an option, since the computational effort would go beyond the scope of modern server systems. To expand the scope of the model, the validation should be extended to other ballistic load cases.

VII. CONCLUSIONS

The material model developed in [16] has some shortcomings regarding the simulation of handgun projectiles (e.g. 7.62×39 mm). Although previously found to provide accurate results for hypervelocity impact of aluminum spheres, the existing model and dataset was found to significantly underestimate the composite performance under impact conditions driven by through-thickness shear performance (ballistic impact of fragment simulating projectiles). The model was found to exhibit premature through thickness shear failure as a result of directional coupling in the modified Hashin-Tsai failure criterion and the large discrepancy between through-thickness tensile and shear strength of UHME-PE composite. As a result, premature damage and failure was initiated in the through-thickness shear direction leading to decreased ballistic performance. By de-coupling through-thickness tensile failure from the failure criteria and discretizing the laminate into a nominal number of kinematically joined sub-laminates through the thickness, progresses in modeling the ballistic response of the panels was improved.

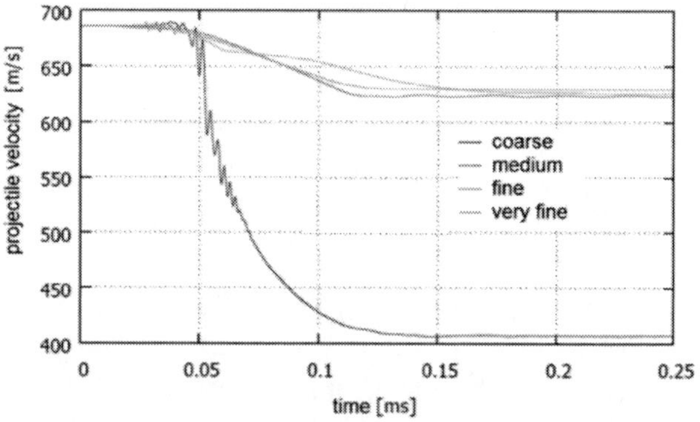

Figure 14. Convergence analysis: comparison of the projectile velocity (7.62×39 mm bullet) at different mesh sizes.

A major difficulty in the numerical simulation of fiber composites under impact is the detection of failure processes between fiber and matrix elements as well as between the individual laminate layers (delamination). One promising approach is the use of "artificial" inhomogeneities on the macroscale.

This paper is based on Ramezani and Rothe [29]. New approaches make it possible to increase the accuracy of the simulation results. The previous concept was not valid for all projectiles/calibers. An alternative model has been developed to overcome these difficulties. Using sub-laminates and inhomogeneities on the macroscale, the model does not match the real microstructure, but allow a more realistic description of the failure processes mentioned above. The numerical model proposed a sub-laminate discretisation of the laminate in order to better model delamination failure. For this to occur, the sub-laminates are joined together using bonded contacts where failure is initiated based on a combined normal and shear stress criterion. Such approach is known to be mesh-dependent and has been replaced by fracture energy based failure (mode I, II and III) [30]. Most finite element models of fibre-reinforced composite today capture interlaminar failure through zero thickness cohesive elements which accounts for both damage and fracture mechanics (using tractionseparation laws), though this is not available in the hydrocode used in this work.

This work also demonstrated how a small number of well-defined experiments can be used to develop, calibrate, and validate solver technologies used for simulating the impact of projectiles on complex armor systems and composite laminate structures. Ballistic trials can be used as the basis of an iterative optimization process. Numerical simulations are a valuable adjunct to the study of the behavior of metals subjected to high-velocity impact or intense impulsive loading. The combined use of computations, experiments and high-strain-rate material characterization has, in many cases, supplemented the data achievable by experiments alone at considerable savings in both cost and engineering man-hours.

VIII. Future Work

Generally, the field of ballistic and penetration mechanics is extensive due to the unlimited combination of targets and threats. The response of targets is different depending on the projectile size, geometry, material and impact velocity. The scope of this work was restricted to the most common threats (where FSPs are used as a representative surrogate), however understanding the penetration and failure mechanisms of the material impacted by different projectiles (spherical and ogive) can also be valuable. This work also only considered normal impacts (the worst case scenario), however attacks experienced on the front line are almost always at an oblique angle (large or small). Understanding how UHMW-PE composite responds to obliquity is important and deserves attention.

References

[1] J. Van Dingenen, "Gel-spun high-performance polyethylene fibres," in High Performance Fibres, pp. 62–92, 2001.

[2] B. Russell, K. Karthikeyan, V. Deshpande, and N. Fleck, "The high strain rate response of ultra-high molecular-weight polyethylene: From fibre to laminate," in International Journal of Impact Engineering (60), pp. 1–9, 2013.

[3] L. H. Nguyen, The Ballistic Performance of Thick Ultra High Molecular Weight Polyethylene Composite. RMIT University, 2015.

[4] P. M. Cunniff, "Dimensionless parameters for optimization of textile based body armor systems," in 18th International Symposium on Ballistics, pp. 1303–1310, 1999.

[5] J. Zukas, Introduction to hydrocodes. Elsevier Science, 2004.

[6] G.-S. Collins, An Introduction to Hydrocode Modeling. Applied Modelling and Computation Group, Imperial College London, 2002.

[7] P. Fröhlich, "FEM Application Basics," Vieweg Verlag, September 2005.

[8] H.-B. Woyand, FEM with CATIA V5. J. Schlembach Fachverlag, 2007.

[9] D. B. Segala and P. V. Cavallaro, "Numerical investigation of energy absorption mechanisms in unidirectional composites subjected to dynamic loading events," in Computational Materials Science 81, pp. 303–312, 2014.

[10] S. Chocron et al., "Modeling unidirectional composites by bundling fibers into strips with experimental determination of shear and compression properties at high pressures," in Composites Science and Technology 101, pp. 32–40, 2014.

[11] C. J. Hayhurst, S. J. Hiermaier, R. A. Clegg, W. Riedel, and M. Lambert, "Development of material models for nextel and kevlar-expoxy for high pressures and strain rates," in International Journal of Impact Engineering 23, pp. 365–376, 1999.

[12] R. A. Clegg, D. M. White, W. Riedel, and W. Harwick, "Hypervelocity impact damage prediction in composites: Part I—material model and characterisation," in International Journal of Impact Engineering 33, pp. 190–200, 2006.

[13] W. Riedel, H. Nahme, D. M. White, and R. A. Clegg, "Hypervelocity impact damage prediction in composites: Part II—experimental investigations and simulations," in International Journal of Impact Engineering 33, pp. 670–80, 2006.

[14] M. Wicklein, S. Ryan, D. M. White, and R. A. Clegg, "Hypervelocity impact on CFRP: Testing, material modelling, and numerical simulation," in International Journal of Impact Engineering 35, pp.1861–1869, 2008.

[15] ANSYS. AUTODYN Composite Modelling Release 15.0. [Online]. Available from: http://ansys.com/ [retrieved: May, 2017].

[16] T. Lässig et al., "A non-linear orthotropic hydrocode model for ultra-high molecular weight polyethylene in impact simulations," in International Journal of Impact Engineering 75, pp. 110–122, 2015.

[17] C. J. Hayhurst, J. Leahy, J., M. van der Jagt-Deutekom, and P. Kelly, "Development of Material Models for Numerical Simulation of Ballistic Impact onto Polyethylene Fibrous Armour," in Personal Armour Systems Symposium, pp. 5–8, 2000.

[18] K. Herlaar, M. van der Jagt-Deutekom, and M. Jacobs, "Finite element simulations and experiments of ballistic impacts on high performance PE composite material," in 22nd International Symposium on Ballistics, pp. 1040–1047, 2005.

[19] C. Ong, C. Boey, R. S. Hixson, and J. O. Sinibaldi, "Advanced layered personnel armor," in International Journal of Impact Engineering 38(5), pp. 369–383, 2011.

[20] U. Heisserer and H. Van der Werff, "The relation between Dyneema fiber properties and ballistic protection performance of its fiber composites," in 15th International Conference on Deformation, Yield and Fracture of Polymers 3, pp. 242–246, 2012.

[21] L. H. Nguyen et al., "Numerical Modelling of Ultra-High Molecular Weight Polyethylene Composite Under Impact Loading," in Procedia Engineering 103, pp. 436–443, 2015.

[22] J. Zukas, T. Nicholas, H .Swift, L. Greszczuk, and D. Curran, Impact dynamics. John Wiley & Sons, 1982.

[23] C. E. Anderson, J. S. Wilbeck, J. D. Walker, K. A. Dannemann, S. A Mullin, and S. Chocron, "Short Course on Penetration Mechanics - Lecture Notes," presented at the Southwest Reseach Institute, San Antonio, USA, 2013.

[24] D. E. Carlucci and S. S. Jacobson, Ballistics: Theory and Design of guns and ammunition. CRC Press, 2008.

[25] G. Johnson and W. Cook, "A constitutive model and data for metals subjected to large strains, high strain rates and high temperatures," in 7th International Symposium on Ballistics, pp. 541–547, 1983.

[26] D. Steinberg, Equation of state and strength properties of selected materials. California, 1996.

[27] L. Meyer and M. Mayer, "New Strain Rate Dependent Material Model for Fiber Reinforced Composites," in Society of Experimental Mechanics 3, pp. 149–158, 2010.

[28] A. Ramezani and H. Rothe, "Influences of Meshing and High-Performance Computing towards Advancing the Numerical Analysis of High-Velocity Impacts," in International Journal on Advances in Systems and Measurements, Volume 9, Numbers 3 & 4, 2016, ISSN 1942-261x , S.142-153.

[29] A. Ramezani and H. Rothe, "Numerical Simulation and Experimental Model-Validation for Fiber-Reinforced Plastics Under Impact Loading - Using the Example of Ultra-High Molecular Weight Polyethylene," The Eighth International Conference on Advances in System Simulation (SIMUL 2016) IARIA, Aug. 2016, pp. 17-25, ISBN 978-1-61208-442-8.

[30] Y. Mi, M. Crisfield, G. Davies, and H. Hellweg., "Progressive delamination using interface elements," in Journal of Composite Materials, 32(14), pp. 1246–1272, 1998.

Hybrid Modeling Approach to Investigate the Impact of Boarding Patients on Unit Performance

Leila Keshtkar, Wael Rashwan, Waleed Abo-Hamad, Amr Arisha
3S Group, College of Business
Dublin Institute of Technology (DIT)
Dublin, Ireland
email: leila.keshtkar@mydit.ie, wael.rashwan@dit.ie, wabohamad@dit.ie, amr.arisha@dit.ie

Abstract— **Overcrowding of Emergency Departments (EDs) is an issue that adversely affects patient safety, quality of care, and patient experience. In attempt to mitigate this risk, the National Acute Medicine Program (AMP) in Ireland has introduced a fast track medical unit, namely Acute Medical Units (AMU), designed to accommodate medical patients presenting to the ED with certain severity levels. Surprisingly, less than 50% of ED medical patients can get access to this unit. In partnership with a leading Irish hospital in Dublin, a hybrid simulation model has developed to investigate the underlying factors that limit patients' access to AMU. Discrete event simulation is used to model the process while cross-boundary interactions with other neighbor units such as ED and inpatient wards are explained using a system dynamics approach. Integrating the two simulation approaches show that boarder patients (i.e., patients waiting to progress) slow performance significantly. Decisions regarding capacity expansion are not the answer to this problem! Staffing and adequate resource leveling seem to have a better impact on patient flow.**

Keywords - Hybrid simulation; Boarding patients; AMAU; Healthcare management.

I. INTRODUCTION

Healthcare organizations worldwide are challenged to meet growing demands on Emergency Departments (EDs). Extra pressures are due to reduce costs, improve outcomes, and be more patient-centered while controlling the cost.

ED overcrowding is a serious issue that adversely affects patient safety, quality of care, and patient satisfaction[1]. One of the main identified factors to ED overcrowding is boarding, in which admitted patients from the ED spend long periods awaiting the availability of inpatient beds [2]. Consequently, less ED resources are available for new emergency patients [3]. The bottleneck of inpatient boarding naturally will increase Patient Experience Time (PET) for both admitted and discharged patients [3]. As a result, the quality of care, patient safety and satisfaction goals are affected by ED boarding and crowding. Hospital management is ultimately looking for ways to reduce ED overcrowding and boarding patients [4], however due to system complexity, they worry about the impact of any interventions on patient flows and equally budget.

Discrete Event Simulation (DES) modeling approach has a proven track record of success when it comes to system variability understanding. The boarding problem is multi-dimensional and has macro and micro impactful decisions. DES models are effective to simulate the process in details while incorporating the patient-resource relationships [5]. Nevertheless, this problem requires higher-level modeling capabilities. Hybrid Simulations (HS) seem to provide better insights into complex systems because they offer a more holistic approach to system analysis [6]. This means less assumptions and better accuracy to outcomes [7]. Therefore, this paper is presenting an integration of two simulation approaches in a unified framework to support decision-makers in the partner hospital [8]. Literature has indicated that HS can contribute to significant improvement of patient scheduling in outpatient clinic setting [9], redesigning and implementing new healthcare facilities [10], and model the complexities of emergency department [11]. Simulation models have been used to study patients boarding problems and their implications on patient experience. The trade off between increasing physical capacity of the ED and reducing admitted patient boarding times was examined in [12], while impact of inpatient boarding on the ED efficiency was explored in [13]. Reports from literature have revealed that not many studies have considered the hybrid approach between System Dynamic (SD) and DES in healthcare applications.

This paper presents a hybrid simulation model (i.e., DES-SD) to investigate the impact of patients boarding problem on the ability of patients to access other units in the hospital such as the Acute Medical Assessment Unit (AMAU). The proposed hybrid model considers the horizontal integration to the up/downstream departments (i.e., intra-departmental and inter-departmental interactions). DES model offers a better representation of the process complexity in details including patients flow, AMAU operations, and underlying relationships with other supporting units in the hospital. On the other hand, SD model is responsible for the cross-boundary interactions outside the AMAU, which allows a holistic view to represent the interaction among system components.

The remaining sections of this paper is organized as follows. A background about the project is given in the next section. A detailed description of developing the hybrid model then follows. Data collection, analysis and experimentation are presented. Finally, section VI concludes the paper.

II. PROJECT BACKGROUND

The Hospital under study is a public, adult teaching hospital that holds more than 520 beds. The hospital has a 24-hour "on-call" Emergency Department (ED) that serves over 45,000 adult patients annually. The department has officially, 23 monitored trolley space. Recently, the hospital has opened two more new units to offer possible alternative treatment routes for patients: An Acute Medical Assessment Unit (AMAU) and a Short Stay Unit (SSU). The capacities of the AMAU and SSU are 11 trolleys and 24 beds respectively. The AMAU works as a 12-hour unit; it opens from 9:00 – 21:00, but only accepts patients till 18:00 to allow beds to be available for the next day. The SSU works as a short stay ward, on a 24/7 basis, for acute medical patients who need to be admitted to the hospital, and whose length of stay is estimated to be less than five days.

AMAUs are resourced by physicians and a dedicated multidisciplinary medical and support teams and the only access to the AMAU is through the ED [14]. After patients are triaged and assigned a triage category according to the Manchester Triage System (MTS) that uses a five-level scale for classifying patients per their care requirements [15]. The triage nurse usually contacts the AMAU consultant or registrar so that they can accept or reject the case. Patients routed to the AMAU are those medical patients triaged as category 2 or 3 (i.e., very urgent and urgent patients respectively) who do not require resuscitation or isolation facilities. These patients only transferred to the AMAU if a trolley is available. Patients presented in these units will get to see a senior medical doctor, who should be able to treat and/or discharge patients, within almost one hour of admission. The two units along with the emergency department share resources among them, and share some resources with the hospital. When the AMAUs were first introduced, an improvement was witnessed in the increase of the proportion of patients discharged within 24 hours and also by decreasing length of stay and overall medical bed day usage [14]. However, AMAU unit under this study is facing two types of boarding problems: ED boarding and internal boarding. In ED boarding case, patients had occupied between one to six AMAU trolleys for maximum 12 hours. On the other hand, internal boarding occurs when patients in AMAU require a hospital bed in another downstream unit (e.g., medical words or SSU) for further treatment. AMAU unit opens from 9am to 6pm. Over a 6-month period, the number of medical patients presented to the ED with triage category 2 and 3 is 3753, however only 40% of these patients got access to the AMAU with an average patient experience time (i.e., The total time from patient entrance to AMAU until s/he exit the unit) of 4.45 hours. Therefore, a collaborative study was conducted with the hospital and the national acute medical program to investigate the underlying factors that restrict patients' access to AMAU specially patients boarding issues.

III. HYBRID MODEL CONCEPTUALIZATION

Analysing the patient boarding problem in AMAU necessitate integrating with downstream and upstream facilities that show high interdependency, in particular, ED and in-patient wards. A better understanding of the problem and its implications could be accomplished when system integration is to considered. Therefore, a hybrid simulation model between SD and DES is developed to address the consequences of patient boarding problem in the AMAU. The upstream component is the ED, which is the demand source of the AMAU while the downstream components model the patient disposition. In fact, patient disposition refers to two cases in AMAU: First, the patients who are waiting for beds in other units to release AMAU trolleys. Second, patients have been transferred to the AMAU overnight in order to free-up ED's blocked trolleys. Patient's flow in the AMAU is modeled using a DES in order to simulate the the unit activities and processes in details, taking into account the resources interaction. Downstream and upstream hospital operations are explained in SD model, which enables manager to envisgae the impact of changes using feedback loops between the different activities. The two simulation models are running simultaneously (Figure 1), and the information is exchanged from both models in the run time with a parallel interaction.

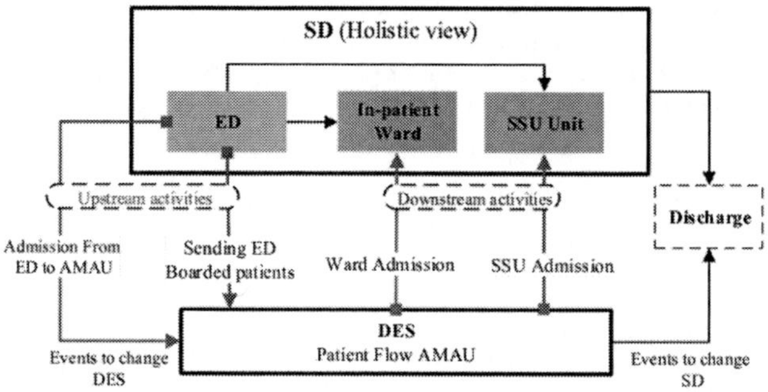

Figure 1. The interaction between the DES and SD models.

A. *AMAU patient flow(DES)*

Upon arrival at the ED and registration, walk-in patients (self-referral or GP referral) remain in the waiting area to be triaged. When a patient's name is called, depending on triage staff availability, the patient is assessed by a triage nurse. Based on patient condition and triage assessment by MTS criteria, each patient is assigned a clinical priority (triage category). Then, based on their severity level, medical patients can be directed to either the ED or the AMAU. A medical patient is eligible for the AMAU path if s/he arrives between 9:00 a.m. and 6:00 p.m. (i.e., the unit's admission hours) and if the patient is triaged either a category two or three. Once these requirements are met, the triage nurse calls the AMAU's consultant to check the availability of a trolley for the patient. The patient goes back to the ED path if a trolley is unavailable. The majority of patients in the AMAU are medical patients, accounting 96% of patients presented to the unit.

Following the triage process, a patient who is directed to AMAU will be registered in the AMAU's system, interviewed by a nurse where his blood pressure and vitals are measured then s/he would wait for a doctor to assess the patient. Next, the AMAU doctor will discuss the case with the unit's consultant who would then either ask for more tests, request an opinion, or decide whether the patient needs to be admitted or discharged. AMAU's consultant from a medical/surgical speciality doctor can confirm whether a patient should be admitted or not. Alternatively, the consultant may wish to refer the patient to a colleague for a second opinion based on the medical condition. These are the primary care stages, which are relevant for all AMAU's patients, whether they are discharged from or admitted to hospital. Secondary patient stages are steps involved in the care of some, but not all patients such as diagnostics (e.g. MRIs and CTs). In the flowchart of AMAU steps (Figure 2) is shown.

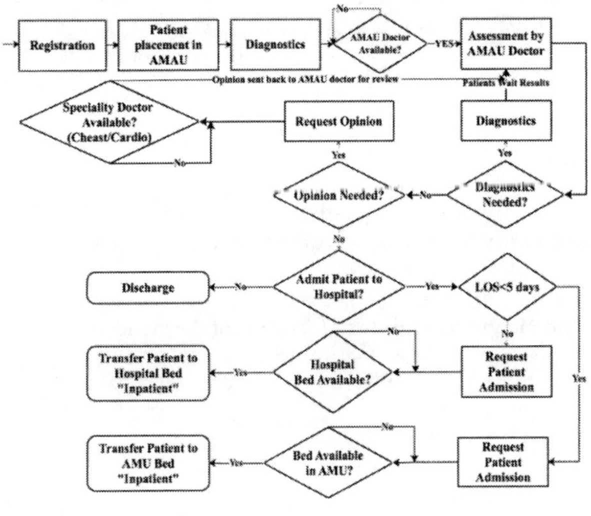

Figure 2. Patient's flow in AMAU

B. SD model

The casual loop – developed by Vensim software (Figure 3) – can be conceptualized regarding two main areas: the community area and the hospital area (ED, AMAU, and inpatient wards). Regarding the community, patients are presented to the ED from the surrounding catchment area and then discharged back to the community. The rate of patient arrivals depends on a variety of factors and characteristics of the surrounding catchment area. The rate of discharge back to the community depends on the bed occupancy, which is a function of the patient's length of stay (LOS) in the hospital. The factors affecting both arrival rate and the average LOS are not considered in this model, and they are represented as aggregate parameters. To reduce the pressure on the ED, medical patients can be dispatched to the AMAU pathway subject to the AMAU's trolley availability. The majority of the patients (75%) presented to the ED are discharged back to the community after receiving their treatment. If further inpatient care is required, patients wait in the ED for an inpatient bed. The rate of admission depends on the bed management and hospital bed occupancy. Due to the high bed occupancy of inpatients beds, patients that need inpatient care are boarded (delayed) in the ED while blocking ED trolleys.

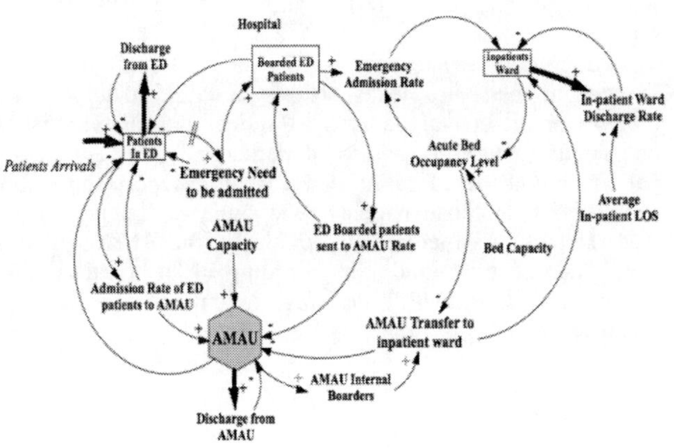

Figure 3. A Simplified causal loop diagram

A similar situation occurs in the AMAU when patients require further stay in the hospital and needed to move to other downstream units such as the SSU or inpatient beds. To free-up ED's blocked trolleys, the ED management transfers some patients to the AMAU overnight. This management practice moves the ED bed blocking partially from ED to the AMAU. Consequently, the AMAU has an average of 3.2 blocked trolleys due the transferred ED boarded patients. The situation becomes worse when it combined with the AMAU boarded patients. In turn, these limit access to the AMAU and subsequently increase the pressure on the ED.

IV. DATA COLLECTION AND ANALYSIS

A. Data sources

The data collected for this project utilized both quantitative and qualitative data types. The quantitative data are collected from the historical data of ED logs, electronic patient records (EPRs) from the ED's IT system, and direct observation. The direct and indirect time per activity and staff Rota are not stored in the IT system and were collected from interviews and observations. The qualitative data such as patient pathways, conceptual modeling have been gathered through observation, interviews, and focus groups.

B. Data analysis

Data are collected retrospectively for six months for patients who are presented to ED and AMAU between January 1^{st,} 2014 and June 30^{th,} 2014. A total of 20,493 anonymous patient records from ED and 1,520 anonymous patient records from AMAU have been collected through the hospital's information system, which is used by the staff (e.g., administrators, doctors, and nurses) to record data about each patient through the stages of their care. 23% of the patients arrived by ambulance, and 77% are walk-in patients. Of the total patients, 90% of patients are new patients, and 10% are unscheduled return. Referral from GP with a letter represents 70% of patients while 23% are self-referred.

Patients differ according to the medical complaints and severity of their care needs, so it is essential to understand their different arrival patterns to reflect the characteristics and needs of various groups of patients. In this study, the patients are clustered based on the triage category to be able to differentiate those patients who will be directed to the AMAU path. As mentioned previously, the AMAU in this study facing two kinds of boarding: ED boarding and internal boarding. In ED boarding, patients occupy between one to six AMAU trolleys (Figure 4) for maximum 12 hours.

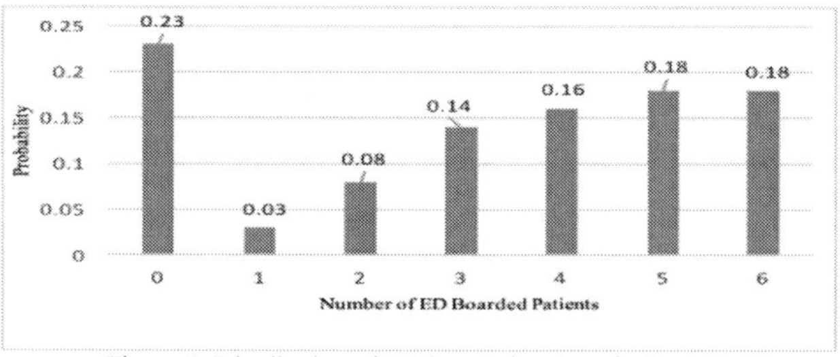

Figure 4. Distribution of ED boarded patients in the AMAU.

In internal boarding case, patients in AMAU are waiting to get inpatient ward beds or SSU beds in order to release AMAU trolleys.

C. *Verification and validation*

Conceptual models for both patient flow and causal loop diagrams have been documented and validated by hospital's senior clinicians and senior nursing staff. The validated conceptual models along with the analysis of empirical data were used to develop the hybrid simulation model using AnyLogic software platform. Once the models are completed, the verification and validation were carried out all the way through the development phases of the model. Visual tracking was used to verify the model logic to ensure that patients follow the correct care path as expected. The following Key Performance Indicators (KPIs) were used for the AMAU: the average of total patient experience time (PET), the average of total waiting time (TWT) and patient access (i.e., the total number of patients enter the AMAU). The main reason for choosing patient access as one of main KPIs is that increasing patients access to the AMAU can mitigate overcrowding in ED [14]. The simulation model is validated (Table. I) using face validation and comparison testing. This is to ensure that the actual PET within the AMAU is reflected by the model when it runs for twenty-four weeks period.

TABLE I. MODEL VALIDATION

KPIS	Base Scenario	Real Data	Difference%
Avg. PET(Min)	276.79	267.6	3.4
Avg. Patient access	1710	1520	11.1

V. SCENARIO ANALYSIS AND DISCUSSION

The simulation results of the baseline model show that on average 1710 patients could access to AMAU unit at any six months. In fact, in the current situation, AMAU works on 9 hours/ 5 days; from 9:00 am to 6:00 pm. According to the baseline only 40% of medical patients of ED could access to AMAU. However, the target of ED managers is to increase the flow percentage in order to absorb most if not all medical patients who attend to the ED during its opening hours. The average PET of the baseline – presented in Table II – is currently 276.8 minutes and patients normally wait 98.2 minutes in AMAU.

TABLE II. SIMULATION RESULTS FOR BASE SCENARIO

KPIS	Baseline Scenario
Avg. PET(Min)	276.79
Avg. TWT (Min)	98.24
Avg. Patient access	1709.80

A. *Scenario Design*

The simulation scenarios are designed (Table. III) to identify the factors that contribute to PET and patient access to AMAU and consequently ED overcrowding. Three factors are considered: ED boarded patients, internal boarded; and the number of trolleys in the AMAU.

TABLE III. SIMULATION VARIABLES FOR BASE SCENARIO,

	Control Variables		
	ED Boarders	***Internal Boarders***	***Number of trolleys***
Base Scenario	Yes	Yes	11
Scenario 1	Yes	Yes	17
Scenario 2	No	Yes	11
Scenario 3	Yes	No	11
Scenario 4	No	No	11

For the first two factors, a value of 'Yes' and 'No' means the existence or the absence of the corresponding factor respectively. For example, Scenario 1 is similar to the baseline with both ED boarding and internal boarded patients considered, however, AMAU trolleys are increased from 11 to 17. This is to investigate the effect of increasing the physical capacity of AMAU only. On the other hand, Scenario 2 is designed to examine the effect of having no ED boarders while keeping other variables the same as the baseline (i.e., same number of trolleys with internal boarders).

B. *Result Analysis*

Increasing the AMAU physical capacity (Scenario 1) results in 30% increase in patient access with an insignificant effect on PET (increased by 0.7%) and TWT (increase by 7%). Despite adding extra trolleys (Table. IV) improve the patient access, it has insignificant effect on PET and TWT. On the other hand, unlocking ED boarders (i.e., Scenario 2 is assuming constant inpatient beds availability for ED patients) has resulted in a significant increase patient access to the AMAU by 25.9% (i.e., 1710 to 2152 patients). Such increase is attributed to an increase of availability of AMAU trolleys as patients do not have to wait in the unit. However, there is no significant change in PET for AMAU patients (1.9% decrease).

TABLE IV. SIMULATION RESULTS FOR SCENARIO 1 AND SCENARIO 2.

KPIS	Base	Scenario 1		Scenario 2	
		O/P[a]	*+/- (%)*	*O/P[a]*	*+/- (%)*
Avg. PET(Min)	276.8	278.85	0.7	271.5	-1.9
Avg.TWT(Min)	98.2	105.08	7.0	96.8	-1.4
Avg. Patient access	1710	2224.0	30.1	2152	25.9

a. O/P: simulation output; +/- : percentage of increase/decrease relative to the base scenario.

Scenario 3 seems more effective in comparison to Scenario 2 (Table. V), in which patient access increase from 1710 patients to 2337 patients and TWT decrease from 98.2 minutes to 51.8 minutes as well as 9.2% reduction in PET.

TABLE V. SIMULATION RESULTS FOR SCENARIO 3 AND SCENARIO 4.

KPIS	Base	Scenario 3		Scenario 4	
		O/P[a]	*+/- (%)*	*O/P[a]*	*+/- (%)*
Avg. PET(Min)	276.8	251.4	-9.2	285.8	3.2
Avg.TWT(Min)	98.2	51.8	-47.2	87.5	-10.9
Avg. Patient access	1710	2337	36.7	3052	78.5

a.O/P: simulation output; +/- : percentage of increase/decrease relative to the base scenario.

Scenario 4 is the ideal situation in the system with no ED boarding and no internal boarding. In this scenario, there is a noticeable increase by 78.5% in patient access and 10.9% decrease in TWT. However, PET has increased by 9 minutes, which is mainly because the number of patients entered into the unit is doubled. All the internal queues in the AMAU were analyzed in order to gain insights regarding the increase in PET. Three main bottlenecks were discovered due to the increased number of patients who can access the AMAU: access to the SSU; the number of AMAU consultants; and finally, the number of required porters. As a result, different combinations of the four basic scenarios (Table. VI) were designed

TABLE VI. SIMULATION SETTINGS FOR SCENARIOS 5 – 11.

Scenarios	Control Variables					
	ED Boarders	*Internal Boarders*	*SSU beds*	*NP[b]*	*NC[c]*	*NT[d]*
Base	Yes	Yes	24	1	1	11
Scenario 5	No	Yes	36	1	1	11
Scenario 6	No	Yes	48	1	1	11
Scenario 7	No	Yes	24	2	1	11
Scenario 8	Yes	No	24	2	1	11
Scenario 9	Yes	No	24	3	1	11
Scenario 10	No	No	24	2	1	11
Scenario 11	No	No	24	1	2	11
Scenario 12	No	No	24	2	2	11

(b.NP: number of Porters, c.NC: Number of Consultants, d.NT: Number of Trolleys)

In Scenario 5 and 6 there are no ED boarders, and the number of SSU beds has been changed from 24 to 36 (50% increase) and 48 (100% increase) respectively. By increasing 50% of SSU beds, patient access from the ED to the AMAU has increased from 1710 patients to 2667 patients (Figure 5) with a slight increase in PET and TWT (Figure 6) compared to the baseline model. In Scenario 7, there are no ED boarders, but another porter added to the AMAU which resulted in a 30.9% increase in patient's access and 20.7% reduction in TWT. Therefore, increasing SSU beds is not as effective as increasing one porter to the AMAU. Scenario 8, is also designed to increase one porter with no internal boarder. The results of this scenario show that patients access increased by 51.2% along with a noticeable decrease in TWT by 74% (from 98.2 minutes to 25.5 minutes). Adding more porters (Scenario 9) does not have further improvement on the performance.

In Scenario 10, a full relaxation scenario (i.e., no ED boarders and no internal boarders) by adding another porter has resulted in a considerable decrease in TWT by 61.2%. In contrast, adding one more consultant to the AMAU with full relaxation (with only one porter) resulted in only 21.3% decrease in average TWT. In last relaxation scenario (i.e., Scenario 12) the combination of adding one porter and one consultant resulted in increasing the number of patients entered to the AMAU from 1710 patients to 3615 patients with an 81.5% decrease in TWT and 20.6% decrease in PET. To conclude, Scenario 12 seems to have the best impact on KPIs.

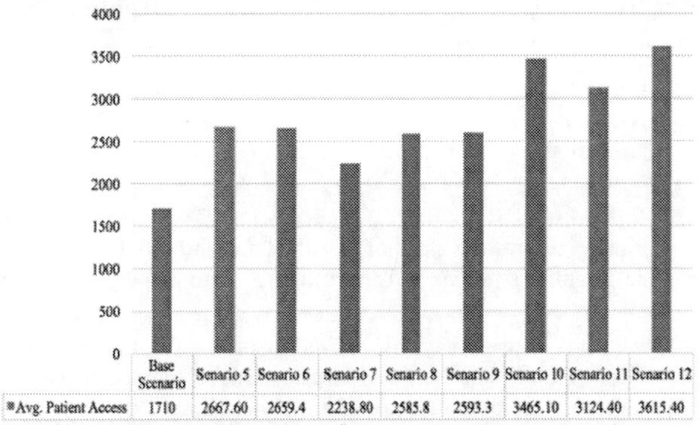

Figure 5. Comparing patient access in scenario 5 to scenario 12

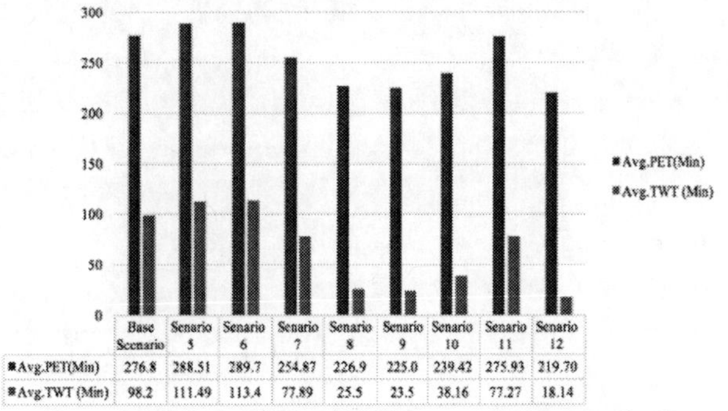

Figure 6. Comparing PET and TWT in scenario 5 to scenario 12

VI. CONCLUSION

Overcrowding is one of the key problems in Emergency Department (ED) of hospitals. It often has a negative effect on patients and unit performance. Acute Medical Assessment Units (AMAUs) is a new unit that is designed to reduce pressures on EDs by serving particular categories of ED patients. However, with time passing, this unit suffers from boarding issues – patients who are waiting for decisions.

A hybrid simulation model (DES-SD) has developed to examine the impact of boarding on AMAUs overall performance. The DES has used to model the patient flow in details incorporating AMAU and its relationships with other supporting units in the hospital such as ED, Wards and SSU. On the other hand, SD has looked at cross-boundary interactions outside the AMAU. Results show that improving the flow between up and downstream enhance patient access and resource utilization. Nevertheless, the original approach to this issue was to increase unit physical capacity. Adding AMAU's bed capacity will not have a significant impact on performance variables in comparison to adding extra staff. Particular resources (e.g., consultants and porters) seem to be impactful especially if less or no boarding problem exists.

Finally, the hybrid modeling approach has enabled the hospital managers to gain insights to the dynamism embedded in the system and also identify bottlenecks that hinder the performance. Future work intends to consider interaction between variables. In addition, Design of Experiment (DOE) module in order to examine factor sensitivity will be included.

REFERENCES

[1] W. Abo-Hamad and A. Arisha, "Simulation-based framework to improve patient experience in an emergency department," Eur. J. Oper. Res., vol. 224, pp. 154–166, Jan. 2013.

[2] J. M. Pines, R. J. Batt, J. A. Hilton, and C. Terwiesch, "The financial consequences of lost demand and reducing boarding in hospital emergency departments," Ann. Emerg. Med., vol. 58, pp. 331–340, 2011.

[3] B. A. White et al., "Boarding inpatients in the emergency department increases discharged patient length of stay," J. Emerg. Med., vol. 44, pp. 230–235, 2013.

[4] E. S. Powell et al., "The relationship between inpatient discharge timing and emergency department boarding," J. Emerg. Med., vol. 42, pp.186–196, 2012.

[5] J. Zulkepli and T. Eldabi, "Developing Integrated Patient Pathways Using Hybrid Simulation," AIP Conf. Proc. vol.1782, 2016, pp.040022, doi: 10.1063/1.4966089.

[6] E. Tillal, B. Mariusz, and S. brailsford, "Hybrid Simulation: Historical Lessons, Present Challenges and Futures," Proceedings of the 2016 Winter Simulation Conference, IEEE Press, 2016, pp. 1388–1403.

[7] K. Chahal and T. Eldabi, "A Generic Framework for Hybrid Simulation in Healthcare," Proc. 28th Int. Conf. Syst. Dyn. Soc., 2010, pp. 1-16.

[8] S. K. L. Brailsford, Sally C., L. Churilov, "Treating ailing emergency departments with simulation: An integrated perspective,"Health science simulation., pp. 25–30, 2003.

[9] R. E. Giachetti, E. A. Centeno, M. A. Centeno, and R. Sundaram, "Assesing the Viability of an Open Access Policy in an Outpatient Clinic: A Discrete Event and Continuous Simulation Modeling Approach ," in Proceedings of the 2005 Winter Simulation Conference, 2005, IEEE Press, pp. 2246–2255.

[10] T. R. Rohleder, D. P. Bischak, and L. B. Baskin, "Modeling patient service centers with simulation and system dynamics," Health Care Manag. Sci., vol. 10, pp. 1–12, Nov. 2006.

[11] N. Ahmad, N. A. Ghani, A. A. Kamil, and R. M. Tahar, "Modelling the complexity of emergency department operations using hybrid simulation," Int. J. Simul. Process Model., vol. 10, pp. 360–371, 2015.

[12] R. K. Khare, E. S. Powell, G. Reinhardt, and M. Lucenti, "Adding More Beds to the Emergency Department or Reducing Admitted Patient Boarding Times: Which Has a More Significant Influence on Emergency Department Congestion?," Ann. Emerg. Med., vol. 53, pp. 575–585.e2, 2009.

[13] A. E. Bair, W. T. Song, Y. C. Chen, and B. A. Morris, "The impact of inpatient boarding on ED efficiency: A discrete-event simulation study," J. Med. Syst., vol. 34, pp. 919–929, 2010.

[14] W. Rashwan, H. Heba, and A. Arisha, "An Integrated Approach of Multi-objective Optimization Modeling for Evaluating New Supporting Program in Irish Hospital," Proceedings of the 2016 Winter Simulation Conference, IEEE Press, 2016, pp. 1904-1915.

[15] J. G. Cronin, "The introduction of the Manchester triage scale to an emergency department in the Republic of Ireland," Accid. Emerg. Nurs., vol. 11, pp. 121–125, 2003.

Internet of Things Simulation Tools: Proposing Educational Components

Majid Bayani
School of Informatics
National University of Costa Rica
Heredia, Costa Rica
mbayani@una.cr

Jeffrie Saenz
School of Informatics
National University of Costa Rica
Heredia, Costa Rica
jeffrie.saenz.rodriguez@est.una.cr

Alberto Segura
School of Informatics
National University of Costa Rica
Heredia, Costa Rica
alberto.segura.gutierrez@una.cr

Brayan Mora
School of Informatics
National University of Costa Rica
Heredia, Costa Rica
brayan.mora.morera@est.una.cr

***Abstract*— Internet of Things (IoT) refers to a developing and prevalent trend which provides connectivity between a huge number of objects (things) by using innovative features of the Radio Frequency Identification and Wireless Sensor networks technologies. As IoT develops, it is being expanded in magnitude and scope, reshaping the context of human life. Education is one of the most popular areas in our life where IoT can have an influence on. The educational process can be implemented and tracked by making use of the IoT objects and devices. In this work, an educational component is proposed in order to include it in the IoT simulation toolkits. A four-block module containing educative objects is designed and proposed. The module includes the smart elements, such as smart backpack, IoT school check in, smart desk and whiteboard. The final model design includes the procedures, methodology, block design and functions of each element. The paper shows that the IoT educational components can provide a novel and flexible virtual platform which can take advantage of the IoT features in the learning system.**

Keywords-Internet of Things(IoT); Smart desk; Smart book; Educational components;Web of Things(WoT);Smart objects; Smart whiteboards; Smart backpack.

I. INTRODUCTION

The basic idea of Internet of Things (IoT) is a new model based on the presence of a variety of objects like Radio Frequency Identification (RFID) tags, sensors and actuators that are able to interact with each other [1]. Internet of Things is considered the internetworking of smart physical objects that are enabled to collect and exchange data through the unique IPv6 addressing schemes. Also, it refers to the use of smartly connected objects, agent and devices to manage data obtained by embedded sensors in the machines and other physical-virtual objects. Based on the recommendation of The Global Standards Initiative on the Internet of Things (IoT-GSI) [7], IoT has been defined as the global infrastructure for the information society that can facilitate the interconnecting of the physical and virtual things based on the RFID and Wireless Sensor Network technologies. IoT-GSI also emphasized on establishing a Study Group on IoT and its applications, in order to promote an integrated methodology for the development of technical standards related to the IoT objects [2] [3] [4] [5].

The range of IoT applications (few applications are currently developed [6]) and the driving technologies, are expanded form the smart-cities to the complex IoT systems. IoT applications can embrace all human-object activities such as the smart home & cities, online-business, smart environment, security & emergencies, smart transportation, smart energy consumption, smart industrial process and education.

More than 50 billion sensor devices will be connected through the Internet by 2020 and a huge number of users will interact with each other over the many smart areas in different forms of the services, programs or applications. [14]. IoT devices provide connectivity for the objects, and systems, Machine-to-Machine (M2M), machine to object and object to object that implies a complex topology between devices. It means that it is required to design the objects with specific feature and capacity such as a small processor, memory, radio and software [9] [10]. The implementing of a complex topology for interconnecting between large numbers of devices is not simple to design. In these cases, simulation of the functions is required to study the scenarios before implementing them. In addition, the connectivity between objects is affected by their geographical features such as the location, their capabilities, and quality of the communications [13].

The huge number of smart IoT objects are deployed over the sensor field and can be controlled remotely through the Internet. But, sometimes implementation of the IoT infrastructure is complicated to administrate due to inaccessible distribution fields such as volcano, wild jungle or even underwater deployment places [11] [12]. Based on the mentioned reasons, simulating the process and functions for IoT scenarios is required.

Simulating the events, functions, and platforms allows the designers to survey a problem at different levels of abstraction. This approach at a higher level of abstraction permits the developers to better understand the object interactions within a complex topology [15].

The IoT implementation field is a large space complex system and it contains lots of objects. Testing the applications running on the high density of physical objects is possible just by using a flexible platform in the labs. On the other hand, real implementation of an IoT scenario is challenging since complex IoT environments are dynamic. Hence, simulation modeling of the IoT scenarios is a proper answer to this paradigm [16].

This paper is organized as follows: after giving a brief description around the main topic, a state of the art related to the previous IoT simulation studies is explored in the second section. The third section broadly discusses the case study model of the proposed components along with the IoT basic system architecture, technologies that support IoT and main blocks of the system design. Finally, a concise conclusion and future work will be described in the fourth section.

II. RELATED WORK

In order to provide smart services, modeling of the IoT environments is a big challenge due to the existing difficulties in designing heterogeneous environments, nodes, devices and wireless technologies [13]. On the other side, monitoring an event without the central administration is another challenge for identifying, observing the events and detecting the critical system components in time [17]. For these reasons, currently, in the real-time heterogeneous IoT environments, there exist very limited models and simulators. For example, Moschakis and H. Karatza [18] offer several simulation concepts for IoT environments. Sotiriadis et al. in [19] present a SimIoT derivative version of Sim-IC framework. SimIoT introduces an innovative level of security for IoT connected devices along with a very deep vision of the IoT behavior structure [20]. A fault model for dynamic IoT system is introduced by Ivanovitch Silva et al. in [21] with a novel perspective. Khan and Manate [22] [23] introduce an innovative infrastructure and coordination techniques for the large scale IoT infrastructure. MicroGrid [24] elaborates a platform for the basic simulation experiments, performing in the grid positions. DGSim [25] also provides a particular framework for scheduler implementation of various grid resource management in a simulation architecture. Finally, Belli et al. [26] present a Web of Things testbed tool. They claim WoT enables developers to design and evaluate easily, smart services and applications in a real IoT- environment.

Currently, IoT concepts and designs, as well as the communication technology, are involved in almost all human-machine activities. In fact, IoT comprises all macro human/object activities; among them, education is one of the most visible applications that IoT can be involved in. Also, it can be said that education is one of the most perceptible undertakings in the human life and is facing several challenges of technology development [8][27]. Simulation of the educational process implemented by IoT technology is one of these challenges. However, there exist several general-purpose IoT simulators such as Cisco packet tracer (recently added the IoT features) which can be used in simulating IoT process with the educational purposes [28]. But, in the most of IoT simulators, educative objects are not present.

The main idea in this work is to propose a novel model design related to the educational components in order to give a proper awareness to the designers with the purpose of incorporating IoT elements into the simulators. A basic model of the educational IoT component will be presented in the following section.

III. CASE STUDY MODEL

In this section, firstly, a basic IoT structure will be described as well as technologies such as Radio Frequency Identification (RFID) and Wireless Sensor networks (WSNs) that support IoT. In the second step, an IoT scenario will be discussed with a concise explanation of the proposed model.

A. *The IoT Basic system Architecture*

The most common basic IoT system architecture is shown in Figure 1. Based on Figure 1, a basic IoT architecture is divided into three layers. They are application, network and perception layers [29].

1) The application layer is responsible for providing smart services to the users through an interface.

2) The network layer is responsible for providing communication between the network devices and objects, cabling, clouding system, and a data local processing unit. A gateway connection point is in charge of obtaining the information which are sensed by sensors of the perception layer.

3) The perception layer includes the physical sensors, objects or actuators.

A small sensor processing system includes the event sensing, local storing, data and controllers. These units build the perception layer.

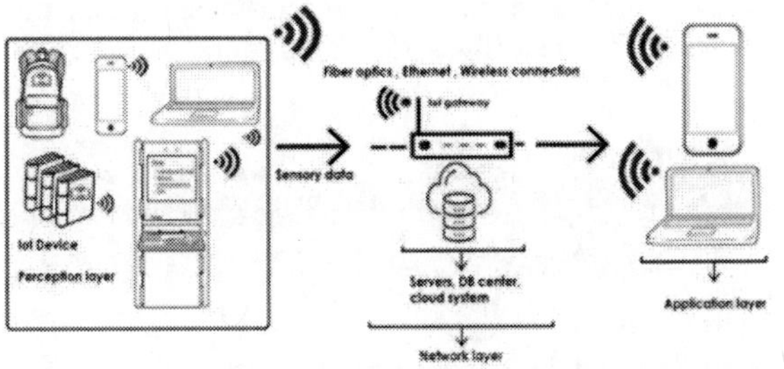

Figure 1. A simple architecture of IoT scenario

B. *Technologies that drive IoT*

1) RFID Sensor System

Figure 2 shows a basic RFID system architecture. The RFID readers detect the sensory data or receive the energy from the tag-pasted object and send information to a private cloud system for more processing or decision taking.

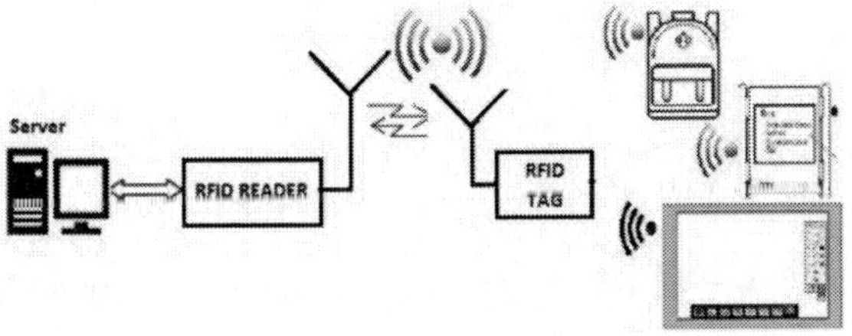

Figure 2. Block diagram of a typical RFID system

2) Wireless Sensor Network

As Figure 3 demonstrates, a group of tiny sensors distributed over a field can build a non-centralized network to sense an event and send the data back to a sink point (gateway) in order to monitor the area or further analysis related to the events [30].

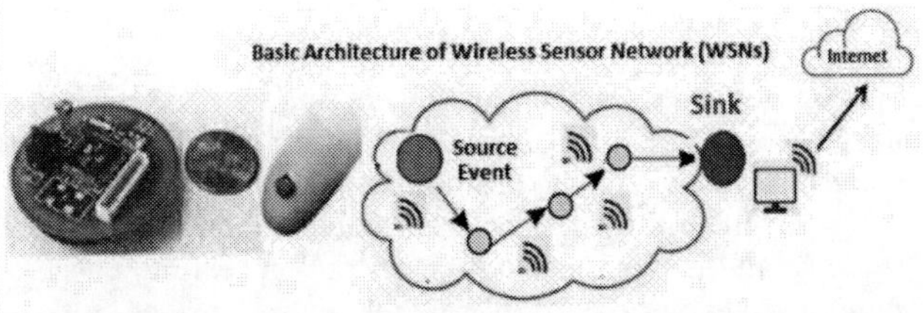

Figure 3. A Basic Wireless Sensor Network Structure

C. *The Main blocks of the Module*

The main blocks of the proposed model are shown in Figure 4.

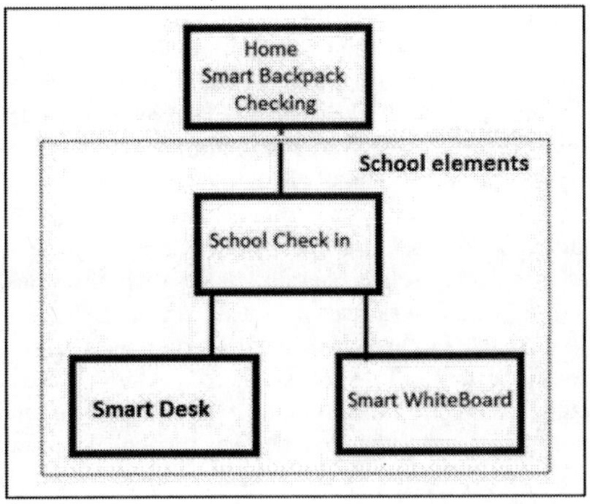

Figure 4. Main blocks of the proposed model

The proposed module consists of four separated blocks: Home smart backpack, school check in, smart desk and whiteboard. Based on the model, firstly, a pre-check of backpack content is carried out at home by students, parents or even a teacher. Mainly, this block is designed for schedule checking. After performing the pass-through authentication process, the user can check the diary agenda. The books or documents are RFID/WSN sensor labeled and will be identified when they are going inside or outside of the backpack. The movement of the RFID-labeled objects generates some control messages that will be sent through the IoT network to a smartphone or a display device for further analysis and collaborative actions.

Another component is the school check-in block that includes a two-phase IoT authentication process. This block is designed for getting access to the main school system menu by students or teachers. The menu for the students is different from the teachers. In this case, a user can have access to the personalized option designed for teaching or administrative objectives. The administrative menu is related to the managerial correspondences and functions, schedule of the semester, student list, etc.

Homework, exams, quizzes, projects, educational materials, evaluation results, and reports of the student will be available in the educational menu.

A second fingerprint authentication is employed for detecting the authority level of each user physically, in order to link the user to its educative profiles, correctly. The second physical authentication is used for user detection and connecting students to the options which are designed specifically for them, as well as their profiles. When the learners´ fingers touch the authentication device, the IoT system identifies if the user is registered in the database (DB) and the type of the user. The students can get access to the first level permission of the main menu designed for the learners. This menu contains many educative or (administrative) options for students such as: the actual semester program and enrolled courses, financial and scholarship status, smart homework, projects, smart exams, evaluation results, etc. The student users can touch any options of the menu and can find the personalized exam, quiz or any projects designed by instructors.

After passing the first checking level, the learners can look for the related class numbers that were registered in the main system. Last two blocks are related to the class activities. In a typical class, students have their own desks that sit on it. Each desk has a sensor for authentication (fingerprint or RFID card). So, each learner uses a smart unique desk and table. The desks are connected wirelessly or by a cable connection to the main IoT system. The smart desks can interact with other IoT devices through a gateway and a small private cloud system, sending or receiving the control messages. In the following, each component, its connections and functions will be analyzed in detail.

1) Home Smart backpack checking:

This component is related to the smart IoT backpack element. First of all, a RFID element and a WSN sensor is pasted on the backpack.

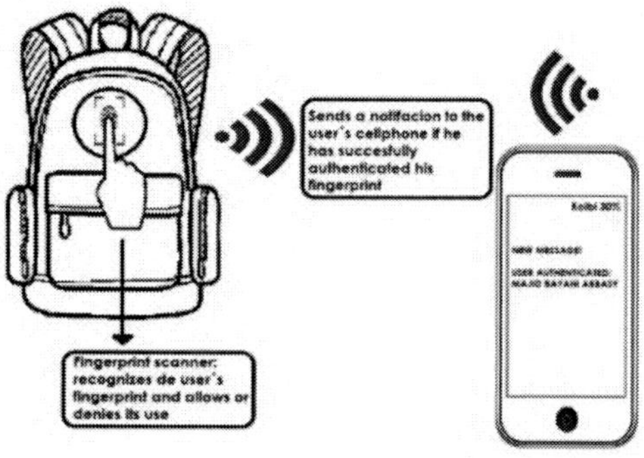

Figure 5. Backpack authentication

The process of authentication is performed through scanning the sensor (RFID or ID card) (Figure 5). This process is an essential security process to protect the unauthorized access to the smart backpack. As Figure 6 demonstrates, after checking the authorization the smart backpack is on ready mode and open status. The reader scans each object that goes into the backpack, sending the signal to the smart phone. The sensory data will be transferred through the IoT gateway to a private cloud system storing the information and control signals.

This element is designed as a flexible system that can scan all physical objects tracking, inside and outside of the backpack.

The sensory data are stored in a small cloud server, communicating with a display device such as a smartphone or a laptop through the internet informing the student parents or the same user. The users arrange this process based on their scheduling.

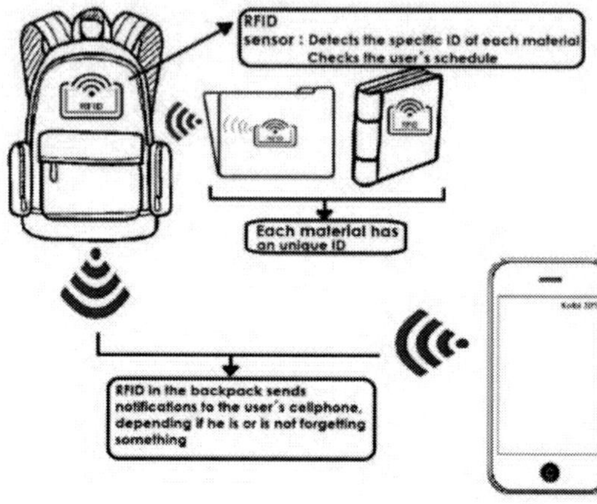

Figure 6. Backpack components

2) School check-in

Based on the main blocks topology, in the first phase of the school check-in, the people should authenticate themselves through presenting any physical identity such as the fingerprint, RFID card or the cellphone interaction with the central entrance terminal. Based on the registered information, the system can detect the validity or type of user. They can be a teacher, student or an administrative member of the institute.

Figures 7 and 8 show that after passing this phase, the user can get access to the personalized main menu. For example, if the user is a student, the options that appear on the screen will be available, exclusively, for the students. In the second phase, the student should perform the second IoT level of validity process. After verifying the user authority, once the user touches any option, more personalized functions for this particular user will be accessible. For example, if the user is a learner and touches the smart homework, a specific homework for this user, uniquely, will open to get access to that content. In this way, the users can have access to the several facilities by this terminal which is connected to school data base (DB).

Email notification is one of these facilities for both students and instructors. In this sub-option service, a web of thing (WoT) service provides the email service for the student and teacher users. They can observe a short list of the updated email box with related subjects and degree of urgency for future email checking.

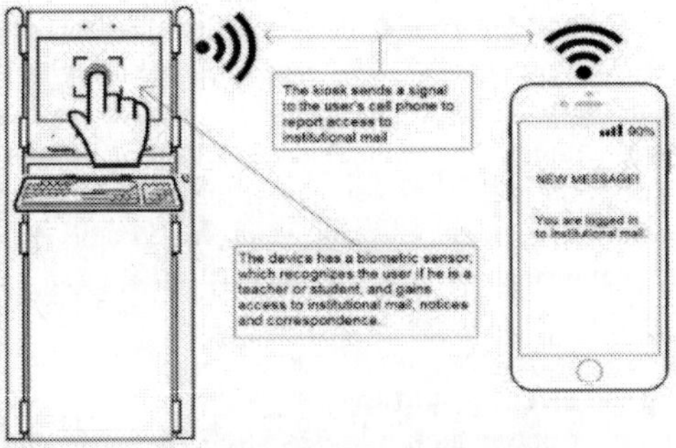

Figure 7. School check-in components

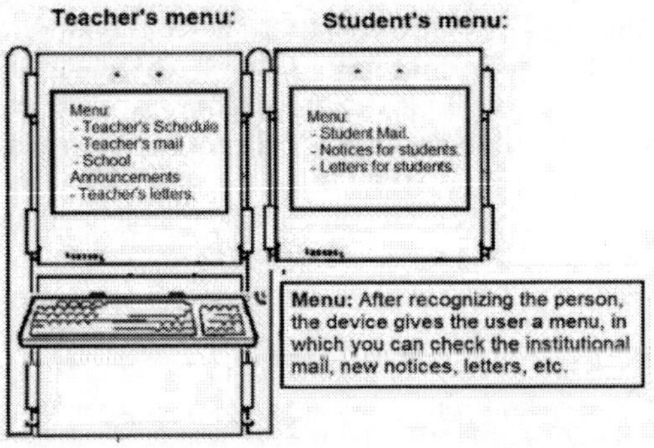

Figure 8. School check in second security level authentication

The third section is related to the smart desk component. The user can enter the smart class looking for preconfigured desks. The class is equipped with the smart IoT devices such as smart desk, smart board, etc.

3) Smart Desk

Each student has a preconfigured smart desk equipped with the IoT sensor detection. Figures 9 and 10 show a scenario in which the smart desks interact with the users.

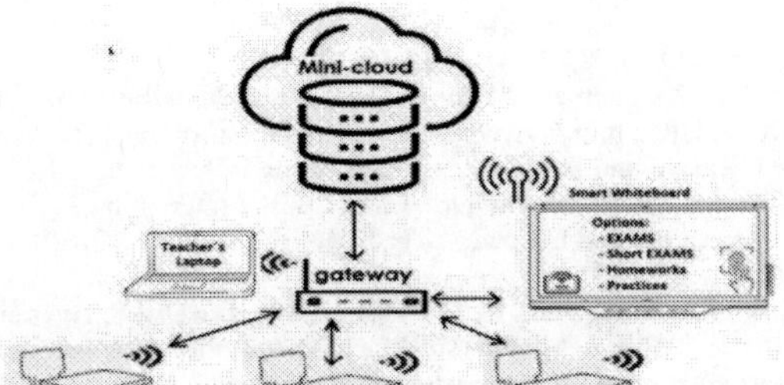

Figure 9. Smart Desks

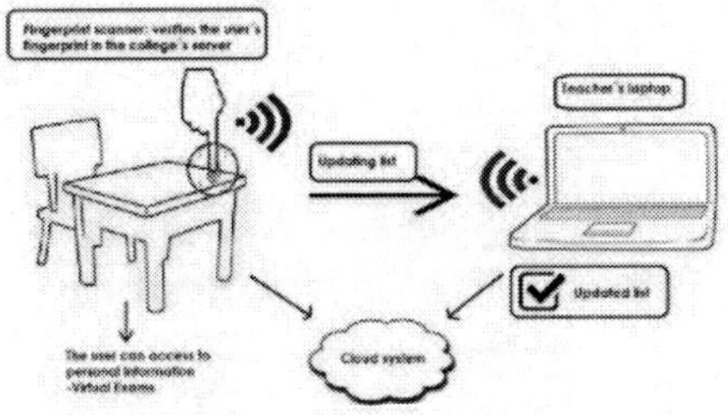

Figure 10. Smart Desk Authentication

Based on Figures 9 and 10, when the users pass the authentication process by checking fingerprint, RFID ID card or a cellphone interaction, they can use the facilities of the smart desks. IoT desks can connect to the network via wireless or cable connection. They can interact with the smart whiteboards as well as the teacher device. Once the users demonstrate the required authority, they can have access to the main system and offered services. For example, they can receive what the instructor is writing on the whiteboard and see it on their laptops. They can also interrupt the professor's lecture (configuration and permission needed) and write enquiries or questions.

The smart desks can be employed for attendance checking list in a secure method. This is an IoT secure way to send the list to a mini-cloud system. The professors can generate a report of the list by using the data stored in the cloud system.

As IoT can implement and use the WSNs, all WSN sensors will be activated and a mini monitoring system can track graphically the user nodes, in a real time mode.

The last component of the module is a smart IoT whiteboard that will be discussed in the following section.

4) Smart Whiteboard

This block contains the authentication IoT elements, and users can check the security validity, physically (Figure 11). A Web of thing (WoT) system software connected to the whiteboard collects the sensory data sending them to a private cloud system.

The users can have access to their personalized facilities built in the smart whiteboard. The educator can touch the menus and get access to the educational services that they need.

A menu with several options appears on the screen and users can select any option or service that needed to proceed. As the validity checking is a physical IoT process, different profiles for instructors can be defined in the main WoT system. For example, the professor of a particular course can get access to all packages related to that course. In this form, the IoT technology provides multi-discipline area platforms for different courses, purposes or users. Similarly, the student users can obtain and get the services after the validity check that is provided only for the students. They can interact with the whiteboard IoT system through their smartphones to send and receive the messages, questions, images, text, or even send an interrupting message during the instructor's lecturing.

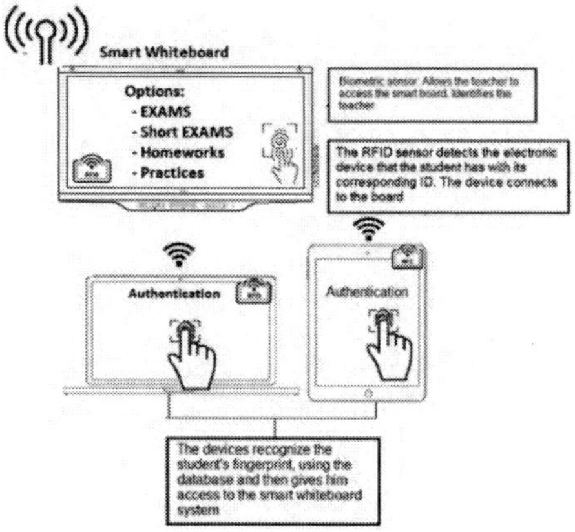

Figure 11. IoT smart Whiteborad components

Figure 11 is a graphical demonstration of a smart IoT whiteboard structure. Based on the Figure 11, the learners can interact with the whiteboard. The smart whiteboard has the capacity of dividing in several areas: student area, messaging, questions, and lecture areas. In this way, in a real time mode, the learners can exchange information with the teacher and vice versa. The instructor can receive the messages and queries from the students and answer them. The students can see the answers on their laptops or computers. Both students and teachers can validate physically their identities through a RFID ID-card taking advantage of the IoT authentication feature.

IV. CONCLUSION AND FUTURE WORK

Many times, implementing the complex procedures in a real mode is difficult and performing a process for the innovative phenomenon is converted into a big challenge. The solution for these cases is "simulating the process". IoT technology is involving in all aspects of the human life. It can provide a platform and many facilities in many areas such as in education. This paper presented a novel application of IoT, offering an *educational IoT module* with physical-machine object authentication. The main idea in this work is proposing the educational components for IoT simulation toolkits. These elements are smart backpack, IoT check-in system, and two more elements; smart desk and whiteboard that are practically used in the smart IoT class. In case of the smart backpack, the objects (books) will be WSN/RFID labeled which can facilitate a real-time monitoring of the object tracking. This system helps the parents (or the same user) to check the user's activities. The check-in school system is another IoT system that eliminates the web authentication process just by using a physical authentication. The user performs the check-in process before entering the classroom. The two-level physical security system increases safety of the system. The users based on their predefined profile can get access to their options. The second component is a smart desk. The users log in physically to have access to the services and interact with other objects such as a smart whiteboard. The idea of proposing this novel component is to inherit all benefits that IoT can provide for a typical education scenario. Internet of things can remove the physical existence limitation and increases the accessibility to several educational recourses and tools, anytime, anywhere improving the effect e-learning.

IoT and related technologies such as RFID and WSN can elaborate a flexible collaboration platform through connecting the objects. And also, it can offer a more secure system by eliminating the traditional web-based authentication process by using the physical authentication.

This work is considered as a first step to take to involve the IoT concepts in the educational objects. Connectivity, collaboration and scalability are some of the advantageous attributes of the IoT that are inherited by any IoT-based learning system. Based on this reality, our future work will be focused on implementing tangibly the proposed module in order to study the impact of applying an IoT-based structure on the learning system performance.

REFERENCES

[1] R. Parashar, A. Khan, and Neha, "A Survey: The Internet of Things", International Journal of Technical Research and Applications, e-ISSN: 2320-8163, vol. 4, Issue 3, 2016, pp. 251-257.

[2] M. Friedemann and C. Floerkemeier, "From the Internet of Computers to the Internet of Things," Informatik- Spektrum, vol. 33, Issue 2, pp. 107–121, April 2010.

[3] M. Weiser, "The Computer for the 21st Century," Scientific American. Bibcode: 1991SciAm.265c.94W, vol. 265, Issue 3, 1991, pp. 94–104.

[4] Silicon Labs, "The evolution of wireless sensor networks," URL: http://www.silabs.com/Support%20Documents/TechnicalDocs/evolution-of-wireless-sensor-networks.pdf, 2013.

[5] A. Wood, "The internet of things is revolutionizing our lives, but standards are a must, " Theguardian.com. Guardian. Retrieved 31 March 2015.

[6] C.A. Vázquez, M. Mejía and R. Pinto, "Modeling Student Engagement by means of nonverbal behavior and Decision trees," IEEE International Conference on Mechatronics, Electronics and Automotive Engineering (ICMEAE), pp. 24-27, November 2015, DOI: 10.1109/ICMEAE.2015.56.

[7] IoT-GSI, "Internet of Things Global Standards Initiative," February 2012, URL: http://www.itu.int/en/ITU-T/gsi/iot/Pages/default.aspx.

[8] M. Bayani and E. Vilchez, ""Predictable Influence of IoT (Internet of Things) in the Higher Education," International Journal of Information and Education Technology, vol. 7, no. 12, 2017, pp. 914-920.

[9] J. Höller, V. Tsiatsis, C. Mulligan, S. Karnouskos, S. Avesand and D. Boyle, "From Machine-to-Machine to the Internet of Things: Introduction to a New Age of Intelligence," Elsevier, 2014, ISBN 978-0-12-407684-6.

[10] M. Bayani, G. Marin and G. Barrantes, "Performance e Analysis of Sensor Placement Strategies on a Wireless Sensor Network," IEEE Fourth International Conference on Sensor Technologies and Applications, Sensorcomm2010, ISBN: 978-0-7695-4096-2, 2010, pp. 609-617.

[11] J. Williams, "Internet of things: Science Fiction or Business Fact?" Harvard Business Review Analytic Services Report, pp. 2-9, December 2014.

[12] D. Evans, "The Internet of Things: How the Next Evolution of the Internet Is Changing Everything," Cisco Corporation, April 2011.

[13] G. D'Angelo, S. Ferretti and V. Ghini, "Simulation of the Internet of Things," IEEE International Conference on High Performance Computing & Simulation (HPCS), Austria, 18-22 July 2016, pp. 1-8.

[14] D. Lund, C. MacGillivray, V. Turner, and M. Morales, "Worldwide and Regional Internet of Things (IoT) 2014–2020 Forecast: A Virtuous Circle of Proven Value and Demand," International Data Corporation (IDC), #248451, May 2014.

[15] B. P. Zeigler, "Object-Oriented Simulation with Hierarchical, Modular Models," Intelligent Agents and Endomorphic Systems Boston, Massachusetts, Academic Press, ISBN: 978-0-12-778452-6, 1990.

[16] J. Engblom," Internet of Things Automatic Testing- Using Simulation," INTEL company, Wind River Blog Network, URL://blogs.windriver.com/wind_river_blog/2014/11/internet-of-things-automatic-testing-using-simulation.html.

[17] S. Dhouib et al., "Papyrus for IoT – A Modeling Solution for IoT," CEA, LIST, Laboratory of Model Driven Engineering for Embedded Systems, 91191, Gif-sur-Yvette CEDEX, 2016, URL: https://ido2016.sciencesconf.org/122755/document.

[18] M. Ioannis and H. D. Karatza, "Towards scheduling for internet-of-things applications on clouds: a simulated annealing approach. Concurrency and Computation: Practice and Experience," vol. 27, no.8, 2015, pp.1886–1899.

[19] S. Sotiriadis, N. Bessis, E. Asimakopoulou, and N. Mustafee, "Towards simulating the internet of things," 28th IEEE International Conference on In Advanced Information Networking and Applications Workshops (WAINA), 2014, pp. 444–448.

[20] S. Sotiriadis, N. Bessis, N. Antonopoulos, and A. Anjum, "Simic: Designing a new inter-cloud simulation platform for integrating large-scale resource management," IEEE 27th International Conference on In Advanced Information Networking and Applications (AINA 2013), 2013, pp. 90–97.

[21] S. Ivanovitch, R. Leandro , D. Macedo , L. Affonso, "A dependability evaluation tool for the Internet of Things," Computers and Electrical Engineering, vol. 39, no.7, 2013 , pp.2005-2018.

[22] A.M. Khan, L. Navarro, L. Sharifi, and L. Veiga, "Clouds of small things: Provisioning infrastructure-as-a-service from within community networks," IEEE 9th International Conference on in Wireless and Mobile Computing, Networking and Communications (WiMob), 2013, pp. 16–21.

[23] B. Manate, TF Fortis, and V. Negru, "Optimizing cloud re-sources allocation for an internet of things architecture," Scientific International Journal for Parallel and Distributed Computing, Scalable Computing: Practice and Experience Journal," vol. 15, no. 4, 2014, pp. 345–355.

[24] H.J., Song, X. Liu, D. Jakobsen, R. Bhagwan, R., X. Zhang, K. Taura and A. Chien, "The microgrid: A Scientific tool for Modeling Computational grids," SC '00: Proceedings of the 2000 ACM/IEEE Conference on Supercomputing, DOI: 10.1109/SC.2000.10028, November 2000.

[25] A. Iosup, O., Sonmez, and D. Epema, "DGSim: Comparing grid resource management architectures through trace-based simulation," In Euro-Par 2008-Parallel Processing, Springer, 2008, pp. 13-25.

[26] L. Belli, S. Cirani, L. Davoli, A. Gorrieri, M. Mancin, M. Picone, and G. Ferrari, "Design and Deployment of an IoT Application-Oriented Testbed," IEEE Computer Society, Computer, Vol. 48, no. 9 , pp. 32-40, September 2015, doi:10.1109/MC.2015.253.

[27] M. Selinger, A. Sepulveda and J. Buchan, "Education and the Internet of Everything: How ubiquitous connectedness can help transform pedagogy," Cisco Consulting Service and Cisco EMEAR Education team, October 2013.

[28] W. Werapun, "Packet Tracer 7.0: IoTs workshop, Introduction to Cisco IoTs," URL:https://werapun.com/packet-tracer-7-0-iots-workshop-17d4763f696.

[29] P. Sethi and S. R. Sarangi, "Internet of Things: Architectures, Protocols, and Applications," Journal of Electrical and Computer Engineering, 2017, Article ID 9324035, 25 pages, https://doi.org/10.1155/2017/9324035.

[30] M. Bayani, Y. Alpizar, O. Ramirez, I. Ulate, and R. Gamboa, "Radio communication range effects on a flat wireless sensor network performance," IEEE 36th Central American and Panama Convention, DOI: 10.1109/CONCAPAN.2016.7942365, November 2016.

Future Tasks of Lightweight-Polymer Combat Helmets

Henrik Seeber, Arash Ramezani, Hendrik Rothe
Chair of Measurement and Information Technology
University of the Federal Armed Forces
Hamburg, Germany
Email: henrik.seeber@hsu-hh.de, ramezani@hsu-hh.de, rothe@hsu-hh.de

Abstract—**In the military and police sector, the endangerment for the forces has risen over the last decades. Especially police forces are facing new threats due to increased terrorist activity in western European cities and a rising propensity to violence. This development makes it necessary to provide state of the art protection for patrol officers. This includes helmets made of ultra-high molecular weight polyethylene (UHMWPE) to lower the overall weight of equipment and increase the combat value of the forces by providing more comfort and possibilities for attachments. However, at the moment these types of helmets are not ready to provide the required level of protection against projectiles. The intention of this paper is to provide background information about those new threats and to mention first ideas how to tackle the emerging problems of current UHMWPE combat helmets.**

Keywords-applied research; fiber-reinforced plastics; optimization; armor systems; ballistic trials.

I. Introduction

Combat helmets are a key factor in personal protection for military and police forces. Rapidly changed threats on missions, especially for police patrol officers [5] and soldiers in stabilization missions [1], prove that protection needs a new ability profile. This work in progress provides background information to specify the problems and first ideas how to solve these problems. The overall aim is to create a ballistic combat helmet that meets the union of test center for armored materials and constructions 3 (Vereinigung der Prüfstellen für Angriffshemmende Materialien und Konstruktionen 3) (VPAM 3) regulations and the technical directive "System Ballistic Helmet" 5/2010 [2].

A. *Structure of the Paper*

The paper is structured as follows. In Section II, there will be brief information about the history of combat helmets and their materials through time. In Section III, threats for ballistic protection will be mentioned. Section IV is about the disadvantages of current UHMWPE combat helmets and Section V is about the advantages of lighter polymer combat helmets. In the final section, Section VI, the aim will be concretized and explained.

II. History

Combat helmets have a long tradition. Before the invention of gunpowder, they were used as a protection against blunt trauma and cuts. They were designed to deflect, e.g. a sword, so there was less residual energy on the head. Later on, helmets were mainly worn for pageantry and unit recognition until the First World War began.

A. *Combat Helmets in the 20th Century*

Due to the massive use and increased lethality of artillery, the German forces introduced the "Steel Helmet Modell 1916" in 1915. All fractions introduced nearly the same helmet models in mode of action at this time, which were made out of basic steel. These helmets were only able to stop the primary threat of that time: fragmenting projectiles of artillery bombs, they were not able to stop bullets because of the available materials. During the Second World War, the U.S Military introduced the M1 in 1942, which was made out of "Hadfield steel". This helmet was used by the German armed forces until the 1990s. Problems with this type of steel helmet occurred because the helmets were too heavy and reduced the view, hearing and mobility of the wearer. The M1 was followed by a very new generation of combat helmets, which was made of aramid. Aramid was the first synthetic bulletproof material and was invented in the 1960s by DuPont.

B. *Combat Helmets in the 21st Century*

As a replacement of the M1, the German armed forces introduced the "Combat Helmet, Ground Forces" made of aramid. In addition, they used the new retention system "NOSHA", which provided a better shock absorption and air circulation. The next stage of development was – again – a totally new material: the ultra-high molecular weight polyethylene fibers (UHMWPE). With hybridization techniques, the U.S Military developed a new generation of combat helmets in 2010, the so-called "Future Assault Shell Technology" (FAST). The German armed forces also use FAST with the name "Combat Helmet Special Forces". Also, FAST helmets were added to the concept "Infantry of the Future" (see Figure 1) [6]. Moreover, this generation has

Figure 1. FAST helmet with the concept "Infantry of the Future" [6].

improvements at the retention system with a multi-pad and four-point retention system. In addition to the reduced weight, the FAST helmet provides higher comfort.

III. NEW THREATS

A. *Changed Threats for Police Forces*

Threats for police forces and the military have changed a lot over the last decades. Police forces face international terrorism, especially in western European cities. More and more, terrorists are military trained and equipped with military weapons and gear. Time is the most crucial point in chaotic situations, so patrol officers have to engage first [6]. Only a combination of ballistic vests and ballistic helmets provides the necessary level of protection in such situations. Especially patrol officers are facing unpredictable threats on duty so their helmets have to provide protection against multiple threats. Apart from ballistic threats, hits with blunt and sharp weapons, fire and chemicals are common threats for them. The willingness of patrol officers in Baden Wurttemberg to wear their helmets also in common situations like brawls and skirmishes make it necessary to provide good shock absorbing attributes against blunt trauma [5].

B. *New Threats for Military Forces*

But also, military forces are facing changed threats. Statistics of the American Operations in Afghanistan and Iraq show that head and neck wounds are increasing. The distribution of wounds shows that 30% of all wounds are in the head and neck area (based on injuries/treatments from hospitalization, including persons who died of wounds) [1]. The main threats at patrol missions are improvised explosive device (IED) attacks and ambushes with assault rifles. Due to the increased use of IEDs, blast associated head injuries, e.g., fragments, have increased compared to gunshot wounds. Furthermore, the characteristics of the fragments have changed compared to mortar and artillery shells. This can lead to a different impact behavior. In addition, blunt traumatic injuries have increased because they are linked to blast events. Nevertheless, blunt trauma is also associated with noncombat situations like vehicle crashes, parachute drop accidents or falls. Common blunt trauma threats have an impact velocity of 6.1m/s, which is equal to a drop of 1.9m [1]. The primary ballistic threat is caused by assault rifles of type AK-47 (7.62x39-mm) and owing to the increased close combat situation pistols emerging as threats, for example Makarov (9x18-mm) or Tokarev (7.62x25mm). Altogether, the America Department of Defense locates the main threat of infantry weapon at 5.56-mm and 7.62-mm rounds at muzzle velocity from 735m/s to more than 800m/s. This corresponds approximately VPAM 6 to VPAM 7 [1].

IV. DISADVANTAGES OF ACTUAL UHMWPE COMBAT HELMETS

A. *Back-face Deformation*

Back-face deformation is one of the main problems of the actual UHMWPE combat helmets. On the one hand, the material has very good attributes against bullet penetration. On the other hand, the energy of the bullet is not well dispersed (see Figure 2). This leads to the so-called back-face deformation, the material indent and the residual energy appeals on the head. For German police helmets, the residual energy has a maximum tolerance limit of 25 Joule [5]. The residual energy could lead to possible head injuries like long linear skull fractures or closed head brain trauma. At the moment, it is unclear whether the injuries occur from the deforming of the helmet onto the head or from acceleration loads transmitted through the helmet padding to the head. In addition, the test methodology with clay to display back-face deformation is not totally linked to head injuries. The human skull behavior in such situations is inadequately represented in the actual test methodology with clay. Especially in the area of back-face deformation there is a lot of potential for necessary improvements.

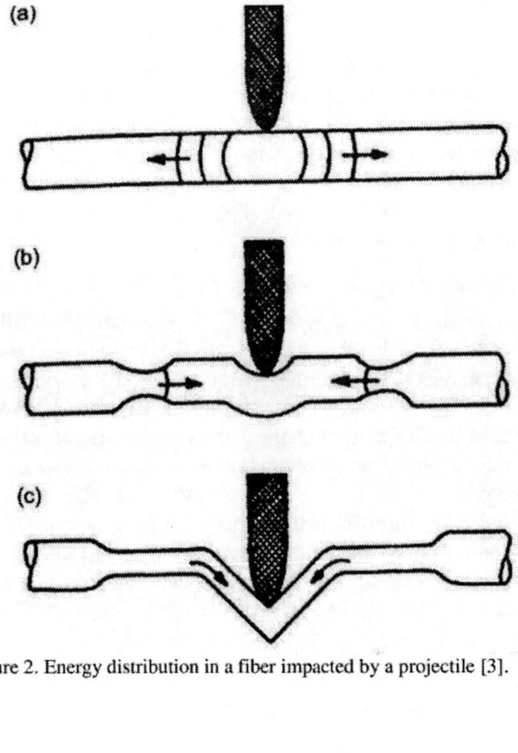

Figure 2. Energy distribution in a fiber impacted by a projectile [3].

B. *Blunt impacts*

In addition, the current generation of UHMWPE combat helmets have deficits with blunt impacts. The current combat helmets can only absorb impacts with a velocity of 3m/s or 45J drop energy [1]. As mentioned earlier, common blunt traumas occur with a velocity of 6.1m/s. In fact, blunt traumas occur especially in noncombat and training situations. Therefore, there needs to be an improvement, because most of the time the wearer of the helmet is in such a situation.

V. COMBAT HELMET AS MODULAR HEADGEAR SYSTEM

Combat helmets will evolve from a device only used for protection to a multi useable platform to increase the survivability and efficiency of the wearer. This includes basic attachments like active ear protection, flashlights or counter weights to provide a stable weight balance. Moreover, the helmet platform can be used to increase the leading ability of the group by adding integrated voice radio, a head up display with important mission information or health sensors to monitor the group vital functions. This would increase the situational awareness of the group leader and would lead to an overall increase of safety during missions. Also the combat value of every solider or policeman can be increased by adding feeder plates for night vision, the ability to wear protective masks against warfare agent or attaching standardized rails like MIL-STD 1913. Of course, the possibilities are limited due to the weight the wearer can handle over the duration of the mission. So, if the combat helmet weighs as little as possible, there are more possibilities for attachments and this leads to earlier mentioned advantages.

VI. AIM OF THE PROJECT

First of all, the aim is to create a UHMWPE combat helmet, which meets the regulations of the police institute of the German police academy in Muenster, this regulation is based on the technical directive "System Ballistic Helmet" (Technische Richtlinie "Gesamtsystem Ballistischer Schutzhelm") [2] of 5/2010. That implies that the project has the focus on police helmets.

A. *Threats Which the Helmet has to Withstand*

The main focus of the research is on the ballistic attributes of the helmet. So the helmet has to provide protection against soft-core projectiles 9mmx19 fired by small arms and machine pistols. This is comparable to VPAM 3. Overall, our aim is also to meet the regulations of VPAM 4 to compete with the current generation of titanium helmets and provide a state-of-the-art alternative [6]. The mentioned titan helmet, which is actually used, by the state of Baden Wuerttemberg is the "Hoplit" model by Ulbrichts Witwe GmbH (see Figure 3). As mentioned, earlier protection against blunt trauma is also a challenge for combat helmets. The residual energy has to be lower than 25 Joule.

Figure 3. "Hoplit F" by Ulbrichts Witwe GmbH [5]

B. *Constructional Problems*

At the moment, the material has a reliable protection against projectile penetration. Also, the material in a possible helmet shape provides a reliable protection. It has to be verified in which areas the protection is effective. Especially near the edges of the calotte, it is possible that the protection efficiency is much lower compared to the central areas. The actual titanium helmets have an efficiency distance of 10mm to the edges. All in all, these helmets provide an effective protection area of 90% [5]. As with aramid helmets, which have a much lower protective area, the fiber structure of the UHMWPE could also be a crucial point to provide a protection area as big as titanium helmets [4].

C. *Possible Solutions*

The main problem is back-face deformation. The residual energy dispensation of the material is too low in the current configuration. Now three possibilities to increase the dispensation have to be tested. Varying the direction of the material layers may mitigate the deformation. This has to be balanced between penetration and deformation of the material. The best penetration protection is provided when the layers are rotated by 90 degrees. Another idea is to use energy-absorbing materials under the calotte and as helm pads to reduce the residual energy. So, this means to integrate strictly the inlay into the helmet. Another possibility is to use two calottes, the first one as a ballistic shell and the second one as a shell to disperse the residual energy and to add absorbing material between the shells. The next step would be to precise the ideas and test their efficiency. After this, a combination of ideas could reduce the residual energy to a value lower than 25 Joule. Finally, the aim is to meet the regulations of VPAM 3.

VII. CONCLUSION

There are three main risks for ground forces: the main blast, blunt trauma and ballistic threats. Especially ballistic threats are challenging the UHMWPE helmets because of a high amount of residual energy. This leads to back-face deformation, which could result in live risking head injuries. In addition, this characteristic of injuries appears with blunt traumas. Some of the mentioned ideas could also lower the risk of blunt traumas even if the main challenge is to reduce back-face deformation. Moreover, an advantage of lighter helmets is, in addition to more comfort, the ability as a multi role carrier for attachments. This ability could improve the survivability and efficiency of the wearer. Nevertheless, the focus is to reduce back-face deformation to meet the regulations of VPAM 3. Possible ideas are to verify the direction of the layers, using energy-absorbing materials for the helmet inlay or using two decoupled shells with energy absorbing materials in between. Therefore, a combination or balance between the mentioned ideas is necessary. This means that the first step is to test how we can construct such a helmet with these possible solutions integrated. After this, ballistic tests are necessary to get an overview over the efficiency and how practical the solutions are. Especially the findings relating to the test methodology of the Review of Department of Defense Test Protocols for Combat Helmets [1] could be implemented into the test cycle. To conclude, back-face deformation is current the main problem of UHMWPE helmets due to the residual energy transmitted through the inlay. As mentioned in Section IV, also, the test methodology, to investigate the relation between back-face deformation and head injuries, has to be beheld and then maybe adjusted.

REFERENCES

[1] Committee on Review of Test Protocols Used by the DOD to Test Combat Helmets, "Review of Department of Defense Test Protocols for Combat Helmets". Washington: The National Academies Press, pp. 8–24, 2014.

[2] Police Institute of the German Police Academy in Muenster, Technical Directive "System Ballistic Helmet" (Technische Richtlinie "Gesamtsystem Ballistischer Schutzhelm"). Muenster, pp. 10-16, 5/2010.

[3] I. G. Crouch, L. Arnold, A. Pierlot, and H. Billion, "Fibres, textiles and protective apparel" in "The Science of Armour Materials". Amsterdam: Elsevier, p. 271, 2017.

[4] T.Tam and A.Bhatnagar, "High-performance ballistic fibers and tapes" in "Lightweight Ballistic Composites: Military and Law-Enforcement Applications", Second Edition. Amsterdam: Elsevier, pp. 1-30 and 210-214, 2016.

[5] Polizei Praxis. Ballistic Helmets for Patrol Officers (Ballistischer Schutzhelm für Streifenpolizisten). [Online]. Available from: http://www.polizeipraxis.de/themen/arbeitsschutz-in-der-polizei/detailansicht-arbeitsschutz-in-der-polizei/artikel/ballistischer-schutzhelm-fuer-streifenpolizisten.html [08.01.2017].

[6] J. Weisswange, Protection for the "Main"-Weapon, Modern Combat Helmets (Schutz für die "Haupt"-Waffe, Moderne Gefechtshelme). [Online]. Available from: http://www.esut.de/fileadmin/user_upload/EST916 Schutz_fuer_die_Hauptwaffe_Moderne_Gefechtshelme.pdf [08.01.2017].

Numerical Simulation and Analysis of Enzyme-Catalysed Substrate Conversion in a Microbioreactor

Linas Petkevičius and Romas Baronas

Faculty of Mathematics and Informatics,
Vilnius University, Naugarduko st. 24, Vilnius, Lithuania
Email: {linas.petkevicius, romas.baronas}@mif.vu.lt

***Abstract*—The paper presents a non-linear mathematical model for digital simulation of an enzyme loaded porous microreactor. The model is based on a system of reaction-diffusion equations, containing a non-linear term related to the Michaelis-Menten kinetics, and involves three regions: the enzyme microreactor where the enzyme reaction as well as mass transport by diffusion take place, a diffusion limiting region (the Nernst layer), where only the mass transport by diffusion takes place, and a convective region, where the analyte concentration is maintained constant. Assuming well stirred conditions, the influence of the thickness of the Nernst layer on the behaviour of the product emission, as well as the impact of the diffusion modulus and the Biot number has been numerically investigated. The simulation results showed that the Nernst layer must be taken into consideration when modelling micro-size bioreactors. The digital simulation was carried out using the finite difference technique.**

Keywords*—*reaction-diffusion; Michaelis - Menten kinetics; microbioreactor; CSTR.

I. INTRODUCTION

Continuous-flow stirred tank reactors (CSTR) are common in chemical industries [1][2]. Although a stirred tank is a usual construction of industrial enzyme reactors, the effectiveness and optimal construction of CSTR remain open to study [3][4]. Specifically, further research is needed due to the application of the immobilized enzymes, such as biocatalysts, on a manufactoring scale that requires to use the reactors of different types, including CSTR [5][6][7].

A CSTR often refers to a model used to estimate the operation parameters when using a continuous agitated-tank reactor to reach a specified output [6]. In the last few decades, immobilized enzyme reactor models have evolved significantly with wide range of applications in food industry [8], waste cleaning [9], bacteria cells immobilization [10][11]. Rapid progress was noticed in integrating microfluidic reactors and biocatalytic reactions [12]. The combination of miniaturized technologies and microfluidics allows to increase the bioprocess efficiency. However, coupling microreactors and biocatalysis is highly complex, requiring an integrated approach addressing biocatalyst features, reaction kinetics, mass transfer and microreactors geometry [12][13].

Mathematical models have been widely used to investigate the kinetic peculiarities of the enzyme microreactors [7][12]. Models coupling the enzyme-catalysed reaction with the diffusion in enzyme microreactors are usually used. Since containing catalytic particles, the analyte in CSTR is well stirred and set in powerful motion, the mass transport by diffusion outside the microreactors is usually neglected [13][14]. In practice, the zero thickness of the diffusion shell (layer) can not be achieved [15]. We consider an array of identical spherical microreactors placed in a CSTR shown in Figure 1 [6], where area Ω_m denotes a microreactor, Ω_d denotes surrounding diffusion shell and Ω_c is a convective region.

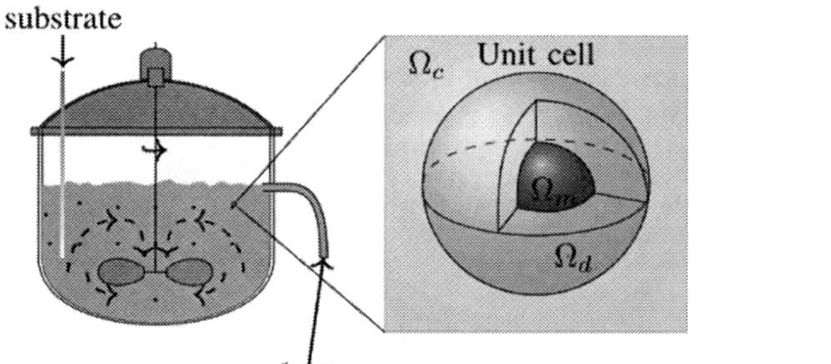

Figure 1. Continuous stirred tank reactor with enzyme-loaded microreactors (pellets) and a zoomed unit cell to be modelled.

The goal of this work was to investigate the dependencies of the internal and external diffusion limitations on the yield of the reaction product, modelled by reaction-diffusion equations, containing a non-linear term related to Michaelis-Menten kinetics [6][7][16]. The model involves three regions: the enzyme microreactor, where the enzyme reaction, as well as the mass transport by diffusion take place, a diffusion limiting region, where only the mass transport by diffusion takes place, and a convective region, where the analyte concentration is maintained constant. Due to a strong non-linearity of the reaction term, the computer simulation was carried out using the finite difference technique. [17].

The rest of the paper is organised as follows: in Section II, the mathematical model and microbioreactor characteristics are described; Section III formulates a dimensionless model and derives the main parameters of the bioreactor; Section IV describes the numerical model and the simulator; in Section V, results of numerical experiments are presented, and conclusions close the article.

II. MATHEMATICAL MODEL

We consider an array of identical spherical microreactors placed in a continuous ideally stirred-tank reactor [6]. Assuming a uniform distribution of the microreactors in the tank and a relatively great distance between adjacent microreactors, the spherical unit cell was modelled by an enzyme-loaded microreactor (pellet) and a surrounding diffusion shell (the Nernst diffusion layer). The principal structure of the tank containing uniformly distributed microreactors and a unit cell are presented in Figure 1, where Ω_m denotes a microreactor (MR), Ω_d stands for the diffusion shell and Ω_c is a convective region.

In the enzyme-loaded MR layer we consider the enzyme-catalyzed reaction

$$\mathrm{E} + \mathrm{S} \underset{k_r}{\overset{k_f}{\rightleftharpoons}} \mathrm{ES} \xrightarrow{k_{\mathrm{cat}}} \mathrm{E} + \mathrm{P}, \tag{1}$$

where the substrate (S) combines reversibly with an enzyme (E) to form a complex (ES). The complex then dissociates into the product (P) and the enzyme is regenerated [18][19].

Assuming the steady-state approximation, the concentration of the intermediate complex (ES) does not change and may be neglected when modelling the biochemical behaviour of the microreactor [6][19][20]. In the resulting scheme, the substrate (S) is enzymatically converted to the product (P),

$$\mathrm{S} \xrightarrow{\mathrm{E}} \mathrm{P}. \tag{2}$$

A. Governing Equations

Assuming the symmetrical geometry of the microreactor and homogenised distribution of the immobilized enzyme inside the porous microreactor, the mathematical model can be described in one-dimensional domain using the radial distance.

Coupling enzymatic reaction in the microreactor (region Ω_m) with the one-dimensional-in-space diffusion, described by Fick's second law, and assuming the steady-state for a system (2) lead to the following governing equations of the reaction-diffusion type ($0 < r < R_0$):

$$D_{S,m}\frac{1}{r^2}\frac{\partial}{\partial r}\left(r^2\frac{\partial S_m}{\partial r}\right) = \frac{V_{\max}S_m}{K_M + S_m}, \tag{3a}$$

$$D_{P,m}\frac{1}{r^2}\frac{\partial}{\partial r}\left(r^2\frac{\partial P_m}{\partial r}\right) = -\frac{V_{\max}S_m}{K_M + S_m}, \tag{3b}$$

where r stands for space, $S_m = S_m(r)$ and $P_m = P_m(r)$ are the concentrations of the substrate and the reaction product in the microreactor, respectively, R_0 is the radius of the microreactor, $D_{S,m}$ and $D_{P,m}$ are the diffusion coefficients, $V_{\max} = k_{cat}E_0$ is the maximal enzymatic rate and $K_M = (k_r + k_{cat})/k_f$ is the Michaelis constant (see Figure 2(a)).

In the Nernst diffusion layer Ω_d only the mass transport by diffusion takes place:

$$D_{S,d}\frac{1}{r^2}\frac{\partial}{\partial r}\left(r^2\frac{\partial S_d}{\partial r}\right) = 0, \tag{4a}$$

$$D_{P,d}\frac{1}{r^2}\frac{\partial}{\partial r}\left(r^2\frac{\partial P_d}{\partial r}\right) = 0, \quad r \in (R_0,\ R_1), \tag{4b}$$

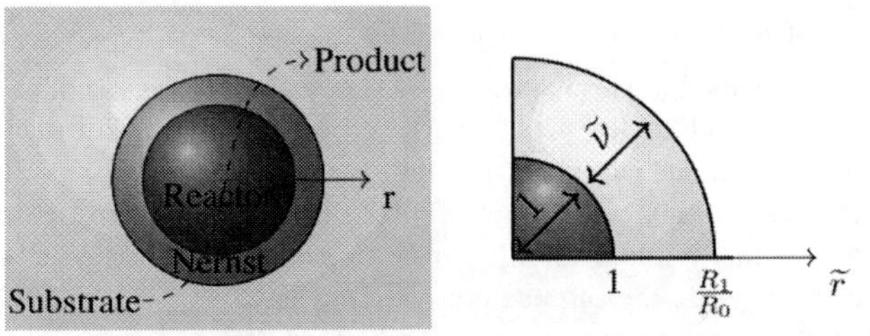

Figure 2. Principal structure of the unit cell consisting of a microbioreactor and the Nernst diffusion shell (a) and non-dimensionalized regions (b).

where $S_d = S_d(r)$ and $P_d = P_d(r)$ are the concentrations of the substrate and the reaction product in the diffusion shell, respectively, $D_{S,d}$ and $D_{P,d}$ are the diffusion coefficients of the materials in the bulk solution, R_1 is the radius of the unit cell.

B. Boundary Conditions

Fluxes of the substrate and the product through the stagnant external diffusion shell is assumed to be equal to the corresponding fluxes entering the surface of the microreactor,

$$D_{S,m}\left.\frac{\partial S_m}{\partial r}\right|_{r=R_0} = D_{S,d}\left.\frac{\partial S_d}{\partial r}\right|_{r=R_0}, \tag{5a}$$

$$D_{P,m}\left.\frac{\partial P_m}{\partial r}\right|_{r=R_0} = D_{P,d}\left.\frac{\partial P_d}{\partial r}\right|_{r=R_0}. \tag{5b}$$

The formal partition coefficient ϕ is used to describe the specificity in concentration distribution of the compounds between two neighboring regions [6][21],

$$S_m(R_0) = \phi S_d(R_0), \quad P_m(R_0) = \phi P_d(R_0). \tag{6}$$

Due to the symmetry of the microreactor, the zero-flux boundary conditions are defined for the center of the microreactor ($r = 0$),

$$D_{S,m}\left.\frac{\partial S_m}{\partial r}\right|_{r=0} = 0, \quad D_{P,m}\left.\frac{\partial P_m}{\partial r}\right|_{r=0} = 0. \tag{7}$$

According to the Nernst approach, the shell of thickness $\nu = R_1 - R_0$ remains unchanged with time [15][17]. Away from it, the solution is in motion and is uniform in concentration. Due to the continuous injection of the substrate into the stirred tank and washing off of the product, the concentration in the convective region remains unchanged:

$$S_d(R_1) = S_0, \quad P_d(R_1) = 0. \tag{8}$$

The thickness ν of the Nernst diffusion shell depends upon the nature and stirring up the buffer solution. Usually, more intensive stirring corresponds to the thinner diffusion layer (shell).

C. Microbioreactor Characteristics

In many industrial processes, especially in the production of low-value added products like biopesticides, bio-fertilizers, bio-surfactants ect. [9], it is important to continuously improve the yield and/or productivity [7]. The productivity is important, since this ensures an efficient utilization of the production capacity, i.e., the bioreactors.

The yield of the desired product on the substrate is one of the most important criteria for design and optimization of bioreactors. The economic feasibility of the process is expressed by the yield factor as the ratio of product formation rate and the substrate uptake rate [6][7].

The bioreactor construction is efficient enough when the product emission is relatively large with given substrate amount used. The product emission rate $\bar{E}_{P,O}$ can be calculated by an integration of the product flux over the outer surface of the diffusion shell [7],

$$\begin{aligned}\bar{E}_{P,O} &= \int_0^{2\pi}\int_0^{\pi} D_{P,d}\frac{\partial P_d}{\partial r}\Big|_{r=R_1} R_1^2\sin(\theta)d\theta d\varphi \\ &= 4\pi R_1^2 D_{P,d}\frac{\partial P_d}{\partial r}\Big|_{r=R_1}.\end{aligned} \qquad (9)$$

The average consumption $\bar{C}_S$ of the substrate over the whole microreactor can be calculated as follows:

$$\begin{aligned}\bar{C}_S &= \int_0^{R_0}\int_0^{2\pi}\int_0^{\pi}\frac{V_{\max}S_0}{K_M+S_0}\sin(\theta)d\theta d\varphi r^2 dr \\ &= \int_0^{R_0} 4\pi\frac{V_{\max}S_0}{K_M+S_0}r^2 dr \\ &= \frac{4}{3}\pi V_{\max}R_0^3\frac{S_0}{K_M+S_0}.\end{aligned} \qquad (10)$$

The yield factor γ for the microreactor system, as well as for the entire tank reactor shown in Figure 1, can be defined by the ratio of the product emission rate to the substrate consumption rate,

$$\gamma = \frac{\bar{E}_{P,O}}{\bar{C}_S}. \qquad (11)$$

The yield factor is equal to unity ($\gamma = 1$) when whole the consumed substrate is converted to the product and the whole the product eluted into the bulk (convective region Ω_c). The microbioreactor is absolutely inefficient ($\gamma = 0$), if no product falls into the bulk.

III. Dimensionless Model

In order to define the main governing parameters of the two compartment model (3)-(8), the dimensional variable r and unknown concentrations $S_m(r), P_m(r), S_d(r), P_d(r)$ are replaced with the following dimensionless parameters:

$$\begin{aligned}&\tilde{r} = \frac{r}{R_0},\quad \tilde{S}_m = \frac{S_m}{K_M}, \\ &\tilde{P}_m = \frac{P_m}{K_M},\quad \tilde{S}_d = \frac{S_d}{K_M},\quad \tilde{P}_d = \frac{P_d}{K_M},\end{aligned} \qquad (12)$$

where $\tilde{r}$ is the dimensionless distance from the microreactor center and $\tilde{S}_m(\tilde{r}), \tilde{P}_m(\tilde{r}), \tilde{S}_d(\tilde{r}), \tilde{P}_d(\tilde{r})$ are the dimensionless concentrations. Having defined dimensionless variables and unknowns, the following dimensionless parameters characterize the domain geometry and the substrate concentration in the bulk:

$$\tilde{\nu} = \frac{\nu}{R_0},\quad \tilde{S}_0 = \frac{S_0}{K_M}, \qquad (13)$$

where $\tilde{\nu}$ is the dimensionless thickness of the Nernst diffusion layer (see Figure 2(b)), $\tilde{S}_0$ is the dimensionless substrate concentration in the bulk solution. The dimensionless thickness of the microreactor equals one.

The governing equations (3) in the dimensionless coordinates are expressed as follows ($0 < \tilde{r} < 1$):

$$\frac{1}{\tilde{r}^2}\frac{\partial}{\partial\tilde{r}}\Big(\tilde{r}^2\frac{\partial\tilde{S}_m}{\partial\tilde{r}}\Big) - \sigma^2\frac{\tilde{S}_m}{1+\tilde{S}_m} = 0, \qquad (14a)$$

$$\frac{D_{P,m}}{D_{S,m}}\frac{1}{\tilde{r}^2}\frac{\partial}{\partial\tilde{r}}\Big(\tilde{r}^2\frac{\partial\tilde{P}_m}{\partial\tilde{r}}\Big) + \sigma^2\frac{\tilde{S}_m}{1+\tilde{S}_m} = 0, \qquad (14b)$$

where σ is the Thiele modulus or the Damköhler number [7][22][23] defined as:

$$\sigma^2 = \frac{V_{\max}R_0^2}{K_M D_{S,m}}. \qquad (15)$$

The governing equations (4) take the following form ($1 < \tilde{r} < 1+\tilde{\nu}$):

$$\frac{D_{S,d}}{D_{S,m}}\frac{1}{\tilde{r}^2}\frac{\partial}{\partial\tilde{r}}\Big(\tilde{r}^2\frac{\partial\tilde{S}_d}{\partial\tilde{r}}\Big) = 0, \qquad (16a)$$

$$\frac{D_{P,d}}{D_{S,m}}\frac{1}{\tilde{r}^2}\frac{\partial}{\partial\tilde{r}}\Big(\tilde{r}^2\frac{\partial\tilde{P}_d}{\partial\tilde{r}}\Big) = 0. \qquad (16b)$$

The matching conditions (5), (6) and (8) become:

$$\frac{\partial\tilde{S}_m}{\partial\tilde{r}}\Big|_{\tilde{r}=1} = \frac{D_{S,d}}{D_{S,m}}\frac{\partial\tilde{S}_d}{\partial\tilde{r}}\Big|_{\tilde{r}=1} \qquad (17a)$$

$$\frac{\partial\tilde{P}_m}{\partial\tilde{r}}\Big|_{\tilde{r}=1} = \frac{D_{P,d}}{D_{S,m}}\frac{\partial\tilde{P}_d}{\partial\tilde{r}}\Big|_{\tilde{r}=1}. \qquad (17b)$$

$$\tilde{S}_m(1) = \phi\tilde{S}_d(1),\quad \tilde{P}_m(1) = \phi\tilde{P}_d(1). \qquad (18)$$

$$\frac{\partial\tilde{S}_m}{\partial\tilde{r}}\Big|_{\tilde{r}=0} = 0,\quad \frac{\partial\tilde{P}_m}{\partial\tilde{r}}\Big|_{\tilde{r}=0} = 0, \qquad (19a)$$

$$\tilde{S}_d(1+\tilde{\nu}) = \tilde{S}_0,\quad \tilde{P}_d(1+\tilde{\nu}) = 0. \qquad (19b)$$

The dimensionless factor σ^2 essentially compares the rate of enzyme reaction ($V_{\max}/K_M$) with the diffusion through the enzyme-loaded microreactor ($D_{S,m}/R_0^2$). If $\sigma^2 \ll 1$, the enzyme kinetics controls the bioreactor action. The action is under diffusion control when $\sigma^2 \gg 1$.

The Biot number β is another dimensionless parameter widely used to indicate the internal mass transfer resistance to the external one [24][25],

$$\beta = \frac{D_{S,d}R_0}{D_{S,m}(R_1 - R_0)}. \qquad (20)$$

When the Biot number is small, the effect of the external diffusion is the most marked. As the Biot number increases the effect of the external diffusion becomes less important.

The diffusion module and the Biot number are widely used in analysis and design of different bioreactors [25]. The experiment conducted by Kont et al. [10] proved the external mass-transfer limitations to be negligible for $\beta > 1$ using the first order kinetics model of CSTR and packed-bed reactors (PBR), which conducted condition (8). Typically, designers seek for bioreactors acting in the reaction-limited regime, since in this case reaction and diffusion occur on different time scales [26].

IV. Digital simulation of experiments

The non-linearity of the governing equations prevents us from solving the boundary value problem (14)-(19) analytically, hence the numerical model was constructed and solved using finite difference technique [17]. An explicit scheme was used; however since Michaelis-Menten non-linearity, further construction of equations was used:

$$D_{C,m} \cdot \frac{1}{r^2}\frac{\partial}{\partial r}\left(r^2 \frac{\partial C_m^n}{\partial r}\right) = \pm \frac{V_{\max} C_m^n}{K_M + C_m^{n-1}},$$

where $C = S, P$. Tridiagonal matrix was constructed from the equations. In the numerical simulation, scheme was run until the following loss becomes very small:

$$\mathcal{L} = ||S^n - S^{n-1}||_{l^2} + ||P^n - P^{n-1}||_{l^2} < \epsilon,$$

where decay rate value $\epsilon = 10^{-14}$ was used over l^2 norm. An explicit finite difference the scheme was built on a uniform discrete grid with 128 points in space direction [16]. The simulator has been programmed by the authors in C++ language [27].

The numerical solution of the mathematical model (14)-(19) was validated by using exact analytical solutions known for very special cases of the model parameters [22][25][6][16]. At such low concentration of the substrate as $S_0 \ll K_M$, the non-linear reaction rate in equations (3) reduces to the first order reaction rate. In very opposite case, when the substrate concentration S_0 to be measured is very high compared to the Michaelis constant K_M ($S_0 \gg K_M$), the reaction term reduces to the zero order reaction rate $V_{\max}$.

V. Results and discussion

To investigate the effects of the geometry and catalytic activity of the microreactor, the reactor action was simulated and the yield factor was calculated for very different values of the Biot number β, the Thiele module σ and the substrate dimensionless concentration S_0.

A. Concentration profiles

Figure 3 shows the profiles of the product concentration P calculated from the microreactor model (14)-(19) changing the Thiele module σ as well as the Biot number β, and keeping unchanged the following model parameters:

$$D_{S,m} = D_{P,m}, \quad D_{S,d} = D_{P,d}, \quad \phi = 0.5, \quad \widetilde{\nu} = 1. \qquad (21)$$

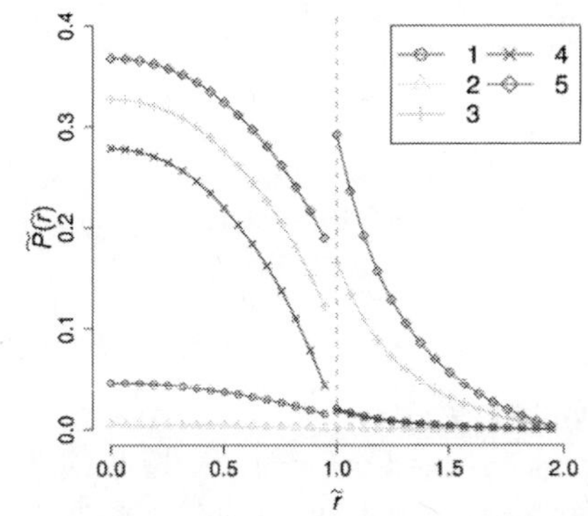

Figure 3. Concentration profiles of the product in the microreactor simulated at the substrate concentration $\widetilde{S}_0 = 1$ and different values of the Thiele module σ^2: 0.1 (2), 1 (1), 10 (3-5), as well as the Biot number β: 0.5 (5), 1 (1-3), 10 (4), the other parameters are as defined in (21). Dashed line shows boundary between the microreactor and the diffusion layer.

One can be seen in Figure 3, that low Thiele modulus values $\sigma < 1$ or high Biot number values, which means that the species passes the Nernst diffusion layer fast, give the concentrations approach to straight line because of linearity of governing equations in the area $r \in (1, 1 + \widetilde{\nu})$. On the other hand, high Thiele modulus values ($\sigma^2 > 10$) lead to significant differences in concentration distribution across the outer boundary of the microreactor.

B. Impact of the substrate concentration

To investigate the dependence of the yield factor γ on the substrate concentration $\widetilde{S}_0$, γ was calculated by simulating the microreactor action at three characteristic values of the Thiele module σ^2: 0.1, 1 and 10, as well as at three values of the Biot number β: 0.5, 1 and 10. The effect of the substrate concentration was investigated in a wide range of $\widetilde{S}_0$ values $[10^{-3}, 10^3]$. Calculation results are presented in Figure 4.

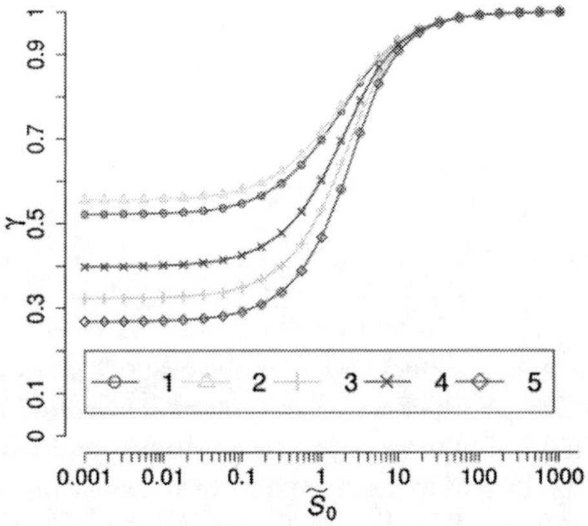

Figure 4. The yield factor γ vs. the substrate concentration $\widetilde{S}$. The notation and values of the parameters are the same as in Figure 3.

One can see (Figure 4) a non-linear impact of the substrate concentration on the yield factor.

As a function of $\widetilde{S}_0$, the yield factor γ is a monotonous increasing function with limit of one. At low concentrations of the substrate $\widetilde{S_0} < 1$, the yield factor increases with decreasing the Thiele modulus and increasing the Biot number β.

The yield factor γ is, practically, invariant to changes in the substrate concentration $\widetilde{S_0}$ when the Michaelis-Menten kinetics approaches the first order ($\widetilde{S_0} \ll 1$) or zero order kinetics ($\widetilde{S_0} \gg 1$). At intermediate values of $\widetilde{S_0}$, when the kinetics changes from the first to zero order, the yield factor γ noticeably increases with increasing the substrate concentration. Increasing the substrance concentration does not influence the increase in the product yield for $\widetilde{S_0} > 100$.

C. *Impact on product rate*

Figure 5 presents the dependence of the product emission rate on the thickness of the Nernst diffusion layer. Values of $\bar{V}_{P,0}$ were calculated changing the dimensionless thickness $\widetilde{\nu}$ of the Nernst diffusion layer from $10^{-0.5}$ up to $10^{0.75}$. At lower values of $\widetilde{\nu}$ the two compartment model (14)-(19) reduces to a notably simpler one layer model [22][25]. The reactor behaviour at larger values of $\widetilde{\nu}$ is not so important due to the product emission at very low rate.

As one can see in Figure 5, the rate $\bar{V}_{P,0}$ is a decreasing function of $\widetilde{\nu}$, which confirms a hypothesis about the importance of the Nernst layer for the reactors productivity [25]. The decrease in $\bar{V}_{P,0}$ with increasing $\widetilde{\nu}$ is especially noticeable at relatively high substrate concentrations ($\widetilde{S_0} = 10$, curve 4), as well as high values of the Thiele module ($\sigma^2 = 2$, curve 2), i.e. in the case of the first order kinetics or when the reactor is under the diffusion control.

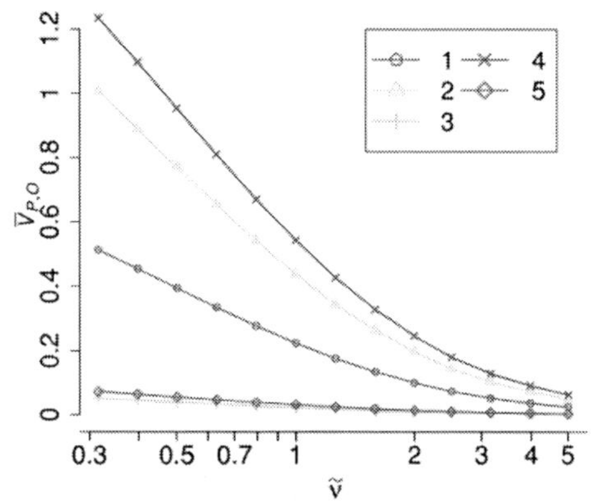

Figure 5. The product emission rate $\bar{V}_{P,0}$ vs. the dimensionless thickness $\widetilde{\nu}$ of the Nernst diffusion layer at $\widetilde{S_0}$: 0.1 (5), 1 (1-3), 10 (4), σ^2: 0.1 (3), 1 (1, 4, 5), 2 (2), the other parameters are as defined in (21).

The impact of the thickness $\widetilde{\nu}$ on the product rate $\bar{V}_{P,0}$ gives us tendencies on thickness $\widehat{\nu}$ selection. However, reducing the thickness of Nernst layer is a serious problem. Since microreactor is soaking and mixing to create layer and zero thickness of the diffusion shell can not be achieved [15], the impact of other model parameters on the microreactor efficiency is also important.

D. *Impact of the Biot number*

To investigate the dependence of the yield factor γ on the Biot number β, the factor γ was calculated at different values of the Thiele module σ^2 (0.1, 1 and 10) and the substrate concentration $\widetilde{S_0}$ (0.1, 1 and 10), changing the Biot number in a range of $[10^{-1}, 10^2]$. The results of the calculations are depicted in Figure 6.

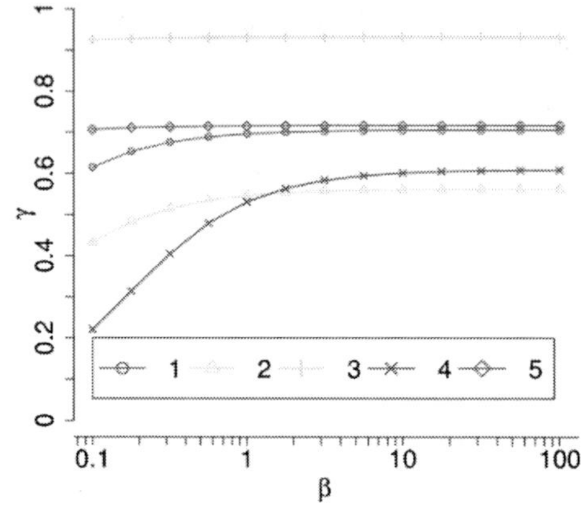

Figure 6. The yield factor γ vs. the Biot number β at $\widetilde{S_0}$: 0.1 (2), 1 (1, 4, 5), 10 (3), σ^2: 0.1 (5), 1 (1-3), 10 (4), the other parameters are as in (21).

Figure 6 shows the product yield γ as an increasing function of the Biot number β. However, the yield factor γ rapidly grows only when β values are relatively small ($\beta < 1$), and the reactor action is under the diffusion control ($\sigma > 1$). The yield factor, practically, does not depend on β when the microreactor acts under the enzyme kinetics control ($\sigma < 1$) or the substrate concentration is high ($\widetilde{S_0} > 10$). On the other hand, the Nernst diffusion layer may be neglected when the Biot number is higher than around 20 [25][28].

E. *Impact of the Thiele Module*

The dependence of the yield factor γ on the Thiele modulus was investigated by calculating the factor γ at different values of the Biot number β, as well as of the substrate concentration $\widetilde{S_0}$ and changing modulus σ from 10^{-3} up to 10^5. Figure 6 shows the yield factor γ as a monotonous decreasing function of σ at very different values of β and $\widetilde{S_0}$.

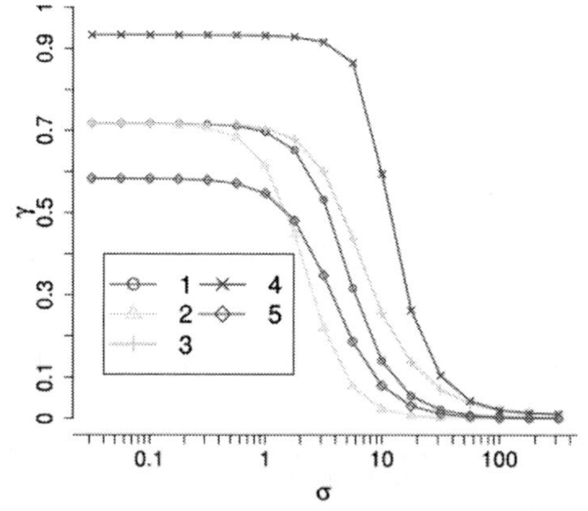

Figure 7. The yield factor γ vs. the Thiele modulus σ at β: 0.1(2), 1(1, 4, 5), 10(3), $\widetilde{S_0}$: 0.1(5), 1(1-3), 10(4), the other parameters are as in (21).

It can be seen in Figure 7 that the yield factor γ, practically, does not depend on σ and approaches to zero when the bioreactor acts notably under the diffusion control ($\sigma > 100$). The yield factor γ is also invariant to changes in the modulus σ when the enzyme kinetics controls the bioreactor action ($\sigma < 0.01$). At mixed conditions when the reactor action is influenced by both the enzyme kinetics and the diffusion, the yield factor γ noticeably decreases with increasing the modulus σ. Figure 7 also shows that the factor γ increases with increasing the substrate concentration (as in Figure 4), as well as when increasing the Biot number β (as in Figure 6).

There are some limitations worth to mention that might be used for the future investigations. First of all, in physical experiments, pellets will not be perfect spheres, which requires modelling more sophisticated domains in 2D and 3D space. Secondly, the system with time dependent characteristics should be considered in the future work.

VI. Conclusion and Future Work

The mathematical model (3)-(8) of the microbioreactor can be successfully used to investigate the behaviour of the catalytic microreactor and to optimize its configuration.

The thickness of the Nernst diffusion layer (shell) noticeably effects the reaction product emission (Figures 5, 6). The production rate $\bar{V}_{P,0}$ as well as the yield especially decreases when the thickness is more than two times greater than the radius of the microreactor, $\widetilde{\nu} > 2$, $\beta < 0.5$. This property becomes important when the size of microbioreactors used in industrial applications continuously reduces, while the Nernst diffusion layer is still often neglected.

The yield of the product increases with increasing the substrate concentration (Figure 4) and with decreasing the Biot number (Figure 6). However, an increase in the substrate concentration becomes ineffective when the enzyme reaction apporaches the zero order kinetics $\widetilde{S}_0 > 10$ (Figure 4). The high yield can be achieved only when the enzyme kinetics controls the bioreactor action $\sigma < 1$ (Figure 7).

Such formulation can be useful to find optimal parameters of such biosystem construction [11]. More importantly, it might improve the design and production of microbioreactors.

More precise and sophisticated computational models, implying the multiple reactions of microreactor, as well as the observed experimental data of the microreactors for model validation are still under development.

References

[1] A. Regalado-Mndez, R. R. Romero, R. N. Rangel, and S. Skogestad, "Biodiesel Production in Stirred Tank Chemical Reactors: A Numerical Simulation," in *New Trends in Networking, Computing, E-learning, Systems Sciences, and Engineering*. Springer, 2015, pp. 109–116.

[2] O. N. Ada and D. T. Sponza, "Anaerobic/aerobic treatment of municipal landfill leachate in sequential two-stage up-flow anaerobic sludge blanket reactor (UASB)/completely stirred tank reactor (CSTR) systems," *Process Biochemistry*, vol. 40, no. 2, pp. 895–902, 2005.

[3] A. Miyawaki, S. Taira, and F. Shiraishi, "Performance of continuous stirred-tank reactors connected in series as a photocatalytic reactor system," *Chemical Engineering Journal*, vol. 286, pp. 594–601, 2016.

[4] M. A. Dareioti and M. Kornaros, "Effect of hydraulic retention time (HRT) on the anaerobic co-digestion of agro-industrial wastes in a two-stage CSTR system," *Bioresource Technology*, vol. 167, pp. 407–415, 2014.

[5] A. J. Straathof and P. Adlercreutz, *Applied Biocatalysis*. CRC Press, 2000.

[6] P. M. Doran, *Bioprocess Engineering Principles*. Academic Press, 1995.

[7] J. Villadsen, J. Nielsen, and G. Liden, *Bioreaction Engineering Principles*. Dordrecht: Springer, 2011.

[8] S. K. Dubey, A. Pandey, and R. S. Sangwan, *Current Developments in Biotechnology and Bioengineering: Crop Modification, Nutrition, and Food Production*. Elsevier, 2016.

[9] J. W. Wong, R. D. Tyagi, and A. Pandey, *Current Developments in Biotechnology and Bioengineering: Solid Waste Management*. Elsevier, 2016.

[10] A. Konti, D. Mamma, D. G. Hatzinikolaou, and D. Kekos, "3-Chloro-1, 2-propanediol biodegradation by Ca-alginate immobilized Pseudomonas putida DSM 437 cells applying different processes: mass transfer effects," *Bioprocess and Biosystems Engineering*, vol. 39, no. 10, pp. 1597–1609, 2016.

[11] D. Cacaval, A. C. Blaga, and A.-I. Galaction, "Diffusional effects on anaerobic biodegradation of pyridine in a stationary basket bioreactor with immobilized Bacillus spp. cells," *Environmental Technology*, pp. 1–13, 2017.

[12] R. Karande, A. Schmid, and K. Buehler, "Applications of multiphasic microreactors for biocatalytic reactions," *Organic Process Research & Development*, vol. 20, no. 2, pp. 361–370, 2016.

[13] F. M. Pereira and S. C. Oliveira, "Occurrence of dead core in catalytic particles containing immobilized enzymes: analysis for the michaelis–menten kinetics and assessment of numerical methods," *Bioprocess and Biosystems Engineering*, vol. 39, no. 11, pp. 1717–1727, 2016.

[14] M. B. Kerby, R. S. Legge, and A. Tripathi, "Measurements of kinetic parameters in a microfluidic reactor," *Analytical Chemistry*, vol. 78, no. 24, pp. 8273–8280, 2006.

[15] J. Wang, *Analytical Electrochemistry*, 3rd ed. Joboken, New Jersey: John Wiley & Sons, 2006.

[16] R. Baronas, F. Ivanauskas, and J. Kulys, *Mathematical Modeling of Biosensors*. Dordrecht: Springer, 2010.

[17] D. Britz and J. Strutwolf, *Digital Simulation in Electrochemistry*, 4th ed., ser. Monographs in Electrochemistry. Springer, 2016.

[18] M. F. Chaplin and C. Bucke, "The large-scale use of enzymes in solution," *Enzyme Technology*, pp. 138–166, 1990.

[19] H. Gutfreund, *Kinetics for the Life Sciences*. Cambridge: Cambridge University Press, 1995.

[20] L. A. Segel and M. Slemrod, "The quasi-steady-state assumption: a case study in perturbation," *SIAM Review*, vol. 31, no. 3, pp. 446–477, 1989.

[21] M. Velkovsky, R. Snider, D. E. Cliffel, and J. P. Wikswo, "Modeling the measurements of cellular fluxes in microbioreactor devices using thin enzyme electrodes," *Journal of Mathematical Chemistry*, vol. 49, no. 1, pp. 251–275, 2011.

[22] T. Schulmeister, "Mathematical modelling of the dynamic behaviour of amperometric enzyme electrodes," *Selective Electrode Reviews*, vol. 12, no. 2, pp. 203–260, 1990.

[23] D. J. Fink, T. Na, and J. S. Schultz, "Effectiveness factor calculations for immobilized enzyme catalysts," *Biotechnology and Bioengineering*, vol. 15, no. 5, pp. 879–888, 1973.

[24] R. Aris, *Mathematical Modeling: a Chemical Engineer's Perspective*. Academic Press, 1999, vol. 1.

[25] M. E. Davis and R. J. Davis, *Fundamentals of Chemical Reaction Engineering*. New York: MGraw-Hill, 2003.

[26] D. A. Edwards, B. Goldstein, and D. S. Cohen, "Transport effects on surface-volume biological reactions," *Journal of Mathematical Biology*, vol. 39, no. 6, pp. 533–561, 1999.

[27] W. T. Vetterling, *Numerical Recipes Example Book (C++): The Art of Scientific Computing*. Cambridge University Press, 2002.

[28] R. Baronas, "Nonlinear effects of diffusion limitations on the response andsensitivity of amperometric biosensors," *Electrochimica Acta*, vol. 240, pp. 399–407, 2016.

A Coupled CFD-FEM Analysis to Simulate Blast Effects on High Security Vehicles Using Modern Hydrocodes

Arash Ramezani, Burghard Hillig, Hendrik Rothe
Chair of Measurement and Information Technology
University of the Federal Armed Forces
Hamburg, Germany
Email: ramezani@hsu-hh.de, burghard.hillig@hsu-hh.de, rothe@hsu-hh.de

Abstract—**The present time is shaped by a variety of religious, political and military conflicts. In times of asymmetric warfare and constantly changing sources of danger from terrorist attacks and other violence based crimes, the personal need for protection continues to rise. Aside from military applications, there is a large area for the use of high security vehicles. Outwardly almost indistinguishable from the basic vehicles, security vehicles are used for protecting heads of state, as well as individuals. To remain state of the art it is necessary for security vehicles to permanently continue to develop protection against modern weapons and ammunition types. It is enormously cost intensive to check any new technology by firing or blasting of real vehicles. Therefore, more and more calculations of new security concepts and materials are carried out by numerical computer simulations. However, product simulation is often being performed by engineering groups using niche simulation tools from different vendors to simulate various design attributes. The use of multiple vendor software products creates inefficiencies and increases costs. This paper will present the analysis and development of an interface between the most common Computer Aided Engineering (CAE) applications ANSYS Autodyn and Abaqus to exploit the advantages of both systems for the simulation of blast effects.**

Keywords-CFD-FEM coupling methods; fully automatic structure analysis; high-performance computing techniques; blast loading; vehicle structures.

I. INTRODUCTION

Since the 1960's, the simulation of physical processes has been a steadily growing and integral part of CAE. Especially, the Computational Fluid Dynamics (CFD) and the discretization of complex models using the Finite Element Method (FEM) have made an impressive development from individual highly specialized applications to the standard of industrial product development. This process was supported by the progressive development of increasingly powerful and less expensive computer hardware. Together with specialized software, a triumph of the simulation of physical processes in everyday technical work has emerged. Positive effects due to the use of simulation tools have been shorter development times, lower production costs, more innovative products, improved security and higher quality. The previous modelling of components and objects of the real world by Computer Aided Design (CAD) software is an important prerequisite for the efficient use of the simulation tools. This has been established as a standard in the automotive industry, so that almost every part of a vehicle can be constructed by using CAD. These complete and realistic vehicle models can be analyzed virtually by available simulation software.

The two leading software providers for CFD / FEM calculations are ANSYS (Canonsburg, USA) and Abaqus FEA from Dassault Systèmes (Vélizy-Villacoublay, France). Although both providers offer software with similar features available, their performance is characterized by different spreads and focuses. For example, Abaqus and CATIA, a CAD software, which is also distributed by Dassault Systèmes, is predominantly used by the automotive industry and provides excellent opportunities for the simulation and modelling of complete vehicles. This includes screwed and adhesive connections. On the other hand, ANSYS offers a wide range of sophisticated simulation capabilities in the field of CFD, which includes the modelling and simulation of explosive detonations and the subsequent propagation of shock waves. The different focuses of the performance of ANSYS and Abaqus yield to a mixed, demand-based use of the software in the research and development area, so that different software is used even within the same company on the same project in different areas of activity. This circumstance is amplified by the fact that product simulations are performed by engineering groups using niche simulation tools from different vendors to simulate various design attributes. Unfortunately the leading software providers avoid the effective interaction of their simulation tools due to mutual competition. This complicates the development effort and results in longer development times in research and industry.

Particularly, in the area of armored security vehicles, it is necessary to remain state of the art and to constantly consider the ongoing development of modern weapon and ammunition types. Experimental tests of the harmful effects of new technologies by blast or impact is associated with enormous time and financial costs.

In order to exploit the full potential of ANSYS and Abaqus, we have developed an interface between these two software platforms [1]. This interface allows an iterative transfer of the blast simulation of ANSYS to the structural mechanic solver of Abaqus, which simulates the effects on the vehicle model and vice versa.

This paper reports on the development of this interface between ANSYS and Abaqus, which will enable combining the strengths of the two leading software providers with the aim of generating synergies that result in short development times and lower costs.

After a brief introduction and description of the different methods of space discretization in Section III, there is a short section on ballistic trials where the experimental set-up is depicted, followed by Section V describing the analysis with numerical simulations. The paper ends with a concluding paragraph in Section VI.

II. State-of-the-Art

A first step in developing an interface between ANSYS and Abaqus has already been reported in [1]. The developed interface allows accessing a set of data and passing them to Abaqus. Python was used as a programming language. ANSYS provides the data records for the interface as .txt files. These files contain data points with Cartesian coordinates, which describe the propagation of shock waves after blasting. The interface takes this data and splits it into separate information. In a further step, the data is stored in a list, linked with the corresponding time points, pressure data and coordinates. It is also possible to use a set of data and to interpolate between the time points to produce a larger data set. After the data has been written and saved in a linked form, the interface retrieves the CAD model. Subsequently, the explosion data can be projected onto a selectable surface of the model. Then, an iterative loop realizes the coupling between CFD and FEM simulations. This approach for a coupled CFD-FEM analysis is called "strong coupling." In another approach, the "semi-strong coupling," a smaller amount of data is used and mathematically interpolated for a sufficient approximation. The third concept is a "weak coupling" solution. Here, neural networks and deep learning can be used to replicate blast effects on different vehicle structures. Until now, the basic functionality of the interface could be validated on different models, including the model of a safety vehicle.

III. Fundamentals of Simulation

In the security sector, the partly insufficient safety of people and equipment due to failure of industrial components are ongoing problems that cause great concern. Since computers and software have spread into all fields of industry, extensive efforts are currently being made in order to improve the safety by applying certain computer-based solutions. To deal with problems involving the release of a large amount of energy over a very short period of time, e.g., explosions and impacts, there are three approaches, which are discussed in [2].

As the problems are highly non-linear and require information regarding material behavior at ultra-high loading rates, which are generally not available, most of the work is experimental and may cause tremendous expenses. Analytical approaches are possible if the geometries involved are relatively simple and if the loading can be described through boundary conditions, initial conditions, or a combination of the two. Numerical solutions are far more general in scope and remove any difficulties associated with geometry [3].

For structures under shock and impact loading, numerical simulations have proven to be extremely useful. They provide a rapid and less expensive way to evaluate new design ideas. Numerical simulations can supply quantitative and accurate details of stress, strain, and deformation fields that would be very expensive or difficult to reproduce experimentally. In these numerical simulations, the partial differential equations governing the basic physical principles of conservation of mass, momentum, and energy are employed. The equations to be solved are time-dependent and nonlinear in nature. These equations, together with constitutive models describing material behavior and a set of initial and boundary conditions, define the complete system for shock and impact simulations.

The governing partial differential equations need to be solved in both time and space domains. The solution over the time domain can be achieved by an explicit method. In the explicit method, the solution at a given point in time is expressed as a function of the system variables and parameters, with no requirements for stiffness and mass matrices. Thus, the computing time at each time step is short but may require numerous time steps for a complete solution. The solution for the space domain can be obtained utilizing different spatial discretization, such as Lagrange [4], Euler [5], Arbitrary Lagrange Euler (ALE) [6], or mesh free methods [7]. Each of these techniques has its unique capabilities, but also limitations. Usually, there is not a single technique that can cope with all the regimes of a problem [8]. The crucial factor is the grid that causes different outcomes. More details are discussed in Section IV.

Due to the fact that all engineering simulations are based on geometry to represent the design, the target and all its components are simulated as CAD models. Real-world engineering commonly involves the analysis and design of complicated geometry. These types of analysis depend critically on having a modeling tool with a robust geometry import capability in conjunction with advanced, easy-to-use mesh generation algorithms [9]. It often is necessary to combine different simulation and modeling techniques from various CAE applications. However, this fact can lead to major difficulties, especially in terms of data loss and computational effort. Particularly the leading software providers prevent an interaction of their tools with competing products. But to analyze blast loading and its effects on vehicle structures, different CAE tools are needed. Therefore, it is important that an interface is provided that allows a robust interaction between various applications. Using a CAD neutral environment that supports direct, bidirectional and associative interfaces with CAE systems, the geometry can be optimized successively and analysis can be performed without loss of data [10].

IV. Materials and Methods

Various approaches are possible when it comes to solving problems that involve the release of large amounts of energy in very short periods of time, which then propagate as shock waves or act as impact on structures. Analytical solutions offer a very powerful way to describe such a process. Unfortunately, their applicability is restricted to problems with simple geometries and few boundary and initial conditions. In contrast, numerical simulations offer much more general applications with complex structures and feasible solutions.

The underlying physical model of numerical simulations is provided by physical conservation laws, the equation of state and the constitutive model. Partial differential equations for the conservation of energy, momentum, and mass form the physical conservation laws. Furthermore, the equation of state combines the internal energy or temperature and the density or volume of a material with the pressure. As a result, changes in the density and irreversible thermodynamic processes such as shock-like heating can be considered. In addition, the constitutive model includes the influence of the material to be simulated and describes the effect of deformation, i.e. changes in shape and material strength properties.

Together, these equations form a set of coupled, time- and location-dependent, highly non-linear equations, which can be solved by computer calculations. The governing partial differential equations need to be solved in both time and space domains. The solution over the time domain can be obtained by an explicit method, which is an iterative method and leads to a step by step solution in the time domain. Software for numerical simulation of shock and impact processes is called a hydrocode [11].

A. Methods of Space Discretization

All existing structural dynamics and wave propagation codes obtain solutions to the Differential Equations (DEs) governing the field by solving an analogous set of algebraic equations. The governing DEs are not solved directly, because currently only a handful of closed-form solutions for DEs are available. The equations of structural dynamics, being a coupled set of rate equations, which account for the effects of severe gradients in stress, strain and deformation, material behavior ranging from solid to fluid to gas, temperatures from room temperature to melt temperature are highly nonlinear and do not lend themselves to closed-form solutions in the general case.

To get a solution over the spatial domain a discretization of the material with a mesh is necessary. FEM uses such a discretization by dividing the problem space into separate elements. These elements can have different shapes: In two dimensions, the shape of quadrilaterals or triangles, in three dimensions hexahedrons and tetrahedrons are usually used. Even complicated geometries can be formed with these elements. Each FEM element has a certain number of nodes, which are located at its corners and have known spatial coordinates. The displacement of these nodes represents the unknowns of the partial differential equations to be solved. There are multiple, different spatial discretization methods related to FEM, such as Lagrange, Euler, Arbitrary Lagrange Euler (ALE) or mesh free methods. Each of these methods can be used independently, but some specific problems need a combination of different discretization methods.

1) Lagrange

The Lagrange method divides an object into a spatial grid where the grid is fixed to the object and moves with it. The material components within an element do not change. If forces are acting on a node, it is displaced, and thus the forces are transmitted to its neighboring nodes, similar to a spring-mass system. This results in deformations of the grid. The nodes of the edge elements of an object remain unchanged so that the boundary and interface conditions can be easily applied. Clear material boundaries are also available so that space outside the material does not require an extra grid and therefore the conservation of mass is automatically satisfied. Figure 1 shows two objects with its mesh as an example of the Lagrange method. Two objects consisting of different materials represented by the colors blue and green before (left side) and after impact (right side). The green object has an initial velocity in the direction of the blue object. The right side of the figure shows the discretization dependent deformation after the impact with the Lagrange solver. The mesh is bound to the objects and divides them into multiple elements. After an impact the objects deform due to the deformation of the elements. A weak point of the Lagrange method is a strong distortion of the mesh in heavily loaded regions, as shown in Figure 1. in the area adjacent to the green and blue object. In general, the Lagrange method is best suited for complex geometries and structures, projectiles and other solids. A disadvantage of Lagrange is the occurrence of strong distortions of mesh element at high loads. Such a distorted element can adversely affect the temporal solution of the simulation since the time step is proportional to the size of the smallest element.

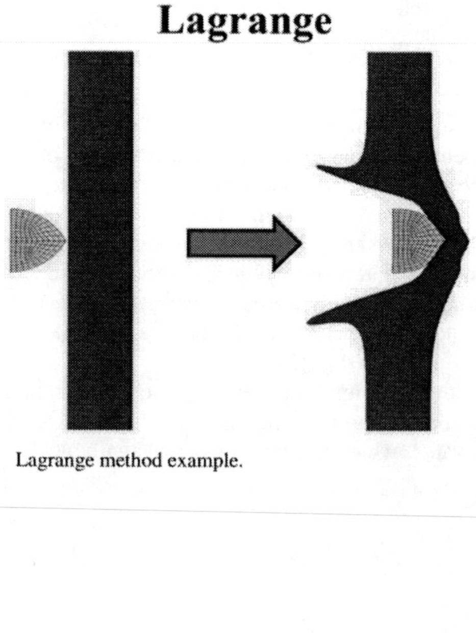

Figure 1. Lagrange method example.

In general the Lagrange method is best suited for complex geometries and structures, projectiles and other solids. A disadvantage of Lagrange is the occurrence of strong distortions of mesh element at high loads. Such a distorted element can adversely affect the temporal solution of the simulation since the time step is proportional to the size of the smallest element.

2) Euler

In the Euler method the coordinates of the nodes are fixed and form the entire mesh of the region to be solved. The material flows through the mesh as a function of time and changes the value of the element, while the spatial coordinates and the nodes remain fixed. This is the reason why no element distortion is possible in the Euler method. In contrast to Lagrange, boundary nodes do not necessarily coincide together with material boundary conditions. Thereby difficulties can arise with the application of boundary and interface conditions. Figure 2. shows two objects and the mesh as an example of the Euler method. Two objects consisting of different materials represented by the colors blue and green before (left side) and after impact (right side). The mesh fills the whole space. The green object has an initial velocity in the direction of the blue object. The right side of the figure shows the discretization dependent deformation after the impact with the Euler solver. The mesh is not bound to the objects like in the Lagrange frame. Instead the mesh fills the whole space with the objects and empty space between them. During the simulation the material of the objects is transported through the mesh of the space. After an impact the mesh stays clear but its content is partly deformed.

In general the Euler method is used to model the propagation of gases and fluids as a result of an explosion or impact. In the investigation of solids, the Euler method has a disadvantageous effect, since additional calculations are needed to transport the stress tensor and the history of the material through the lattice. In this case Euler needs more computing performance and smaller elements to resolve the occurring shock waves.

3) ALE

The Arbitrary Lagrange Euler (ALE) method is a mix of Lagrange and Euler method. ALE allows an arbitrary redefinition of the mesh on each calculation step. Different predefined grid motions can be specified, such as free (Lagrange), fixed (Euler), equipotential, equal spacing and others. As an advantage distortions can be avoided. On the other hand, additional computation steps are necessary to move and to convert the grid. An example of ALE is shown in Figure 3. Two objects consisting of different materials represented by the colors blue and green before (left side) and after impact (right side). The blue object has an initial velocity in the direction of the green object. The right side of the figure shows the discretization dependent deformation after the impact with the ALE solver. In comparison to the pure Lagrange method (Figure 1.), no lattice distortions occur here.

4) SPH

Smoothed Particle Hydrodynamics is a method which is not based on a fixed topological lattice but on a finite set of particles. These particles are embedded to the material similar to the nodes of the Lagrange method, but their connections are not fixed. However, the particles represent not only mass points, but also interpolation points for the calculation of the physical variables. The calculations are based on the data of the neighboring particles and are scaled by a weighting function. Unlike Lagrange, no grid distortion can occur at SPH, since no grid exists. Related to the Euler method, SPH has the advantage that all material boundaries and interfaces are clearly defined. Figure 4 illustrates two objects consisting of different materials in the SPH frame represented colored particles before (left side) and after impact (right side). The green object has an initial velocity in the direction of the blue object. The right side of the figure shows the discretization dependent deformation after the impact with the SPH solver. As seen in Figure 4. two objects consist of small particles in the SPH frame. Their behavior before and after an impacts differs from the solutions in the Lagrange, Euler or ALE frame.

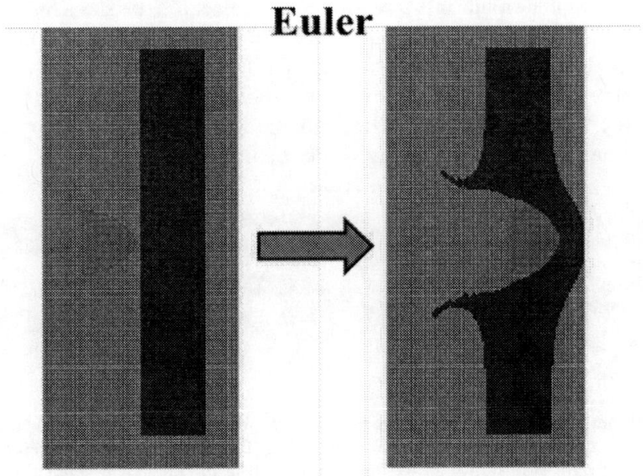

Figure 2. Euler method example.

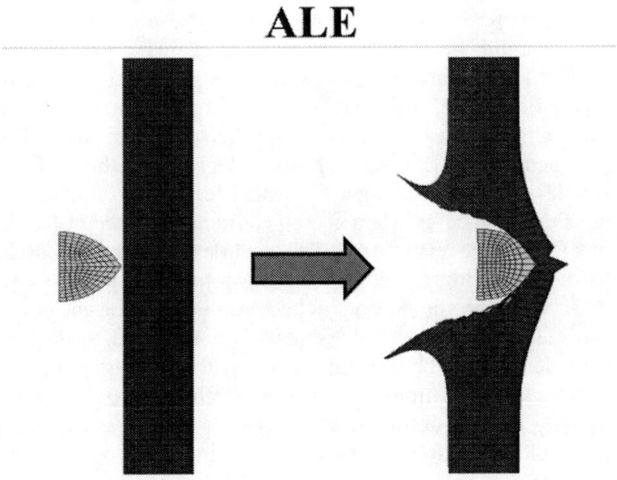

Figure 3. ALE method example.

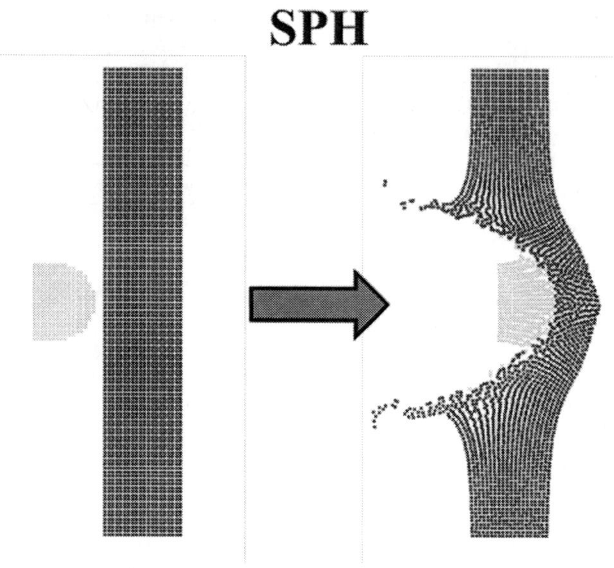

Figure 4. SPH method example.

The SPH method has proven especially useful in the simulation of impact processes on brittle materials [2]. It should be noted that the modelling of the material as particles leads to significantly higher computing effort per time step.

For problems of dynamic fluid-structure interaction and impact, there typically is no single best numerical method which is applicable to all parts of a problem. Techniques to couple types of numerical solvers in a single simulation can allow the use of the most appropriate solver for each domain of the problem.

One of the more important issues, which have to be carefully considered is the issue of mesh size. Different results are obtained if the number of cells per unit length is not adequate. For example, it was found that for penetration studies with eroding long rods, the number of cells on the rod's radius should be at least eleven. The same density of cells should be kept in the target, at least for several projectile radii around its symmetry axis. In order to save computing time, the cell size at farther zones can be gradually increased according to their distance from the symmetry axis. The mesh cell size depends on the specific problem. As an example, a small cell size should be considered in cases where there is a fracture in the projectile or target. It is recommended that while preparing the code for its final runs, the numerical convergence with respect to mesh cell size should be checked. Another important issue, especially when material elements are expected to deform considerably, is the issue of erosion with Lagrangian codes. At large deformations the code may run into trouble when treating heavily deformed elements. The use of the erosion threshold condition is then necessary in order to eliminate elements at a predetermined value of the plastic or geometric deformation. The erosion should be monitored constantly, and when it is too high one should replace the Lagrangian with an Eulerian code.

The goal of this paper is to evaluate an interface between different hydrocodes, computational tools for modeling the behavior of continuous media. In its purest sense, a hydrocode is a computer code for modeling fluid flow at all speeds. For that reason, a structure will be split into a number of small elements. The elements are connected through their nodes (see Figure 5.). The mesh divides the object into small elements connected by its nodes.

The behavior (deflection) of the simple elements is well-known and may be calculated and analyzed using simple equations called shape functions. By applying coupling conditions between the elements at their nodes, the overall stiffness of the structure may be built up and the deflection/distortion of any node – and subsequently of the whole structure – can be calculated approximately [12]. Therefore, several runs are necessary: From modeling to calculation to the evaluation and subsequent improvement of the model.

Hydrocodes, or wave propagation codes, are a valuable adjunct to the study of the behavior of metals subjected to high-velocity impact or intense impulsive loading. The combined use of computations, experiments and high-strain-rate material characterization has, in many cases, supplemented the data achievable by experiments alone at considerable savings in both cost and engineering man-hours.

A large database exists of high-pressure Equation-Of-State (EOS) data. Considerable data on high rate deviatoric behavior exists as well although, unlike EOS data, it is not collected in a few compilations but scattered throughout a diverse literature. Experimental techniques exist for determining either EOS or strength data for materials not yet characterized under high-rate loading conditions.

By contrast, computations with non-metallic materials such as composites, concrete, rock, soil and a variety of geological materials are, in effect, research tasks. This is due to several reasons: lack of definitive computational models for high strain rate–temperature–pressure response; lack of a database for EOS and high rate strength data for such materials; lack of test methodologies for anisotropic materials subjected to high-rate loading.

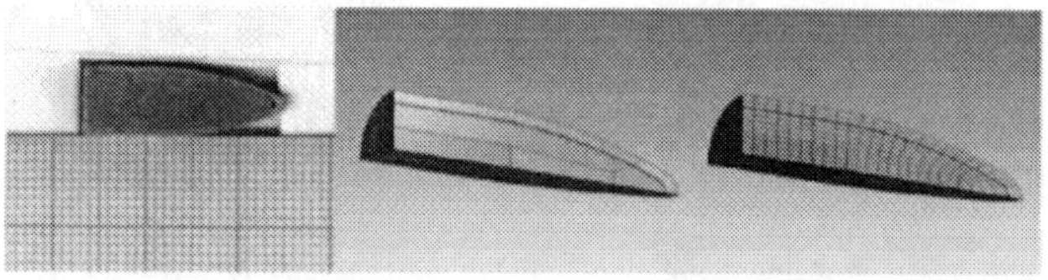

Figure 5. The left side shows the cross-section of a bullet over millimeter paper, which could theoretically divide the bullet into multiple elements. The right side shows an example of a mesh in the numerical simulation. Different parts are color coded in the representation of the bullet.

A large number of ad hoc models exist for explosives, geological materials, concrete and other non-metallics. Many of these lack a firm theoretical foundation. This is an area where considerable research is required, both to devise appropriate test techniques to measure material response under high strain rates, elevated temperatures and high pressures as well as to develop appropriate constitutive models.

B. Interface

In general, an interface connects systems that have different properties with the purpose of exchanging information. For computers, this is mainly the case between software, hardware, peripheral devices and humans. Communication at the interface can be either in one direction, such as a remote control or keyboard, or in both directions, such as a touch screen or a network adapter [13].

In the context of numerical simulation of blast and impact processes, an interface is necessary to ensure an effective coupling of CFD / FEM simulations between the software Abaqus and ANSYS. For our research, ANSYS is to be used to provide data from simulated explosions using Euler-Lagrange coupling. On the other hand, the structure, which is affected by the blasting is simulated by Abaqus. The developed Interface has the task of conveying the data between ANSYS and Abaqus, so that the individual simulation steps can be performed successively with respect to the successive transfer of data.

V. Experimental Section

In computing, an interface is a shared boundary across two separate components of a computer system exchange information. The exchange can be between software, computer hardware, peripheral devices, humans and combinations of these. Some computer hardware devices such as a touchscreen can both send and receive data through the interface, while others such as a mouse, microphone or joystick operate one way only [13].

Coupled FEA/CFD analysis is an alternative technique, where separate FEA and CFD codes are used for solid and fluid regions, respectively, with a smooth exchange of information between the two codes to ensure continuity of blast loading data. The main merit of the approach is to enable users to take full advantages of both CFD and FEA capabilities.

The objective of this work is to develop an interface between ANSYS Autodyn and Abaqus. The software ANSYS is used to solve linear and non-linear problems of structural mechanics, computational fluid dynamics, acoustics and various other engineering sciences [14]. Here, ANSYS will provide data from the simulation of blast effects. The capability to couple Eulerian and Lagrangian frames in ANSYS is helpful in blast field modeling. The Eulerian frame is best suited for representing explosive detonations, because the material flows through a geometrically constant grid that can easily handle the large deformations associated with gas and fluid flow. The structure is modeled with the Lagrangian frame in Abaqus. Abaqus supports familiar interactive computer-aided engineering concepts such as feature-based, parametric modeling, interactive and scripted operation, and GUI customization [15].

First, every possibility of transferring the data from ANSYS outputs to Abaqus inputs has to be detected. A summary of this process is shown in Figure 6.

ANSYS will provide the data by generating a data set for the blast loading. Figure 7. shows the color coding of the shock wave goes from low pressures (0 hPa) in blue to high pressures in red (> 3500 hPa). The last picture shows the shock wave when the simulated vehicle is reached. This data set will include snapshots of given points in time. At this stage there is a data set of five points in time, between 0.0291s and 0.0475s (after detonation). Related to the points in time this data set includes the pressure values with Cartesian coordinates based on the simulation of the spread of explosive materials. A script is coded to read the blast loading data in Abaqus. This script, coded in Python, uses the line interface in Abaqus directly. First, a blast loading data is generated in ANSYS and saved as a normal text file in .txt format. The data set will be split to separate the different types of information. After that, a list will be created to save the data and connect the related time points to the coordinates and pressure values. At this point, there is a possibility to use linear interpolation between the five time points to generate a larger data base. After reading and saving the data set, the script will load the model used for impact tests in Abaqus. A surface of the model must be selected to project the blast data on it.

The goal is to investigate the impact of the blast data on a full vehicle model in Abaqus. This work (in progress) starts with a less complex model to validate the function of the script and the interface itself. The first model was a basic rectangle to be strained by the pressure data. Afterwards, two more complex models were tested successfully. This approach will lead to a surface similar to the silhouette of high security vehicles (see Figure 8.).

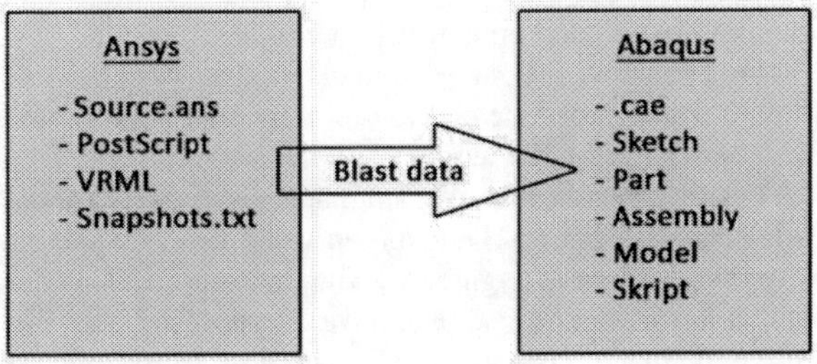

Figure 6. Inputs and outputs for an interface between Ansys and Abaqus. Blast data consisting of several files is exported by Ansys and read via a python script in Abaqus.

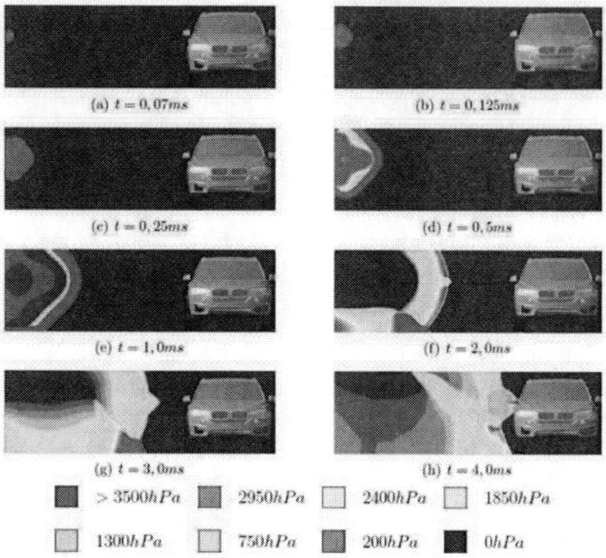

Figure 7. Progressive expansion of a blast in ANSYS Autodyn with a repr-esentation fo a vehicle on the rigth side.

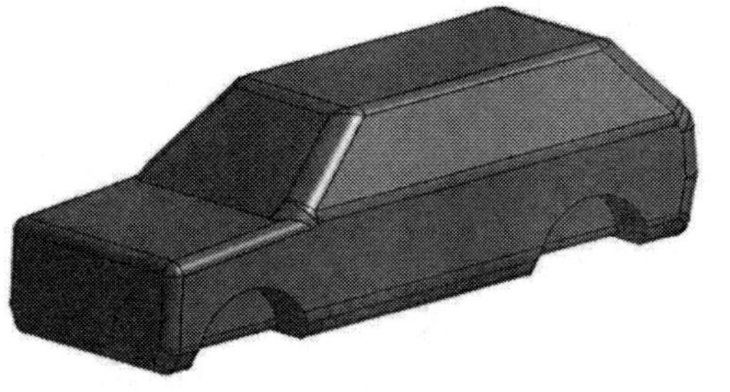

Figure 8. Testing structure in Abaqus with the coarse appearance of a vehicle.

The coupling is realized through an iterative loop between the FEA and CFD simulations, with communications ensuring continuity of shock compression data across the coupled boundaries between the FEA and CFD models. In the coupling process, intermediate individual FEA and CFD solutions are obtained in turn with dynamically updated boundary conditions.

To avoid exceptional deadlock of the individual CFD simulations, appropriate maximum numbers of iterations are assigned for each CFD model.

Testing means that the spatially discretized model is loaded with pressure. The change over time is decisive. An example is shown in Figure 9. . The unarmored SUV model was loaded with a typical explosive charge. The load on the vehicle is made visible by color coding from low strain (blue) to very high strain (red). The deformation on the sheet metal body parts is clearly shown. This data can be used to simply analyze vulnerabilities. The goal is, however, to use complete vehicle models and to carry out realistic investigations.

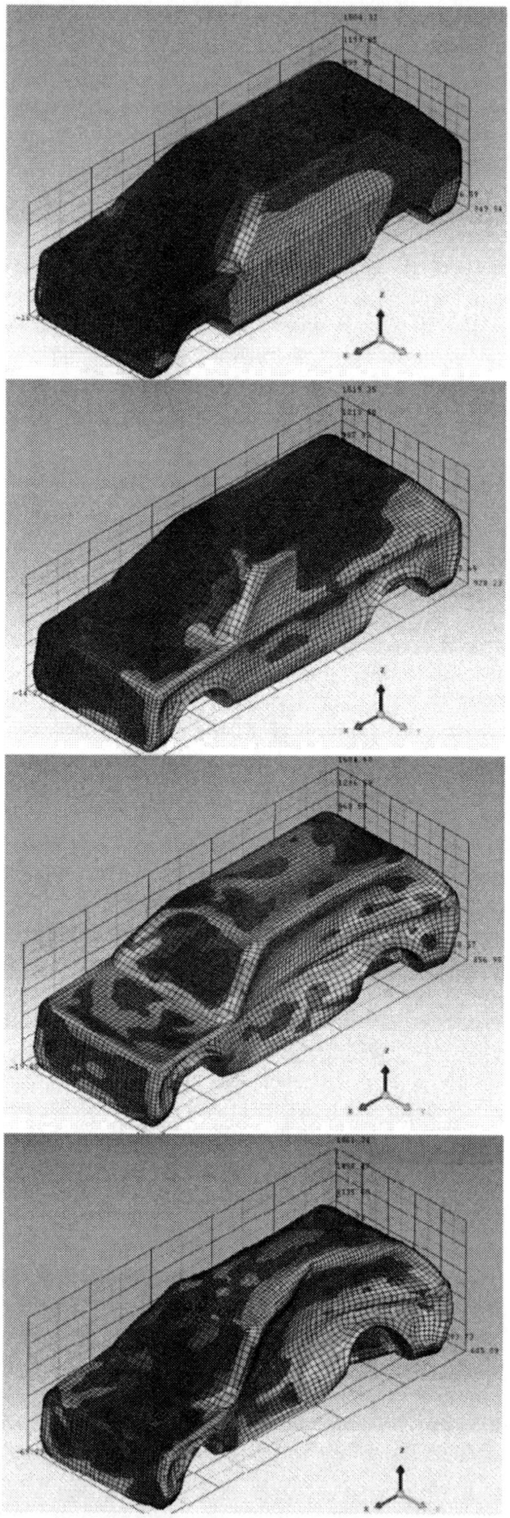

Figure 9. Simulated test structure (unarmed SUV) and deformation process after 3, 5, 10 and 20 ms (images arranged from top to bottom in order of increasing time).

VI. Outlook

There are a variety of approaches in implementing the coupled FEA/CFD analysis. One is generally called "strong coupling," where data have to be transferred between ANSYS Autodyn and ABAQUS in every single time step. A "semistrong coupling" can get along with a smaller set of date, using mathematical interpolation for a sufficient approximation. The third concept is a "weak coupling" solution. Here, neural networks and deep learning can be used to replicate blast effects on different vehicle structures. These approaches are going to be tested in a next step.

Furthermore, a larger blast loading data set has to be created in ANSYS. This will allow a more accurate illustration of blast effects on vehicle structures. Smaller time steps will enable a linear interpolation with a higher accuracy. Different explosives are going to be tested to expand the data base. The next step will be a model for the reflection of blast waves and dynamic changes of pressure values. Using a full vehicle model will provide important information about the behavior of armored structures under blast effects. But to validate the results of the simulation, more ballistic trials are needed. Based on the difficulties of full vehicle model simulations, the implementation of an automatic surface detection has to be taken into consideration. This could be helpful if a large number of different vehicles are investigated. In order to create a user-friendly interface it is possible to generate the script as a plug-in which can be started from the Abaqus user surface directly.

By using pre-defined blast data to create forces as vectors on our vehicle structures, the proposal can be generalized. Then, FEA analysis can be done with other software suites as well. Right now, the concept is not applicable to other systems. This is a major disadvantage and part of our future work. Furthermore, a parallelization of the problem should be considered.

VII. Conclusion and Future Work

A technique for efficiently coupling FEA/CFD for the simulation of blast effects is described. An interface between ANSYS and Abaqus was created to provide blast data sets. The data sets from ANSYS include snapshots from the blast simulation saved at different points in time. The interface is coded in Python and also contains the possibility to use linear interpolation on the data sets.

A good agreement of blast load test data and simulation results was observed. Furthermore, it is shown that the coupled solutions can be obtained in sufficiently short turn-around times for use in design. These solutions can be used as the basis of an iterative optimization process. They are a valuable adjunct to the study of the behavior of vehicle structures subjected to high-velocity impact or intense impulsive loading. The combined use of computations, experiments and high-strain-rate material characterization has, in many cases, supplemented the data achievable by experiments alone at considerable savings in both cost and engineering man-hours.

References

[1] E. Hansen, N. Ehlers, A. Ramezani, and H. Rothe, "Developing an Interface between ANSYS and Abaqus to Simulate Blast Effects on High Security Vehicles," The Eighth International Conference on Advances in System Simulation (SIMUL 2016) IARIA, Aug. 2016, pp. 73-76, ISBN 978-1-61208-442-8.

[2] A. Ramezani and H. Rothe, "Investigation of Solver Technologies for the Simulation of Brittle Materials," The Sixth International Conference on Advances in System Simulation (SIMUL 2014) IARIA, pp. 236-242, Oct. 2014, ISBN 978-61208-371-1.

[3] J. Zukas, "Introduction to Hydrocodes". Elsevier Science, 2004.

[4] A. M. S. Hamouda and M. S. J. Hashmi, "Modelling the impact and penetration events of modern engineering materials: Characteristics of computer codes and material models," Journal of Materials Processing Technology, vol. 56, pp. 847-862, Jan. 1996.

[5] D. J. Benson, "Computational methods in Lagrangian and Eulerian hydrocodes," Computer Methods in Applied Mechanics and Engineering, vol. 99, pp. 235-394, Sep. 1992, doi: 10.1016/0045-7825(92)90042-I.

[6] M. Oevermann, S. Gerber, and F. Behrendt, "Euler-Lagrange/DEM simulation of wood gasification in a bubbling fluidized bed reactor," Particuology, vol. 7, pp. 307-316, Aug. 2009, doi: 10.1016/j.partic.2009.04.004.

[7] D. L. Hicks and L. M. Liebrock, "SPH hydrocodes can be stabilized with shape-shifting," Computers & Mathematics with Applications, vol. 38, pp. 1-16, Sep. 1999, doi: 10.1016/S0898-1221(99)00210-2.

[8] X. Quan, N. K. Birnbaum, M. S. Cowler, and B. I. Gerber, "Numerical Simulations of Structural Deformation under Shock and Impact Loads using a Coupled Multi-Solver Approach," 5th Asia-Pacific Conference on Shock and Impact Loads on Structures, Hunan, China, Nov. 2003, pp. 152-161.

[9] N. V. Bermeo, M. G. Mendoza, and A. G. Castro, "Semantic Representation of CAD Models Based on the IGES Standard," Computer Science, vol. 8265, pp. 157-168, Dec. 2001, doi: 10.1007/ 978-3-642-45114-013.

[10] J. Sarkar, "Computer Aided Design: A Conceptual Approach," CRC Press, December 2014.

[11] C. E. Anderson, "An overview of the theory of hydrocodes," International journal of impact engineering, 5.1-4, pp 33-59, 1987.

[12] G.-S. Collins, "An Introduction to Hydrocode Modeling," Applied Modelling and Computation Group, Imperial College London, 2002.

[13] IEEE 100 – "The Authoritative Dictionary Of IEEE Standards Terms," NYC, NY, USA: IEEE Press, 2000, pp. 574-575, ISBN 0-7381-2601-2.

[14] ANSYS. CAE. *Structures: FEA Simulation*. [Online]. Available from: http://www.ansys.com [retrieved: May, 2017].

[15] Abaqus *Complete Solutions for Realistic Simulation*. [Online]. Available from: http://www.3ds.com/products-services/simulia/products/abaqus/abaquscae/ [retrieved: June, 2017]